Going to War in Iraq

To Janet
for the infinite
gift of her daughter,
and her love,

Going to War in Iraq

When Citizens and the Press Matter

STANLEY FELDMAN, LEONIE HUDDY,
AND GEORGE E. MARCUS

THE UNIVERSITY OF CHICAGO PRESS   CHICAGO AND LONDON

STANLEY FELDMAN is professor of political science and associate director of the Survey Research Center at Stony Brook University.

LEONIE HUDDY is professor of political science and director of the Survey Research Center at Stony Brook University. She is coeditor of *The Oxford Handbook of Political Psychology*.

GEORGE E. MARCUS is professor of political science at Williams College and the author, coauthor, or coeditor of seven books, including, most recently, *Political Psychology: Neuroscience, Genetics, and Politics*.

The University of Chicago Press, Chicago 60637
The University of Chicago Press, Ltd., London
© 2015 by The University of Chicago
All rights reserved. Published 2015.
Printed in the United States of America

24 23 22 21 20 19 18 17 16 15   1 2 3 4 5

ISBN-13: 978-0-226-30406-9 (cloth)
ISBN-13: 978-0-226-30423-6 (paper)
ISBN-13: 978-0-226-30437-3 (e-book)
DOI: 10.7208/chicago/9780226304373.001.0001

Library of Congress Cataloging-in-Publication Data

Feldman, Stanley, author.
    Going to war in Iraq : when citizens and the press matter / Stanley Feldman, Leonie Huddy, and George E. Marcus.
        pages cm
    Includes bibliographical references and index.
    ISBN 978-0-226-30406-9 (cloth : alk. paper) — ISBN 978-0-226-30423-6 (pbk. : alk. paper) — ISBN 978-0-226-30437-3 (e-book)   1. Iraq War, 2003–2011—Public opinion. 2. Iraq War, 2003–2011—Mass media and the war.   I. Huddy, Leonie, author. II. Marcus, George E., 1943– author.   III. Title.
    DS79.767.P83F45 2015
    956.7044'31—dc23

                                                        2015005540

♾ This paper meets the requirements of ANSI/NISO Z39.48-1992 (Permanence of Paper).

Contents

Preface and Acknowledgments

The etiology of any book involves at least one if not several complex tales. Our story begins immediately after 9/11 when Feldman and Huddy, agonizing over recent events, hatched a plan to conduct a national survey on American reactions to the attacks on the Pentagon, the World Trade Center, and the downed airliners, an important project supported by the National Science Foundation that also doubled as an effective form of social science therapy. The plot thickened in August 2002 at the annual meeting of the American Political Science Association in Boston, at which Marcus approached them with a proposal to use their study as the basis for a panel survey focused on the impending Iraq war. This approach, we hoped, would enable us to connect prewar reactions to terrorism from late 2001 and early 2002 with reactions to Saddam Hussein and the war as events unfolded in the latter part of 2002 and into 2003. Once again, we were fortunate to obtain funds from the National Science Foundation to turn an invigorating lunch discussion into a major research project.

The staff at Stony Brook University's Center for Survey Research capably and cheerfully pitched in and interviewed Americans after 9/11, reinterviewed as many of these people as possible some twelve months later, adding a small group of new interviewees, and then interviewed respondents a third time after the war had begun. In this third phase, some respondents were interviewed right after the war's onset and others after President Bush announced (erroneously in hindsight) that the war was over a few months later. This provided us with information on the public's views on Iraq, Saddam, terrorists, the war, and other related issues before, during, and after the war's onset. In brief, it provided us with a successful panel of pre- and postwar views, a rarity in such situations. We assessed the public's views well before anyone had visibly proposed a war in Iraq, examined changes in public opinion as the war was raised and promoted by the nation's leadership, and then finally assessed opinion once the war began. This panel of Americans became the Threat and National Security Survey (TNSS).

Our story continues through a number (more than we like to count) of conferences and meetings of the American Political Science Association, the Midwest Political Science Association, and the International Society for Political Psychology, and sabbaticals, in locales familiar and exotic, in Chicago, Barcelona, Paris, Dublin, Istanbul, and Melbourne, their charms improving the book's quality if not speed of production. Through numerous iterations of analysis and discussion, we discovered something intriguing hidden within our data beyond its immediate focus on the political psychology of terror and affect-laden decision making. We uncovered a powerful link among Democrats between newspaper reading and war opposition. We puzzled over this, had a fruitful discussion with John Mueller (who without knowing it spirited this project forward), and decided that the lack of mobilization among Democrats in the fall of 2002 was a project in its own right. We presented our work to our most highly valued critics and interlocutors, members of the New York Area Political Psychology Workshop. There, spurred on by critical comments from Robert Erikson, James Gibson, Danny Hayes, Richard Lau, Robert Shapiro, and many others, we thought more critically and more deeply about our project as it slowly developed into the current book.

Along the way, a number of people improved immeasurably the quality of this project. Huddy presented findings to the Department of Political Science at the University of Michigan and elicited thoughtful objections from Donald Kinder and other attendees. The three of us met in Cambridge to present our findings to a group at Harvard University and received helpful and probing comments from Stephen Ansohlabehere and others present at the seminar. Huddy and Feldman presented the project at the American Studies Center at the University of Sydney and received helpful comments and reactions from Brendan O'Connor, David Smith, Rodney Tiffen, and others.

We also shared the first draft of our manuscript with several readers and cannot thank enough Tali Mendelberg and Markus Prior who in record time and with customary insight made sharp and very helpful observations that greatly improved the book. James Klurfeld kept us focused on the politics of foreign policy and added vivid journalistic color to our conversations. John Mueller provided intellectual support and thoughtful objections. We also need to thank effusively John Tryneski whose patience (while not infinite) was sufficient to allow us time to ruminate, argue, and rework the manuscript. His razor-sharp judgment placed an earlier version of the manuscript in the hands of two anonymous reviewers whose comments led us to a richer and more focused analysis that dramatically improved the book.

Finally, a number of people deserve thanks for their very direct assistance in collecting or providing the data on which this book is based. Gary Jacobson very generously shared his treasure trove of polls tracking public opinion on the war; Scott Keeter kindly added data from various Pew polls to complete the picture. Grants SES-0201650, SES-9975063, and SES-0241282 from the National Science Foundation made the national survey possible. We also gratefully acknowledge the assistance of Gallya Lahav, Michael MacKuen, and Charles Taber in the first wave of data collection. In addition, we must thank a group of talented graduate students then at Stony Brook University who coded the news and allowed us to see that the patterns in our survey data originated there. Kathleen Donovan, Christopher Johnston, Charles Klahm, Martijn Schoonvelde, and David Wutchiett collected, read, and coded news stories with care, diligence, and good cheer. Their assistance was indispensable to the success of this project.

Stanley Feldman
Leonie Huddy
George E. Marcus
New York, October 2014

The Public Responds to a Possible War in Iraq

Confronting Two Conundrums

"Without debate, without criticism, no Administration and no country can succeed—and no republic can survive." —John F. Kennedy[1]

Introduction

On March 20, 2003, the United States and several of its allies began a military campaign to oust Saddam Hussein as leader of Iraq. The war has been the target of endless discussion, consternation, debate, and analysis. However, the military campaign was preceded by another campaign that is equally worthy of research scrutiny but that has attracted less, far less, analysis than the war itself. In the twelve months or so prior to the war's onset, but beginning in earnest in September 2002, the administration of President George W. Bush designed a political campaign to mobilize public support to help secure congressional approval for military action in Iraq. At first glance, the Bush administration was successful in this second campaign: public opinion polls conducted in the months before the war's onset documented majority support for military action to remove Saddam, and both houses of Congress supported and passed in October 2002 the "Joint Resolution to Authorize the Use of United States Armed Forces against Iraq," commonly referred to as the Iraq War Resolution.

The Bush administration's efforts to sway the American public and members of Congress to support a war in Iraq, its apparent success in promoting dubious claims about Saddam's intentions and Iraq's weapons capabilities, and the failure of the news media to challenge these claims is well-worn territory by now (Bennett, Lawrence, and Livingston 2007; Entman 2004; Hoyle 2008; Isikoff and Corn 2006; Rich 2006; Ricks 2006). The main storyline is familiar: the Bush administration advanced a number of factual claims that were either ill supported or plain wrong; the news media relayed and amplified these claims in the absence of much scrutiny; many congressional Democrats, in an effort to settle the war issue before the 2002 midterm election, voted for the war resolution; and the public, with no credible counterweight to the administration's claims, supported the use of military power to remove Saddam Hussein.

While much in this account is correct, in two crucial respects it is clearly wrong. First, while the news media as a whole may have failed the public by insufficiently challenging the administration's claims concerning Iraq, not all news outlets did so. In recounting a story of broad news media failure in the months before the Iraq War, researchers have overlooked the publication of a series of newspaper articles that got the story right. The existence of these critical newspaper accounts, emanating in part from the Knight Ridder Washington Bureau but also other sources, has been acknowledged sporadically in recent years (Massing 2004; Moyers 2007; Rendall 2006; Ricchiardi 2008; Ritea 2004). But previous public opinion researchers have failed to note this exceptional news coverage, leaving unexamined its potential influence on public opinion.

Second, while many public opinion surveys document majority support for the use of military force in the months before the Iraq War, implicitly linking support to the Bush administration's war advocacy, the administration's efforts in promoting war may have been less successful than this link implies. For one, Republicans supported the war well in advance of September 2002, and their support did not increase even after the administration had launched its pro-war campaign. Moreover, other segments of the American polity, namely, Democrats and independents, became increasingly opposed to war during this time period.

We believe it is important to revisit public opinion in the lead-up to the Iraq War for three reasons. First, we show that a close reexamination of public opinion prior to the war challenges the dominant political science model of public deliberation concerning war, a model in which public opinion is driven by political elites, including the administration, congressional leaders, and partisan politicians. Second, we demonstrate that Americans can sift through complex information on foreign policy and arrive at an independent political judgment under the right conditions.

Third, our analysis of public opinion in the months before the war illustrates that Americans' ability to sensibly evaluate complex information surrounding government policy depends on the existence of an active and critical press, something that is under growing threat at the present time as the news business struggles to establish a stable economic foundation. Our findings challenge much of what constitutes conventional wisdom about the public and the press.

Democracy and Information

Democracy has long provoked conflicting appraisals. These largely emanate from opposing views of the public and its capacity for thoughtful prudent judgment. Thomas Paine's (1776) defense of democracy in *Common Sense* and Abraham Lincoln's (1953, 536) celebration of democracy, in his Gettysburg address, as "government of the people, for the people, and by the people" have democracy as the laudatory vehicle that gives full and proper voice to the public's collective will. Critics of democracy have focused their challenge on what they see as the incapacity of the public to provide sober judgment. H. L. Mencken's (1949, 622) quip that "democracy is the theory that the common people know what they want and deserve to get it good and hard" is representative of a vast opposing literature.[2] Intermediate is the more circumspect construction of Churchill (1947, 7:7566): "Many forms of Government have been tried, and will be tried in this world of sin and woe. No one pretends that democracy is perfect or all-wise. Indeed, it has been said that democracy is the worst form of government except all those other forms that have been tried from time to time."

Our goal is not to assess the virtues and vices of democracy, but rather to answer a more tractable question: What conditions promote, and which undermine, democracy? More specifically, our interest lies in the conditions that allow citizens to evaluate complex political information and make the best decision concerning the future course of government action. We have no illusions about the public. We are acutely aware of the many ways in which human failings undermine the quality of public deliberation (Chong 2013; Taber and Young 2013). Nonetheless a number of institutional factors play a key role in determining how well a democracy functions, including open and competitive elections, laws that protect free expression, active and vigorous contestation between contending parties, and the rise of social movements. The most important factor, however, is the availability of information.

If the public is to influence governmental policy, it must have information. What problems are being pondered by political leaders? How serious are these problems and which are most important? What feasible and practical solutions to such problems are being crafted, discussed, and evaluated by government officials and political elites? What changes to existing policy are being proposed? What are their prospects for success or failure? Information is needed to answer such questions. But such information typically lies outside the daily experiences of most citizens and must be made available from elsewhere. The government and opposing political elites are the primary sources of political facts, arguments, and insights, which then need to be arrayed before the public by an entity such as the press in order to influence everyday political deliberation. If democracy is to be viable, plentiful information must be transparently available to the public so that the public can attend to and make good use of it.

The vital importance of information in a well-functioning democracy leads us to advance two claims. First, while other factors matter, democracy depends on information generated by competing political elites, disseminated and critically evaluated by a free press, and actively used by an engaged electorate. Second, it is more difficult to make democracy work under conditions of war and external threat than under peaceful conditions because the free flow and use of information is often curtailed at such times. The barriers to successful public deliberation are thus high, yet we argue that the public can perform better than these hurdles might imply and conventional wisdom asserts, even when faced with a foreign policy crisis.

Competing Elites, a Free Press, and an Engaged Electorate

We consider three players central to a well-functioning democracy: political parties, the press, and citizens. To more fully understand the conditions under which democracy best operates, we consider each in turn. We turn first to political parties. It is commonly claimed that to function effectively, democracy minimally requires competing elites. Having multiple political parties, goaded by the discipline of recurring elections, ensures that the parties will engage in vigorous public debate about the merits, and demerits, of their respective plans. Visible and vigorous elite debate, debate directed to the citizenry, keeps the public informed and enables citizens to consider partisan claims and counterclaims to arrive at an informed opinion on the credibility of competing proposals.

When this logic is applied to the formation of government policy, it follows that democracy is best served when a policy proposal advanced by one political party is challenged by another to foster spirited and illuminating public debate.[3] This is not to say that partisan disputes are always in a country's best interests. For instance, under conditions of national threat, one political party often joins another in support of a common policy position in a clear demonstration of bipartisanship. This can lead to swift and decisive action, a potential plus. But it can also obscure or weaken the quality of a chosen course of action, a clear negative. A decision by partisans to join forces in a show of bipartisanship and "put country first" can be beneficial under some circumstances, but it can also worsen democratic decision making. Because united political parties have a common stake in overstating the policy's benefits and minimizing its risks, bipartisanship can hide information on any side bargains made to attain consensus, on the full array of costs, and on risks associated with the policy.

An active and free press is the second key player essential to democracy. One task of the press is to accurately convey ongoing debate among political elites to the attending public. But a free press is expected to do more. It is also expected to critically examine the importance and veracity of various claims and counterclaims advanced by partisans, weigh the evidence, and probe the honesty and accuracy of the points and counterpoints. Hence, when a major political decision is placed before the public, the political system can be judged more democratic when the press not only advances the claims of those on different sides of an issue but also vigorously and independently evaluates such claims and related evidence. This process lies at the heart of investigative journalism, which Alex Jones (2009, 5) describes as "the toughest kind of journalism because it not only takes time and great expertise, it must be done in the face of efforts to keep information secret."

Journalists can check factual claims and lay bare uncertain or dubious assertions. They can seek out experts to verify or challenge swirling suppositions and questionable conclusions. They can identify and reach out to opponents, present their alternative perspectives, and examine their arguments and factual claims. The news media can expose the truth by bringing to light clandestine activities, reports, and conversations. The views of the powerless, the reluctant, and the secretive can be sought and conveyed. The more the press scrutinizes government policy in this way, taking actions that lie at the heart of investigative journalism, the more the press can be judged as aiding democratic debate.

Finally, a well-informed public that deliberates over policy choices presented to it by competing political elites is the third essential ingredient in a healthy democracy (Benhabib 1996; Elkin and Soltan 1999; Rawls 1971). Deliberation here means that the public has "agency." Rather than deferring to others, members of the public use their own capacity for autonomous judgment to determine the best course of action. If democracy is meant to empower the public, it follows that a public that exhibits modest engagement and passive acquiescence is less democratic than a public that is thoughtful, critical, and informed (Bennett and Resnick 1990; Ladd 1978; Schattschneider 1960).[4]

Each of these three elements, taken separately, is vital to a functioning democracy. However, we should not conclude that each factor is independent of the others, each a solitary pillar. In the main, those who drafted the Constitution and the Bill of Rights, the first ten amendments to the Constitution, thought of them as intertwined and interdependent. A close reading of the First Amendment of the Constitution makes this interdependence quite clear. Table 1.1 explicates the common thread of freedom, information, and public debate within democracy, interweaving spirited debate and a free press to enable an energetic and competent electorate. This interdependence is evident in the construction of the First Amendment, which is written as one sentence consisting of three sequential clauses. The order of the clauses is meaningful as each clause is also a foundation for the clause that follows.

The authors of the Bill of Rights believed that the competence of the public and the vitality of the new republic would prove to be mutually reinforcing. Democracy requires multiple intertwined supporting elements, including the absence of an established religion and the positive endorsement of the diversity of religious expression, which together provide the foundation for a legally secured "public sphere" (Habermas 1989). This sphere allows for forceful and open public debate and proffers legal protection for political action that might challenge an existing government or its proposed course of action. Remove, or weaken, any of the precedents and the consequent result will diminish an active and assertive electorate.

In sum, democracy is in greater force when elites take different positions on grave policy matters, thereby generating the conditions for public debate. Democracy is in greater force when a free press covers the debate

TABLE 1.1 **The First Amendment and electorate competence**

First Amendment	Our explication
Congress shall make no law respecting an establishment of religion, or prohibiting the free exercise thereof;	An established religion limits by force of law religious expression to positive affirmation of the doctrine of the established church. Such a practice would preclude democratic contestation on any matters that fall under sway of the official religious doctrine. Hence by precluding an established religion and allowing the free exercise of religious belief, individual thought and collective practice are protected and thereby encouraged;
or abridging the freedom of speech, or of the press;	and, more expansively, the consequent freedom of thought can be better and safely expressed and debated in the public realm with the aid of an active and free press;
or the right of the people peaceably to assemble, and to petition the government for the redress of grievances.	so that the people can gather and, when they find common grievance, actively press their government for a favorable resolution.

and probes the claims so as to aid the public in its efforts to arrive at a well-informed opinion. Democracy is in greater force when the engaged public uses elite debate to inform its thoughtful judgment (Fishkin 1991; Warren 1996). And democracy is best served when all three conditions mutually reinforce one another.[5]

The Detrimental Effects of War on Democracy

It has long been understood that war is a robust danger to democracy. Democracy demands wide-ranging and open debate in the making of collective decisions. But war impels reliance on hierarchy and secrecy. Moreover, the normally high status of military service and patriotism are elevated to yet more lustrous levels.[6] During wartime, the military typically asserts more expansive claims to authority, thereby reducing civilian power. Further, war eclipses all other policy claims, which take second place to the demands for national victory.

With respect to information, the claim of a watchful and devious enemy is used to establish wide-ranging schemes of secrecy that often preclude congressional, let alone public, awareness of the true state of affairs (Wills 2010). Democracy presumes equality and, in the American variant, civilian control of the military as well as various checks and balances that empower an independent judiciary to secure the public's political and civil rights. Each of these factors—equality, civilian checks on the military, and judicial power—typically suffers during wartime (Polenberg 1987). Democracy presumes transparency in governmental matters, yet in wartime secrecy is often preeminent. In times of war, claims of national security readily trump concerns about democratic accountability. Democracy presumes the validity of contestation, yet in wartime patriotism can promote obedient subordination to a governing authority and subservience to current political doctrine.

Most of those who had fought to gain independence for the colonies from the rule of King George III, though mindful of the need for security against foreign invasion, nonetheless worried about the risks of a standing army in their new republic. More recently, observing the expansion of the US military to secure victory in World War II, and the manner in which states governed during war, Harold Lasswell (1941, 455) warned of a new world of "garrison states" wherein "the specialists on violence are the most powerful group in society."[7] This warning was amplified by George Orwell (1949) in his novel *1984*. The temptation of elites to use war to secure their authority was and remains a deep concern. At the heart of this warning is the trepidation that given the choice between security and liberty of thought and expression, the public would blindly endorse the former and willingly give up the latter (Fromm 1965).

When people confront an external threat they often find common purpose and comfort in traditional values, thereby securing sufficient solidarity to face the challenge (Feldman 2003; Feldman and Stenner 1997); their national identity is also brought to the fore and intensified, leading to greater conformity around common values and increased support for national leaders (Huddy 2013). While solidarity is of great value in achieving unity of purpose, it is, by its essential nature, antithetical to democratic debate.

Our discussion of democratic principles and practices underscores what is at stake in revisiting the dynamics of public opinion in the lead-up to the Iraq War. We return now to consider the specifics of that case. Conventional wisdom tells us that in the months before the war the Bush administration advanced claims of questionable veracity, that the political opposition failed to say much of anything, that the press was unable or unwilling to investigate the administration's claims, and that because of each of those facts, the public was left without needed information. The end result would seem to reflect poorly on the entire episode.

Going to War: Information and Elite Debate in the Fall of 2002

As the summer months of 2002 came to an end, the war in Afghanistan was ongoing and the impact of the 9/11 terrorist attacks persisted. The major figures in al Qaeda (Osama bin Laden and Ayman al-Zawahiri) and in the Taliban (Mullah Omar) remained at large. Right after the Labor Day weekend the Bush administration announced its new initiative to remove Saddam Hussein from power by any means, including war. During the six-week period from September through mid-October 2002, the administration presented its reasons for using military force in Iraq and, in the end, achieved its goal of securing congressional approval of its new Iraq policy.

On the evening of October 10, the United States House of Representatives voted for the bill known as the "Authorization for Use of Military Force against Iraq Resolution of 2002." The resolution in the House was introduced, jointly, by the Speaker of the House, Republican Denny Hastert, and the minority leader, Democratic congressman Dick Gephardt. The House vote was 296 in favor and 133 opposed. The United States Senate followed suit on the next day. In the Senate, the resolution was introduced, following the pattern of the House, by the two party leaders, Republican senator Trent Lott and Democratic senator Tom Daschle. The vote in the Senate was also one-sided: 77 in favor and 23 against. President George W. Bush signed the joint resolution into law on October 16, 2002. The war against Iraq and the regime of Saddam Hussein would not begin for another five months, but the likelihood of a new war against Iraq to be led and largely mounted by the United States was clear to one and all.

How well did the American political system function during this period? How successfully did American elites generate a debate on the merits of the war? How well did the free press cover that debate? How well did the American electorate engage the issue of whether to adopt or reject the Bush administration's initiative? We examine these questions in detail by focusing on the critical six-week period beginning just after Labor Day 2002 when the Bush administration made public its decision to overturn the Saddam Hussein regime and ending with passage in mid-October of the two bills in the House and Senate authorizing the use of military force against Iraq. We consider the actions of the players in our democratic triumvirate: political elites, the press, and, the public.

Political Elites Fail to Disagree

The Bush administration's campaign to gain public support for a war in Iraq was launched in earnest in early September of 2002. Though there had been talk earlier in the year of the administration's interest in pursuing Saddam Hussein, the campaign to secure public support for the war project was not mounted until after Labor Day. During the summer there was some public discussion of the administration's thinking about Saddam Hussein and his regime (which we discuss in greater detail in chapter 3). On August 15, Brent Scowcroft, the former national security advisor to President George H. W. Bush, published an editorial in the *Wall Street Journal*, questioning the administration's war plans. During the summer other politicians issued public warnings about a possible war. Still only the most attentive of voters would have caught these admonitions. Most members of the public encountered the new White House initiative in early September. The administration strove mightily to secure public endorsement of a war against Iraq during the six-week period between the announcement of this new policy in early September and congressional passage of the Iraq War Resolution in the middle of October.

The public's response to that initiative is the focus of this book. Did the administration secure the public's support for this policy? Or was support confined to certain segments of the population? And if so, why was the administration less than fully successful in its efforts to secure public backing for a war in Iraq?

Political circumstances created less than ideal conditions for the electorate to demonstrate thoughtfulness. If, as we argued above, democracy is at its best when two political parties publicly debate their differences, then a debate between a unified Democratic party, pressing back against the Bush proposal, never really materialized. Most of the major Democratic congressional figures acquiesced on the question of going to war against Iraq, although a minority of Democratic senators argued against the war or at least took issue with the administration's shifting war rationale. In chapters 3 and 4, we will cover the elite debate and the media coverage of that debate in greater detail, but here suffice it to say that there was some challenge to the Bush administration's proposal. The administration faced questions from Republican senator "Chuck" Hagel of Nebraska and from Democratic senators Byrd, Durbin, Feingold, Graham, and Kennedy and other members of the liberal wing of the Democratic Party. Thus, debate was not completely absent. Nonetheless, it is fair to conclude that elite debate over the merits was more muted than full throated. As the vote margins in the House and the Senate demonstrate, Bush's new initiative was better characterized as bipartisanship, backed by near complete Republican and substantial Democratic support, than vigorous partisan debate.

The Press Fails to Critically Evaluate the Administration's Claims

If democracy is at its best when the press actively investigates a proposed policy or course of government action, then its reportage on the administration's claims concerning a war in Iraq is far from exemplary. As in the case of elite debate, the performance of the free press requires detailed consideration. We provide such detail in chapters 3 and 4. Here, we can say that the performance of the press was not as neutered as many critiques have claimed (Rich 2006). Our more complete examination does indicate a robust pattern of uncritical treatment of administration assertions within the news media and a tendency to diminish or ignore critical views on the part of television news and, notably, the *New York Times* on the issue of Iraq's possession of WMD. But our examination shows that regional newspapers, including those owned by Knight Ridder, performed far better than the national televised news and other media sources.

The broad portrait of an uncritical and pro-war press misses this important difference among media outlets and has thus masked the antiwar effects of regional newspapers on American public opinion. Though newspaper readership has steadily declined since 2002, at that time roughly 60% of Americans read a daily newspaper (Cohen 2010). And as we show in chapters 5, and 6, whether members of the public, specifically Democrats and political independents, obtained their news from television or newspapers affected how they understood the administration's claims and whether they supported or opposed the proposed war.

The Public under Threat

Finally, the propensity of publics to "rally to the flag" when faced with an external threat has been well documented (Brody 1991; Gadarian 2010; Groeling and Baum 2008; McCann 1997). And with the public still reeling from the 9/11 terrorist attacks and confronted with the administration's claims that Saddam Hussein had weapons of mass destruction and ties to al Qaeda, the public faced not one but two intertwined external threats. The major leaders of al Qaeda and the Taliban remained free to plot and kill wherever they chose to strike. And the new and sudden re-emergence of Saddam Hussein, purportedly armed with weapons of mass destruction and in alliance with al Qaeda, loomed as a prominent threat to the United States. In confronting two major existential threats during the "war on terrorism," the public had to consider the merits of launching a new war in less than optimal democratic conditions, under duress when circumstances predisposed them to support the administration as an act of national solidarity.

The absence of vigorous political debate should have eased the Bush administration's task of gaining public endorsement for the war. The less than vigorous challenge by much, if not all, of the press ought to have made the task of gaining public support easier still. And a public still shaken by the greatest terror attack in US history and fighting a "war against terrorism" in Afghanistan with the enemy leadership still free should have made some individuals, especially those with authoritarian leanings, even more compliant and ready to endorse the administration's new venture.[8] Taken together then, these factors bode poorly for the existence of a fully informed and reasoned public debate among Americans on the advantages and disadvantages of going to war against Iraq. The expectation that the Bush administration would find it easy to rally broad public support for its objectives in Iraq is further strengthened by the dominant scholarly view of public opinion.

Conventional Expectations: Public Opinion Driven by Elite Influence

Walter Lippmann, before he wrote his classic book *Public Opinion*, worked in the Wilson administration during World War I. There he saw up close how easy it was to create heroes of even the most inept of generals, how easy it was to create a sustained fervor in support of the war, and how easy it was to generate disdain and hatred for the enemy among the American public (Lippmann 1922). He argued that because the public lived far removed from foreign affairs in general, and the execution of war in particular, they were especially reliant on elite messages to shape their responses.[9] Because the public had no direct knowledge of what was happening "out there," on the battlefields or, more generally, in the war, they would have only opinions, opinions given to them by elites. This suggested that however well, or badly, the public mastered domestic policy details, citizens are especially vulnerable to elite manipulation on matters of foreign policy, generally, and war, specifically.

Since that time, research has led scholars of public opinion within mainstream American political science to affirm Lippmann's view that elite opinion is the prime mover of public opinion, and not just on foreign policy (Lenz 2012; Mueller 1999; Page and Shapiro 1992; Zaller 1992). The dominant view in political science has largely portrayed the public as eagerly compliant with elite opinion, at best, and disinterested, ill-informed, and incapable of political judgment, at worst (Bishop 2005; Converse 1970; Ginsberg 1986; Lippmann 1922). This culminates in the prevailing view of public opinion as a "top-down" phenomenon driven largely by powerful elite messages (Brody 1991; McGuire 1969; Zaller 1992).

What has led social scientists to doubt the capacity of an electorate in a representative democracy to function independently of political elites? First, elections and other forms of political participation in several countries in the period between the two world wars suggested that large segments of publics in European societies would choose authoritarian and militant regimes over democratic rule. Fascist regimes emerged between the wars in Spain, Italy, Germany, and, later, Austria, with considerable, if not always generally majoritarian, public support. The universal appeal of democratic rule seemed heavily overestimated by democracy's advocates (Fromm 1965).

Second, the development of survey research in the United States provided scholars with direct access to the political beliefs, attitudes, and values of the "average" American. As survey research began in earnest after World War II, data on the American electorate provided a new blow to the progressive hopes for the spread of democratic rule. Many, indeed most, voters were found to be largely uninformed about public affairs, disinterested in politics, and lacking any deep principles that might organize their political views. Reflecting on the early research, most notably Philip Converse's (1964) influential paper "The Nature of Belief Systems in Mass Publics," Don Kinder (2006, 214) summarized the prevailing conclusion thusly: "By any reasonable standard, Americans are affluent, well educated, and virtually swimming in news of politics. And yet despite these advantages, most Americans glance at the political world mystified by its abstractions and ignorant of its particulars. So it was, according to Converse, nearly a half century ago, and so, by and large, it remains today."

In reflecting on what he has learned about American public opinion in over fifty years of research, Philip Converse came to a similar conclusion even on a matter of direct experience to most voters: the issue of estate taxes. He wrote: "My main concern about the limited information that voters bring to the ballot box is that they are prey to unscrupulous interests who can play off their gullibility" (2006, 323). If the public is so thoroughly ill-informed and gullible to adopt positions directly contrary to their own self-interest, then it is hardly surprising that the public can be easily driven to support war even when supported by claims of only slight merit.[10] From this perspective, then, on the matter of deciding whether to go to war, the public takes its guidance from elites who are in a position to craft persuasive messages (Berinsky 2007; Mueller 1973).

This portrait of a largely passive and receptive public has led many observers to conclude that the public is too trusting and hence unlikely to place brakes on elite inclinations to go to war. Thus, when in 2002 the Bush administration announced its plan to eliminate Saddam Hussein as the leader of Iraq, using all the devices available to a determined president, an effort little challenged by the elected Democratic opposition leaders, an effort not given much searching examination by the press, what options did the public have but going with the call to arms? How could a public confronting such a unified, intense, and largely unchallenged elite message resist?

The formidable power of elite opinion was on full display in the lead-up to the Iraq War. In the fall of 2002 the elected leaders of the Democratic party, mindful of the negative political fallout that accompanied their opposition to the successful Persian Gulf War in 1991, were wary about opposing what was expected to be another easy victory in Iraq. Further, the effects of 9/11 had generated a powerful rally effect lending substantial support to the Bush administration in matters of foreign policy. Indeed three future Democratic leaders, Senators John Kerry, the 2004 Democratic presidential candidate, John Edwards, Kerry's vice presidential running mate, and Hillary Clinton, who competed with Barack Obama for the Democratic presidential nomination in 2008, endorsed the Iraq War Resolution.

The Elite Influence Model

The elite influence model of American public opinion, as we have characterized it above, requires further discussion. Within the elite influence account, the public is seen as largely incapable of independent and competent political judgment and lacks the expertise for, or commitment to, the task of managing political affairs. But it is costly to summarily reject the public in this way as it removes the necessary foundation for legitimate rule: the public's express endorsement of elected leaders. As a result, the elite influence view of public opinion achieves a balance by endorsing the necessary involvement of the public in the electoral process at least sufficient to convey legitimacy to governing elites, but it assigns these popularly elected elites the more challenging task of policy formation and execution (Sartori 1987; Schumpeter 1943).

That leaves us with the specific task of explaining how the public responds to elite policy claims and proposals. That is the question that John Zaller (1992) takes up in his magisterial volume *The Nature and Origins of Mass Opinion*. In his account, the public is cast in the role of audience observing a political spectacle. Building on social psychologist Bill Mc-Guire's (1969) model of persuasion, Zaller (1996) develops an elegant and simple model of public opinion involving three key factors: "the amount and directional thrust of information carried in the mass media, people's differential attention to this information, and people's political values" (Zaller 1991, 84). This boils down to two key psychological processes at the individual level: whether one is exposed to a specific message and whether one accepts the message content.

Zaller names his model the reception-acceptance-sampling (RAS) model of persuasion. Overall, it produces a classic U-shaped curve of message influence or persuasion across different levels of public attentiveness. The least politically engaged remain unexposed and thus immune to elite influence. The most politically engaged are unchanged. Ample research has shown that in the main strong partisans remain loyal to their party by downplaying the arguments and facts advanced by their political opponents (Kunda 1990; Lodge and Taber 2000; Redlawsk 2002). This leaves the moderately engaged political middle, political moderates and independents, as the most readily persuaded by elites, because they are exposed to the ongoing flow of information but lack a strong partisan or ideological basis on which to reject powerful and persuasive political messages.

According to Zaller (1992, 325–28), this process can work effectively to promote democracy but depends on four key ingredients: first, "predispositional differences among the experts paralleling those within the general public" to ensure that citizens accept and reject the correct messages according to their partisan affiliation; second, "institutional incentives" for experts to develop effective policy solutions so that good competing options are presented to political elites; third, a press that covers all viewpoints; and, fourth, politicians who "keep within the parameters of expert opinion." In a recent reevaluation of the RAS model, Zaller (2012) largely sticks with his original conception.

The resultant view of the public is less than flattering. Zaller (1992, 311) concludes his book in this fashion:

> The argument of this book is, on first inspection, scarcely encouraging with respect to domination of mass opinion by elites. Many citizens, as was argued, pay too little attention to public affairs to be able to respond critically to the political communications they encounter; rather, they are blown about by whatever current of information manages to develop the greatest intensity. The minority of citizens who are highly attentive to public affairs are scarcely more critical: they respond to new issues mainly on the basis of the partisanship and ideology of the elite sources of the messages.
>
> If many citizens are largely uncritical in their response to political communications as carried in the mass media, and most of the rest respond mechanically on the basis of partisan cues, how can one deny the existence of substantial elite domination of public opinion?

Zaller (1992, 312) answers his own question with the following normative solution: "The real problem is guaranteeing the existence of an equally vigorous competition among opposing ideas." This brings us back to the partisan and ideological nature of Zaller's model. According to Zaller, the overall volume of elite messages and their partisan balance constitute the "information flow" that reaches the public. If the major political players align behind a single message, then the information flow is "one-sided" or bipartisan. If partisan elites are divided, sending conflicting messages, then the public has the option of choosing between two sides. When the information flow is "two-sided," the movement of public opinion is determined by the weight and balance of the respective partisan messages. We argued earlier that a well-functioning democracy requires just this kind of vigorous partisan debate.

Zaller (1991, 1992) provides a compelling example of this process at work in an analysis of public opinion on the Vietnam War. Americans of all political stripes came to increasingly support the Vietnam War between 1964 and 1966 in a period when it was backed by congressional elites of both parties. In this early phase of the war, the most attentive of citizens strongly supported it because they were most likely to have been exposed to a bipartisan pro-war message regardless of their liberal/conservative ideology or general hawk/dove position on military action. From

1966 onward, however, there was a growing chorus of war opposition from liberal and Democratic elites to which the most attentive were exposed. This generated growing opposition to the war among the best-informed liberals, giving them ammunition with which to counteract conservative pro-war arguments. In contrast, less well-informed liberals continued to support the war because they had not yet been exposed to antiwar arguments. By 1970 the flow of liberal antiwar information had increased further to reach almost all liberals, who now realized that their ideological leaders opposed the war and quickly fell into line behind them. In contrast, conservatives supported the war throughout the entire time period, between 1964 and 1970, with greatest support for the war among those who were paying the most attention to politics and thus exposed maximally to pro-war conservative messages.

Elite Influence and the Iraq War: The Public as Audience

The elite influence model generates specific predictions about pro- and antiwar public opinion in the months leading up to the Iraq War. There was a faint glimpse of a possible war with Iraq in the summer of 2002. The administration was actively discussing the war, but for the most part these discussions occurred outside of the public's view. There had been low-level rumblings by congressional Democrats earlier in the year that the administration was insufficiently consulting with them on war, and some Republican angst surfaced in the summer concerning the wisdom of a war with Iraq (discussed in greater detail in chapter 3). Nonetheless, such utterances and writings remained low profile. The information environment changed dramatically, however, in early September 2002, when the administration launched its campaign to secure public support for the looming war. In the period from September through October 2002, the elite debate was powerfully pro-war on the Republican side and confusingly mixed on the Democratic side, with little antiwar rhetoric from the major Democratic congressional leaders and some more visible opposition from a handful of Democratic senators. As the time to vote on the Iraq War Resolution arrived, most of the Democratic congressional leadership endorsed Bush's initiative for war.

Given muted partisan disagreement over the war, the elite influence model predicts growing support for the war in September and October of 2002 among the major segments of the American electorate: Republicans, Democrats, and independents. The absence of powerful Democratic opposition to a possible war with Iraq at this time should have resulted

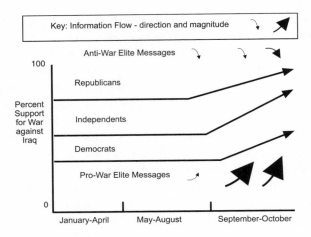

FIGURE I.I Expected dynamics: Elite messages and support for war against Iraq

Note: Readers familiar with the mainstream "normal vote" model developed by Philip Converse and his colleagues (Campbell et al. 1960) will see the similarity between figure 1.1 and the figure that has come to be known in the field as "waves of grain" in Converse (1966).

in modest and stable partisan differences on the war, with greater support for the war among Republicans than Democrats. The elite influence model predicts growing or sustained war support in the fall of 2002 among Republicans and increasing support among Democrats and political independents, especially the most politically attentive who were most likely to be exposed to the administration's pro-war message and would have encountered mixed and confusing signals from leading Democratic politicians. High-profile senators John Kerry, John Edwards, Hillary Clinton, Harry Reid, Joe Biden, and majority leader Tom Daschle voted for the Iraq War Resolution whereas others, including Senators Kennedy, Feingold, Durbin, Graham, and Leahy, and a number of congressional House Democrats, gained media attention as war opponents (we discuss the information environment more fully in chapter 4).

Of course, these are general expectations, and not all Republicans, independents, or Democrats are expected to change their position on the war in response to the administration's pro-war campaign to the degree depicted in figure 1.1. As we have already noted at some length, attentive partisans are the first to be influenced by partisan messages, and we would expect sophisticated Democrats, Republicans, and independents to have been the most attentive and most persuaded by the administration's message and bipartisan support in the first weeks of September 2002. Still, all in all, the aggregate pattern is clear. Given the one-sided nature of partisan elite messages in this prewar time period, public opinion should have moved in the fall of 2002 to greater support for a war to overthrow Saddam Hussein's regime in Iraq.

The Public Responds: Two Conundrums

As we move from early September 2002 to the end of October, we should thus see growing public support for a war in Iraq in synchrony with elite opinion and the broad information flow if public opinion is largely driven by the views of political elites. We are fortunate that the major public polling operations had regularly asked Americans if they would endorse, or oppose, taking military action against Iraq, dating back to the onset of the 1991 Gulf War and continuing thereafter (Everts and Isernia 2005). That polling became especially intense in 2002, beginning well before the summer of 2002 and continuing through the fall and into the winter. Political scientist Gary Jacobson (2007) collected polling data on this core question and has kindly made them available to us. We focus on the period from January 2002 to the end of the year. The public's opinion about whether to support military action against Iraq is displayed in figure 1.2, depicting how Republican, independent, and Democratic public opinion changed over the course of the year.

As expected, we see little movement in public opinion during the first part of the year. But in the summer and early fall the trends depicted in figure 1.2 diverge from those we laid out in figure 1.1. The elite influence model, as shown in figure 1.1, predicts growing public support for military action against Iraq in the fall of 2002 in light of evidence of a heavily one-sided "information flow," the largely unopposed Bush administration campaign to generate public support for the war. But that is not what is evident in figure 1.2.

Here, in table 1.2, are the two conundrums. While exposed to a concerted campaign to drive public opinion, neither Democrats nor political independents responded with greater support for the war. According to elite influence models, both groups should have moved to align themselves with the new call to arms, but they did not. Moreover, declining Democratic support for the war occurred in the absence of strong signals from their partisan leaders about the war. There is even a slight decline in Republican support for the war after the administration's rollout in early

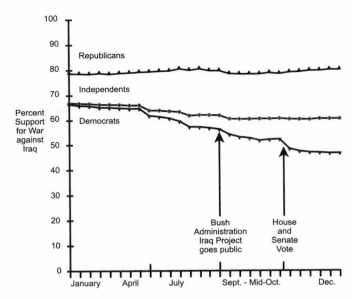

FIGURE 1.2 American public opinion on support for military action in Iraq, by party identification, January to December 2002

Source: Jacobson (2007).
Note: As noted in Gary Jacobson's book (2007), these data are not evenly distributed across the months but are sufficiently spread out to generate the trends depicted above.

September 2002 before support flattens out to end up in mid-December somewhere near its starting point.[11]

Zaller's account is not the only version of an elite influence model. Adam Berinsky (2009) offers a revised account, which he refers to as an elite cue model, to account for the failure of the elite influence model to predict a decline in Democratic support for an Iraq war in the fall of 2002. After reviewing the full array of American wars from World War II to Iraq, he concluded that "a large portion of the citizenry judge the wisdom of war by following the cues provided by trusted politicians" (214). He adjusts Zaller's model to argue that elites can drive public opinion simply by signaling their support or opposition to a given policy—Republican elite support can generate opposition to a policy among rank-and-file Democrats just as Democratic support arouses opposition among rank-and-file Republicans. In the context of the Iraq War, the Bush administration's war support would have been sufficient to generate Democratic war opposition even if Democratic elites were divided on the war. According to

Berinsky, such political signaling could occur independently of the combined bipartisan balance and flow of information, and thus salvage the
elite influence model.[12]

The problem with Berinsky's interpretation is that a bare majority of
Democrats in figure 1.2 continued to support the war in September and
October of 2002 even though it took very little information to understand
that military action in Iraq was being forcefully advocated by President
Bush. If all Democrats needed to know was that George W. Bush strongly
supported military intervention in Iraq in order to conclude they should
oppose the war it is hard to see why Democrats were so divided in the fall
of 2002. Ultimately, we find only very limited and inconsistent support for
this supposition. We address Berinsky's argument more fully in chapter 6
and note here that it leaves largely unexplained declining Democratic
support for the war in the months before its onset. Berinsky's approach
also fails to explain growing opposition to the war among political independents. This leaves unresolved our two conundrums concerning declining Democratic and independent public support for the war in the fall
of 2002.

There have been several other recent modifications of the elite influence model on war-related public opinion. Hayes and Guardino (2013)
uncover evidence of pervasive foreign opposition to the Iraq War on
television and argue that French, German, Iraqi, and other international
leaders influenced well-informed Democrats and independents to oppose

TABLE 1.2 **Two conundrums: Citizens' responses to elite information flows**

The first conundrum
An examination of the support for military action against Iraq among Democratic partisans shows a clear and steady decline that begins before the administration's Iraq policy rollout. That decline occurs in the context of mixed and muted war opposition from congressional Democrats. However, the decline strengthens just as the administration launches its campaign for war in the absence of strong Democratic opposition.

The second conundrum
Support for the war declines among independents in a similar direction to that observed for Democratic partisans. Yet because independents have no ideological or partisan anchors, they should be responsive to the pro-war information flow. Zaller's model asserts that their only protection against elite influence is their political inattention. But inattentive independents, having received no strong antiwar elite messages, should have remained unmoved or shifted toward war support. Thus, it is surprising to find no evidence of an increase in independent support for the war. Indeed, during the summer months there is a modest decline in support, weaker but parallel to that of Democrats.

the war. One problem with this interpretation, however, is that Iraqis were the most vocal antiwar sources on television in Hayes and Guardino's analysis, and it is difficult to view them as a highly credible source for the American public. No matter how good their arguments, Iraqis were a self-interested source of questionable reliability. We also find strong evidence against this interpretation in our data to which we return in chapter 5.[13]

Research on Public Opinion and War

Zaller's model of public opinion dynamics, grounded in elite influence, does not go unchallenged. Within international relations, scholars of war opinion have advanced an alternative perspective that emphasizes the power of events to influence public opinion, an approach that may help to explain why some Democrats and independents increasingly opposed an Iraq war in the fall of 2002. Wars offer a rich field in which to examine the public's ability to respond to events independent of elite-driven claims because they are replete with both costly and beneficial events that require little explanation such as casualties, battles lost, battles won, ground gained, and the destruction of enemy armies and navies. Given evidence that the public increasingly opposes war as casualties mount, supports war as the prospect of victory increases, and is willing to go to war to defend vital US interests and further US foreign policy goals, some political scientists conclude that the public can deliberate independently and capably on matters of foreign policy (Aldrich, Sullivan, and Borgida 1989; Aldrich et al. 2006; Page and Shapiro 1992).

In support of this conclusion, Bruce Jentleson analyzes American opinion on wars that occurred over several decades and finds that the rationale for war, such as a serious threat to national security, typically promotes support for military action (Jentleson 1992; Jentleson and Britton 1998). Richard Herrmann, Philip Tetlock, and Penny Visser (1999) examine public deliberation concerning the use of military force abroad by presenting Americans with different scenarios in a series of experiments. They find that the prevailing political context, including the strength and perceived malevolence of an opponent, is critical to war support.

When taken together, research by Jentleson, Herrmann, and their respective colleagues underscores the power of national threats to shape public opinion. What can be gained or lost in a possible conflict? Is a military conflict worth the investment of time, money, and, most importantly, lives that might be lost? These are sensible questions that were highly germane to the decision of whether to wage war with Iraq in the fall of 2002. The conclusion that the public responds to reasonable features of a foreign policy situation is further endorsed by international relations and political communications scholars. A number of these researchers argue that pragmatic features of a conflict, such as the number of casualties and the prospect of victory, drive public opinion (Gelpi, Feaver, and Reifler 2005; Gelpi, Reifler, and Feaver 2007). Once begun, wars generate casualties. John Mueller's classic volume (1973) considers the impact of events on public opinion and reports that support for war is inversely related to casualty counts. Rising US military casualties, accelerating casualties, or a loss of local military personnel generate opposition to an ongoing war (Gartner 2008; Gartner and Segura 1998; Karol and Miguel 2007; Larson 1996; Mueller 1973). The framing of military casualties and their uneven spread across socioeconomic groups further enhance the influence of casualties on war opinion (Boettcher and Cobb 2006, 2009; Kriner and Shen 2014).

Researchers working from this rational or pragmatic approach to foreign policy opinion are not in complete unanimity; they disagree on the relative effects of casualty counts, whether it is absolute or relative casualty rates that matter more, and to what degree the perception of victory and the degree of threat to US interests affect public opinion. Nonetheless, the pragmatic event-based approach points to the importance of ongoing events and their perceived future trajectory as essential to understanding public opinion. Elites obviously attempt to shape public expectations about the course of a future war, but public support depends ultimately on how a war is seen to play out, what goals it is likely to achieve, and whether it will succeed.

The event-based account of war opinion is credible, has garnered considerable support from international relations scholars, and is consistent with growing isolationism in the American public in reaction to casualties incurred in Iraq, Afghanistan, Somalia, and elsewhere (Aldrich, Sullivan, and Borgida 1989; Aldrich et al. 2006). Overall, this account stresses the public's ability to reason rationally and carefully evaluate ongoing events and related information to shape their support or opposition to war. However, this account is more difficult to apply to the period of interest to us, because war-related events had yet to occur. Nonetheless, in the preamble to war many claims and counterclaims are made about the nature and imminence of national threat, the likelihood of victory, the degree and ferocity of enemy resistance, and the magnitude of military casualties. An event-based model suggests that the public can sift through such claims and counterclaims to determine the necessity of war.

A reasoned or pragmatic account of war-related public opinion thus serves as a viable alternative to the dominant elite influence model, and we give it careful consideration in the coming chapters in an effort to re-solve the conundrums we have outlined concerning public support for a possible war in Iraq in the fall of 2002. Questions about the threat posed to the United States by Saddam Hussein, his involvement in the 9/11 ter-ror attacks, and the degree to which he posed a threat to US allies in the Middle East were paramount considerations in whether to launch a war in Iraq. Information concerning Saddam's connections to al Qaeda, his ca-pacity and inclination to use WMD on the United States or his neighbors, his motives, and other related facts were critical to the determination that the United States needed to deploy military troops in Iraq.

As we have made clear, we believe the data shown in figure 1.2 chal-lenge the presumption that elite influence is the sole and primary mover of public opinion.[14] But that does not mean that we unabashedly adopt an event-based or pragmatic model either. In synch with an event-based model, our explanation of the trajectory of public opinion portrayed in figure 1.2 incorporates the public's (Democrats' and independents') care-ful examination of information, leading us to conclude that the public has some independent capacity for judgment. But we also need to make clear that whether the public engages in a careful examination of events or suc-cumbs to simple elite influence depends on several crucial psychological conditions that influence how information is processed. In the following section, we consider these various factors to better account for the pat-tern of Democratic and independent war support observed in figure 1.2. In providing a brief overview of the psychology of war opinion we hope to shed greater light on the circumstances under which the public follows its partisan elites, resorts to a more independent and careful analysis of the evidence, or does a little of both.

The Political Psychology of Convictions and Political Judgment

The elite influence model conceives of the public as passive and dependent on elite cues, but there is much to be learned about public opinion from political psychologists and psychologists who have studied the process of persuasion and influence. Over the past twenty-plus years, there has been growing consensus that people arrive at political judgments by one of two different pathways. The elaboration likelihood model proposed by Richard Petty and John Cacioppo (1986) provides the first complete account of these two pathways. This approach has consolidated around what has come to be called the dual process model of judgment (Chaiken and Trope 1999; Evans 2008).[15] In one pathway, political decisions are relatively effortless and involve time- and energy-saving shortcuts or heuristics. When information is processed via this pathway, cues are taken from trusted leaders of one's political party, or information is accepted that is concordant with prior beliefs and convictions. Little further scrutiny is given to factual claims, logical consistency, or strength of argumentation. The decision process inherent in the elite influence model is consistent with this pathway and assumes little independent judgment on the part of the public.

The second pathway involves far greater thoughtful effort and much closer scrutiny of factual arguments. When arriving at decisions in this way, people consider information carefully, thereby coming to a decision through the exercise of reasoned judgment. In effect, when using this path, people are exercising what we previously called agency; they are thinking and doing so for themselves.

Thus, when people express a judgment, such as an opinion about an impending war, that judgment can be generated by one of two means. First, most commonly, it could involve little thought and simply mirror the positions adopted by the leaders of one's favored political party or a trusted source such as the president. But secondly, perhaps not so commonly, people can sort through the facts and seek out differing opinions before coming to a measured conclusion. In brief, political judgment can be the result of deliberative reflection.[16] As we will see, this does not necessarily ensure an unbiased decision but it does involve greater mental effort. And without the public airing of competing views, hard-to-obtain factual information, and detailed and well-documented arguments, it is unlikely to be especially productive or lead to positions very different from those that arise through the less effortful use of partisan cues. As we argue below, there is a clear need to examine the way in which the press conveys to the public a range of elite voices, partisan and nonpartisan, and their competing facts and arguments in order to understand the conditions under which citizens are enabled to engage in fruitful reasoning that is independent of political elites.

The path taken by members of the public, and the quality of their reasoning regardless of pathway, depends crucially on motivation (Kunda 1990; Leeper and Slothus 2014): its level, which can be low or high, and its nature, which varies between a desire for accuracy and a defense of one's existing beliefs (for a clear exposition of this model in a political context, see Lavine, Johnston, and Steenbergen 2012). When people are not motivated to think intensely about a political situation, they are likely to succumb to partisan influence as the easy way out. This situation often prevails in politics and is especially pronounced among strongly affiliated partisans. But that is not the only situation in which partisan elites dominate political decision making. Party cues also prevail when people are motivated to think hard about a situation, such as at the moment of a possible war, and are quite satisfied with the position outlined by their partisan elites. Why think hard about something if it is not necessary? This is the situation in which we believe Republicans found themselves in September and October of 2002. President Bush and his top aides indicated the necessity of a war with Iraq, and Republicans followed their lead and supported going to war. Well-informed Republicans should have been most likely to support the war because they learned earlier and more fully of the administration's pro-war stance. When taken together, the best-informed Republicans would have felt most confident in adopting the administration's pro-war position (Taber and Lodge 2006). In this respect, Republicans conform most closely to the expectations of the elite influence model.

However, Democrats found themselves in a very different situation. If their elites had provided a strong pro- or antiwar message, they may also have followed such cues in line with the elite influence model. But that was not the case, as we show in chapters 3 and 4. Some Democratic politicians did raise questions about the war. But not all did so. Thus Democrats confronted a set of mixed signals from their leaders. A majority of Democratic senators and a minority of Democratic members in the House voted to authorize President Bush to use military force in Iraq in the fall of 2002. Other Democratic members of Congress appeared in the news questioning the need for a war. Such mixed signals from partisan elites would have left many Democrats uncertain as to what position to adopt on the war. On one hand, it was supported by the Republican administration, a potential negative cue for Democrats. But at the same time their partisan leaders were providing insufficiently clear guidance. Under these conditions, we believe Democrats shifted from an easy reliance on partisan cues, no longer so evident, to a search for more accurate information that resulted in careful and deliberate thought (Bolsen, Druckman, and Cook 2014).

This does not mean, however, that Democrats eradicated all partisan considerations as they thought about the war, even when motivated to arrive at the "right" position in the absence of clear partisan signals. It is actually very difficult for partisans to eradicate all thoughts of their party when deliberating about politics (Lodge and Taber 2013; Taber and Lodge 2006). With mixed pro- and antiwar signals from Democratic politicians, Democrats may have been inclined to not only seek information but also seek antiwar information and weigh it more heavily in part as a reaction to George W. Bush's strong support for the war (Chen, Duckworth, and Chaiken 1999). As we show in the following chapters, Democrats that did so were empowered by some segments of the press that provided critical examination of the administration's various claims about the necessity and justification for war.

This leaves political independents whose support for the war also declined in the fall of 2002. If independents had simply accepted the predominant elite messaging of this period, in line with the predictions of the elite influence model, they should have followed the Republican pro-war "information flow" and supported the war. Unlike Democrats, they had no specific partisan agenda that could have offered a defense against Republican messaging. But that is not what happened. What might have induced independents to undertake the more deliberate reasoning that would lead them toward war opposition? Our answer is that, like Democrats, some independents who were motivated to seek out and carefully process additional information were exposed to critical and credible information that led them to oppose the war. In many ways, political independents provide the best test of our supposition that in the fall of 2002 a subset of Americans engaged in deliberate information processing that involved the careful consideration of hard-to-find facts and arguments made by experts and other nonpartisan sources. We show in chapter 5 that, with no political agenda and no obvious grudge against George W. Bush or the Republican Party, independents exposed to information critical of the Bush administration became increasingly opposed to the war and doubtful of the administration's claims.

We conclude that many Democrats and independents were stimulated to think carefully about a war in Iraq and progressively opposed the war in September and October of 2002. We demonstrate that this decline was the result of exposure to information that challenged the dominant prowar view. But from where did this information arise? Democrats and independents may have been motivated to seek information critical of the administration's case for war, but this information also had to exist and be readily available. But where?

The Free Press and the Engaged Public

In assessing the dynamics of public opinion, Zaller's parsimonious elite influence model gives ample attention to elites and the public but far too little attention to the media, a weakness which Zaller (2012) has recently acknowledged. The press plays a critical role as a purveyor of elite views; it is also the major conduit from which the public obtains factual information about war, its success or failure, mounting casualties, and the successful defense of national interests. Without the press, the public would lack even the most rudimentary information about foreign policy, or any public policy for that matter. We return to the role of the press here and in far greater detail in chapters 3 and 4 to assess not only its coverage of elite messages in the buildup to the Iraq War, but also the degree to which it conveyed and critically evaluated the administration's factual claims concerning Saddam Hussein, his possession of WMD, links to terrorists, and aggressive intentions toward the United States. In Zaller and Berinsky's shared conception of elite influence, the media's principal task is to convey the full array of elite opinion to the public. The media fails when it favors some views, such as those of the administration, over others. It also fails when it mischaracterizes some elite views, conveys an inaccurate picture of the balance of elite opinion, overreports some elite views, or omits a segment of elite views entirely. In a free society with a commercial market-oriented press, editors and reporters have some considerable but not unconstrained independence in deciding what and how to cover news stories. But in times of war, the press is not free from self- and government-imposed rules concerning national secrecy. As Baum and Groeling (2010) note in thorough detail (discussed at greater length in chapter 3), elites and the press have their respective interests to serve in determining what they wish to reveal to the public.

One way to gauge bias within media coverage is to ask whether the quantity and balance of opinions convey and probe the substance of elite debate. Much of the research on elite and media influence gets at this by indexing the volume of pro and con messages, which typically reflect the positions adopted by politicians in the major parties (Bennett 1990). This creates the foundation for Zaller's elite influence model in which arguments and facts are packaged in partisan bundles with great-est resonance among the best-informed partisans. But under conditions of bipartisanship, the press must go beyond the relatively easy task of indexing and conveying the views of the major political parties to consider other sources of opinion. This may involve seeking out a far wider range of voices and require active investigation.

In this we harken back to Thomas Jefferson. Jefferson is known for many contributions to the founding of the United States. Among those is his consistent and vocal support for a free press as a vital foundation for sustaining a democratic regime. In his view much depends on the press to enable citizens to perform their task of separating the wheat from the chaff. Typical is this statement from a letter to General Lafayette: "The only security of all is in a free press. The force of public opinion cannot be resisted when permitted freely to be expressed. The agitation it produces must be submitted to. It is necessary, to keep the waters pure" (Jefferson 1903–1904, 15:491).[17]

In the context of bipartisan agreement on a possible war with Iraq, advocated by a popular president in the aftermath of a major terrorist at-tack on US soil, a free press required independent and courageous news organizations and journalists who were willing to dig below the surface to assess the administration's claims. As Alex Jones (2009) notes, this task of investigative journalism is most likely to be performed by the print media as exemplified by Bob Woodward and Carl Bernstein's legendary cover-age of the Watergate scandal in the *Washington Post*. It is well known that major newspapers, such as the *New York Times*, were subsequently excoriated for their inaccurate reporting on Iraq's possession of WMD and other matters linked to an impending war with Iraq. Nonetheless, as we will see in chapters 3 and 4, there were substantive differences between how television and print media covered news of the Bush administration's pro-war campaign. And these differences help to solve the conundrum of declining war support among Democrats and independents in the fall of 2002 just when the Bush administration was making its most ardent case for war.

Political Elites, the Press, and the Public: A Roadmap

In this book, we seek to resolve two specific conundrums concerning pub-lic opinion in the lead-up to the Iraq War. Our purpose is twofold: first, to better understand the views of the American public at that time and, second, to shed light on broad theories of public opinion. The established position within political science is that the public has limited capacity to deliberate on key issues of the day and requires the guidance and direction of political elites. As Converse, Zaller, and others argue, democracy depends on the effective contestation of competing elites to enable an otherwise disengaged and ill-informed public to perform the limited task of choosing among contending elites for leadership and to endorse, or reject, various elite initiatives. The dominant account portrays a democratic electorate of limited competence and therefore endorses a very modest role for the public, as consumer of products sold to it by its betters (Sartori 1987; Schumpeter 1943; Mueller 1999). Thus, it largely endorses the older view of publics as readily gulled into whatever programs elites choose to present (Ginsberg 1986; Hobbes 1968; Lippmann 1922; Plato 1974).

Our analysis of the formation of public opinion in September–October 2002 presents a different tale, and one that is in synch with recent political psychology research. The account we offer is one in which the public confronts a challenge: an important and high-stakes issue, a difficult information environment in which a popular administration identifies a threat from a hated former enemy absent much criticism from the opposing political party, and the news media provides largely supportive but occasionally critical coverage of the administration's claims based on diverse sources including the views of nonpartisan experts. Some members of the public perform better than expected, absorbing factual information that leads them to be skeptical of the administration's claims concerning Iraq. In that sense, a subset of the press allowed some members of the public to move from elite reliance and toward self-reliance.

In the six chapters that follow we take up the following challenges. In chapter 2, "The Skeptical Citizen: Public Uneasiness about Waging War in Iraq," we rely on data from the Threat and National Security Survey (TNSS; Huddy et al. 2005), the American National Election Studies (ANES), and polling data from the Pew Research Center for the People and the Press to flesh out Americans' views on the war in the fall of 2002. We confirm the differences in war support among Republicans, Democrats, and independents observed by Jacobson (2007), and go further to reveal even stronger Democratic and independent opposition to the war in response to a broader array of polling questions. The trends laid out in chapter 2 create the foundation for the following chapters. In chapter 3, "Political Leaders Set the Stage for War," we provide an in-depth account of the information environment surrounding the buildup to the Iraq War. We cover in detail the media's reporting on the Iraq war proposal and the arguments and evidence presented by the administration, and discuss differences in the dynamics of television and print news that would lead them to cover the story somewhat differently. In chapter 4, "The News Media Reacts: Channeling and Challenging the Administration," we review how the press covered the specific claims advanced by the Bush administration to sustain its case. We give particular emphasis to media coverage of two major, verifiable factual claims in order to assess the relative quality of media coverage across different news outlets. Chapter 4 includes descriptive data from a content analysis of newspaper and TV stories in September and October of 2002, some months before the Iraq War. Both chapters 3 and 4 provide the media backdrop for resolution of the two conundrums outlined earlier concerning a decline in Democratic and independent support for an impending war with Iraq in the fall of 2002.

Chapter 5, "The Deliberative Citizen Emerges: Democratic and Independent Opposition to the Iraq War," focuses on both conundrums and draws on data from the TNSS and the ANES to analyze Americans' support for the war. This chapter highlights the central role of information in promoting Democratic and independent opposition to the war and the crucial role played by newspapers in conveying that information. The divide between Democrats and Republicans observed in these data is unusual; Americans have generally been reasonably united across partisan lines when considering the prospect of overseas military action in survey data collected over the last half century.

In chapter 6, "Newspaper Content or Newspaper Readers?," we consider whether the greater war opposition found among Democrats and independents who obtained their information from newspapers holds up to numerous alternative explanations. We analyze various possibilities: that the antiwar proclivities of Democrats and independents who read newspapers might have been caused by a preexisting liberal political ideology, pacifist leanings, or higher levels of education. We also contrast Democrats' and independents' support for a war in Iraq with their support for the war in Afghanistan in the aftermath of 9/11 and find that the partisan divide in war support was far less pronounced for Afghanistan. In each instance we find that our conclusions are not much affected by these alternatives.

Finally, in chapter 7, "Citizen Competence Reconsidered," we return to a discussion of the broader implications of our findings for representative democracy. We conclude on a note of measured optimism about citizens' democratic abilities, but we note the critical supporting roles that political elites and the news media must play in setting the foundation for successful citizenship. The widespread discussion of media failure in the lead-up to the Iraq War has missed an important divergence in performance between print and broadcast news coverage, with TV news faring far more poorly. Newspapers did not fare well in all instances and failed the public in major ways during this period, as has been well documented. Nonetheless, some segments of the print media also performed well in ferreting out and amplifying information that cast doubt on the Bush administration's claims concerning Iraq. The current decline of print news sources thus gives us pause, and we consider the implications of a world without print media, or more importantly, without costly and effortful investigative journalism, and end on a sobering note. In such a diminished information environment, democratic citizens will have a difficult time performing competently especially in times of national crisis and threat.

CHAPTER TWO

The Skeptical Citizen

Public Uneasiness about Waging War in Iraq

"The private citizen, beset by partisan appeals for the loan of his Public Opinion, will soon see, perhaps, that these appeals are not a compliment to his intelligence, but an imposition on his good nature and an insult to his sense of evidence."—Walter Lippmann, *Public Opinion* (1922, 368)

In the fall of 2002, there was weak opposition to an Iraq war among leaders in the Democratic Party and whatever opposition existed lacked both political clout and sharp focus. Some Democratic politicians attracted news media attention by raising questions about the war, but these critics did not represent the congressional Democratic leadership, and they did not challenge the administration's facts head-on, complaining instead of insufficient consultation with the administration. In fact, a majority of Democratic senators (58%) and a sizeable minority (39%) of Democratic members of the House of Representatives voted for the Iraq War Resolution in October 2002, including the highest-ranked leaders in both bodies. All in all, rank-and-file Democrats were exposed to a moderately pro-war message from their partisan leaders amid confusing and mixed signals from others within the party. Democratic elites were not strongly pro-war but nor were they especially antiwar either, and their message was far more muddied than the very powerful and unified pro-war message emanating from the Bush administration and Republican leaders.

If Democrats heard a mixed but predominantly pro-war message from their party, independents, who were likely attending to both Democratic and Republican elites, were exposed to a strong pro-war message with overwhelming support from Republican elites swamping the mixed opposition from Democrats. Without any obvious reason to weigh anti-war Democratic critics more heavily than pro-war Republicans, independents were exposed to the full flow of partisan information, which was more pro- than antiwar on balance.

This brings us back to our original questions, posed at the outset of this book: Why did Democrats and independents increasingly oppose the looming war just as the administration intensified its pro-war campaign? The longstanding conventional wisdom, backed by considerable empirical research, is that publics follow where elites lead, especially in times of war, external threat, and patriotic appeal. In the presence of a strong pro-war signal from the administration and the absence of a unified antiwar message from Democratic leaders, rank-and-file Democrats should have supported the war. Yet they did not just resist the administration's pro-war arguments; they increasingly opposed the war in the fall of 2002.

The response of political independents is even more puzzling. While we can argue that Democrats so distrusted the Bush administration that they sought Democratic elites who opposed going to war, independents had, by definition, no such partisan motives. They should have been strongly swayed by the predominant pro-war environment. The standard model of elite influence predicts that independents should have exhibited growing support for war in the fall of 2002, not the decline in support seen in public opinion surveys. Perhaps the proposed Iraq war presented the public with just the kind of dubious partisan entreatments that Lippman, quoted at this chapter's outset, viewed as an insult to the public's sense of evidence.

Public Opinion Data Sources

Close examination of public opinion, provided in this chapter, shows that Democrats and independents were even more opposed to the war in the fall of 2002 than suggested in analyses of public opinion conducted to date (Jacobson 2007; Nacos, Bloch-Elkon, and Shapiro 2011). The public was also attending closely to the war discussion, suggesting a high level of motivation to obtain information and think carefully about the war. To explore more fulsomely public opinion on the war, we turn to data from the Threat and National Security Survey (TNSS), a three-wave national panel study of Americans conducted from 2001 to 2003 (Huddy, Feldman, and Cassese 2007). The first wave occurred in the six months following the 9/11 terrorist attacks (from October 2001 to March 2002) and included questions on reactions to terrorism and the war in Afghanistan.

The second wave assessed opinions toward terrorism and an impending Iraq war and was conducted in October 2002 after congressional debate on the war had ended. The final, third wave occurred after the onset of the Iraq War, between March and June 2003, and dealt with terrorism, the Iraq War, and the war's progress, largely repeating questions included in wave 2. All three waves of the survey included questions on news media consumption patterns. In this chapter, we rely most heavily on data from wave 2 (see the appendix for details on survey methodology).

We also draw on data from the 2002 preelection American National Election Study (ANES) and two national surveys conducted by the Pew Research Center for the People and the Press to verify findings in the TNSS. The TNSS, ANES, and Pew surveys were all conducted at roughly the same time during September and October of 2002.

Americans Follow the Iraq War Discussion

To form opinions about an impending war, or any other political issue for that matter, Americans need information, which can be easy or difficult to acquire depending on the complexity of the information environment. For partisans, it is a relatively simple matter to form an opinion on an issue when deluged with information unambiguously placing the two major political parties on the same or different sides. In this setting, citizens can follow cues emanating from their party without giving much thought to the situation or considering the information very carefully. The public is confronted with a more complex informational setting when one or both parties are internally divided, information is difficult to acquire, the decision is extremely important for national or world affairs, or some combination of these factors exists (Bolsen, Druckman, and Cook 2014). As we note, going to war in Iraq was an exceptionally important issue, raising Americans' motivation to learn about the situation. In addition, Democrats faced mixed and unclear signals from their party, complicating their decision making, removing the motive of party defense as a basis for their decision on the war, and increasing their need for "accurate" and reliable information. The question then is how much attention Americans were paying to the debate over a possible war in Iraq in what was an undeniably complex information environment.

Normally, politics is not the central focus of life for most Americans. But national elections and an impending war draw ample media coverage and necessarily attract public interest. In October of 2002, during and after the congressional debate on the Iraq War Resolution, most Americans were paying at least some attention to the ongoing discussion. When asked, "Over the past week, how much thought have you given to a possible war with Iraq?" three-quarters of the TNSS respondents said that they had given it at least "some" thought and a little over a third said they had thought about it "a great deal." In an early October Pew poll, 88% of Americans said they were following the debate over possible military action in Iraq fairly or very closely.[1] An additional 86% of respondents in the same poll said they had personally given some or a great deal of thought as to whether the United States should use military force in Iraq.

The war was also emerging in conversations held around the water cooler and at the dinner table. Nearly six in ten (57%) TNSS respondents said they had discussed the possibility of war with friends, coworkers, or neighbors at least "somewhat often" and almost one in five said they had discussed it "very often." In early October, 52% of Americans in the Pew poll said they had talked frequently with family and friends about the possibility of a war with Iraq and another 33% had talked about it occasionally. In the fall of 2002, Americans were paying fairly close attention to, and talking about, the ongoing debate over military action in Iraq.

Americans' thoughts and conversations about Iraq occurred in the shadow of 9/11, which continued to weigh heavily on the public. In October 2002, more than nine out of ten (94%) Americans in the TNSS thought that another terrorist attack on US soil was at least somewhat likely. Three out of five (60%) thought it was very likely (something that varied little by partisanship). In addition, many Americans were concerned about the personal effects of terrorism. More than two out of five (44%) respondents thought it was somewhat or very likely that they, a relative, or friend would be the victim of a future terrorist attack (Democrats were somewhat more likely to believe this than were independents or Republicans). As we show in detail in chapter 4, the Bush administration tried to channel concerns about terrorism into war support by linking Saddam Hussein to the 9/11 attacks with accusations of an Iraq–al Qaeda link. The specter of future terrorism thus added another compelling reason for Americans to attend to the debate surrounding Iraq's links to terrorism and possible possession of WMD.

How closely were Americans following news of a possible war? TNSS respondents were asked, "How many days in the past week did you watch the national TV news on ABC, CBS, CNN, FOX, or NBC?" This was accompanied by a similar question concerning the frequency with which respondents read "a daily newspaper." Nearly half (46%) said that they were watching national news seven days a week and an additional 10% watched five to six days a week, leading to a majority (56%) of Americans who watched TV news at least five days a week. Few (14%) had watched no TV news in the past week. Following a long-term trend, fewer people obtained their political information from newspapers. Only a third of TNSS respondents reported reading political news in a newspaper every day, and almost as many said they never read about politics in a newspaper. Thus, in the months before the Iraq War, most Americans were paying some attention to the news, with greater exposure to news on television than in newspapers. Americans consumed news from one of the two sources at least some of the time, and roughly a quarter (23%) said they received daily news from both sources. This leaves a small minority of Americans, only 7%, who said they had not received any news from either TV or newspapers in the previous week. Democrats, Republicans, and independents differed little in their patterns of news consumption.[2] There were virtually no differences in reported TV news viewing; if anything, Republicans reported a slightly higher frequency of newspaper reading than Democrats and independents.

Partisan Differences Emerge

War Support

News media and nonprofit organizations conducted numerous surveys to assess public support for military action against Iraq in the year leading up to the war. In chapter 1, we noted trends in the public's general support for war. In this chapter, we look more closely at a broader range of poll questions on the war to place public opinion in context. This more fine-grained survey of opinion underscores the decline in war support among Democrats and independents in the fall of 2002, a decline which is underestimated by broad survey questions on general war support or opposition (see also Nacos, Bloch-Elkon, and Shapiro 2011, fig. 4.6). In October 2002, TNSS respondents were asked this standard pro- or antiwar question: "How strongly do you favor or oppose U.S. military action against Iraq?" They were then asked two additional questions to gauge more accurately their support or opposition to a war with Iraq: "How strongly do you favor or oppose sending large numbers of U.S. ground troops into Iraq?" and "How strongly do you favor or oppose U.S. military action against Iraq even if it means that U.S. armed forces might suffer a substantial number of casualties?"

Figure 2.1 displays responses to these questions separately for Democrats, political independents, and Republicans on a scale in which −100 indicates 100% opposition to the war and +100 indicates 100% support.[3] Not surprisingly, Republicans were strongly supportive of military action in Iraq in October 2002. Four out of every five (80%) favored US military action, 62% supported sending large numbers of ground troops, and more than seven out of ten (72%) were willing to proceed with war even if there were a "significant number" of US casualties. Republican support for the war was far from unanimous, especially if it resulted in large numbers of deployed ground troops, but there is no question that most Republicans supported the war. In the Pew poll conducted in early October, 80% of Republicans also favored taking military action in Iraq, although this dropped to 71% later in the month.

The picture is very different for Democrats, consistent with national polls conducted at much the same time as wave 2 of the TNSS (Jacobson 2007). In the TNSS, a majority of Democrats (52%) were opposed to military action. In the October Pew polls, Democrats were slightly more supportive than opposed to the war (47% support compared to 44% opposition) early in the month but had shifted to majority opposition just a few weeks later after passage of the Iraq War Resolution (41% support compared to 50% opposition). In the TNSS data, an even higher number of Democrats were opposed to action if it involved large numbers of ground troops (64%) or resulted in substantial casualties (61%). Responses to the TNSS question on general military action in Iraq thus parallel findings from Pew and other national polls conducted in the fall of 2002. The additional TNSS questions underscore that Democrats, when probed on details of the war, were even less enthusiastic about it than indicated by the standard poll question. While Democrats were split on the general question of whether to use military force against Iraq, a significant majority were opposed to such action if it involved large numbers of ground troops or resulted in large numbers of American casualties (both of which eventually came to pass).

Perhaps more surprisingly, independents expressed only tepid support for sending military troops to Iraq. If we look only at the most general question on war support in the TNSS, a majority (52%) of independents appear convinced by the Bush administration's arguments and supported US military action in Iraq. But once again, the Pew polls indicate declining support over time, with independent support slipping from 57% in early October to 50% later in the month. In the TNSS, support also dipped among independents when survey questions raised additional complexities; only 48% of independents supported war if it involved substantial numbers of casualties. And when asked about sending large numbers of ground troops to Iraq, a bare majority, 50% of independents, were *opposed*. Despite being exposed to a strongly pro-war flow of information, many independents, perhaps a majority, were not convinced that the United States should send troops to topple Saddam Hussein's regime.

War opinions do not reveal, however, the full depth of Americans' uncertainty concerning possible military action in Iraq or the degree to which they wanted more information about the situation. In wave 2 of the TNSS, respondents were asked the following question: "Do you think that President Bush has adequately explained his reasons for taking military action against Iraq, or would you like more information?" A majority (63%) of Republicans were satisfied with President Bush's rationale for war, but a majority of Democrats (70%) and independents (63%) and a minority of Republicans (35%) wanted more information. Similar levels of uncertainty are also apparent in the national Pew poll conducted later in October (October 17–22). Respondents were asked, "Do you think George W. Bush has explained clearly what's at stake as to why the U.S. might use military force to end the rule of Saddam Hussein, or do you think he has not explained the reasons clearly enough?" Once again, a majority of Democrats (63%) felt he had not explained this clearly enough. In this instance, a plurality of independents (45%) felt this way[4] along with a minority of Republicans (25%). Pew respondents were also asked, "In your view, has there been too much, too little, or the right amount of discussion of ways to deal with Saddam Hussein other than using military force?" Among the respondents, 62% of Democrats, 46% of independents, and almost four in ten (39%) Republicans felt there had been too little discussion of other options. Figure 2.2 depicts these partisan differences. The numbers suggest that even Republicans felt some uncertainty about the war. Levels of support for the war on the standard pro- or antiwar poll question thus mask considerable public uncertainty concerning the war's rationale.

To further probe opinion on the war, and reveal the full depth of sentiment among Republicans, Democrats, and independents for or against the administration's position, we included several questions in the TNSS on the role of the United Nations. While the Bush administration did not

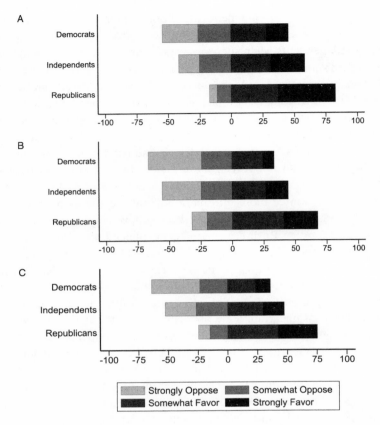

FIGURE 2.1 Partisan differences in war support: *A*, "How strongly do you favor or oppose U.S. military action against Iraq?" *B*, "How strongly do you favor or oppose sending large numbers of U.S. ground troops into Iraq?" *C*, "How strongly do you favor or oppose U.S. military action against Iraq even if it means that U.S. armed forces might suffer a substantial number of casualties?"

Source: TNSS, October 2002.
Note: Entries are the percentages who favor or oppose each policy. Negative numbers indicate the percentage who oppose the war; positive numbers indicate the percentage who support it.

ultimately obtain UN support for military action in Iraq or wait for the UN weapons inspectors to complete their report on WMD, the official position of the administration in the fall of 2002 was to seek UN support. Section 2 of the Iraq War Resolution specifically noted that the president should "strictly enforce through the United Nations Security Council all relevant Security Council resolutions regarding Iraq" and "obtain prompt and decisive action by the Security Council to ensure that Iraq . . .

complies with all relevant Security Council resolutions." It was only after the passage of the Iraq War Resolution in mid-October 2002 that attention shifted to a focus on WMD and UN weapons inspection, a story that reached its zenith in terms of network news coverage in December (Hayes and Guardino 2013).

Two survey questions in the TNSS assessed support for unilateral American action and the need to wait for UN weapons inspections in

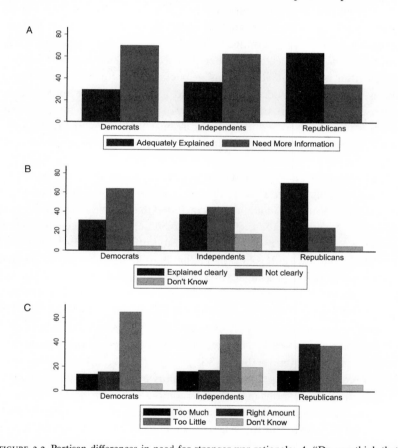

FIGURE 2.2 Partisan differences in need for stronger war rationale: *A*, "Do you think that President Bush has adequately explained his reasons for taking military action against Iraq, or would you like more information?" *B*, "Do you think George W. Bush has explained clearly what's at stake as to why the U.S. might use military force to end the rule of Saddam Hussein, or do you think he has not explained the reasons clearly enough?" *C*, "In your view, has there been too much, too little, or the right amount of discussion of ways to deal with Saddam Hussein other than using military force?"

Source: A, TNSS, October 2002; *B*, Pew, October 17–27, 2002; *C*, Pew, October 17–27, 2002.

Iraq to be completed: "How strongly do you favor or oppose U.S. military action against Iraq without the support of the United Nations?" and "Should the U.S. take military action against Iraq sometime soon, or should the U.S. wait for U.N. weapons inspectors to complete their work in Iraq?" Responses to these two questions are shown in figure 2.3.

Many Republicans supported going to war in Iraq unilaterally. Three out of five (59%) supported military action even if it was not endorsed by the United Nations, although roughly the same number of Republicans (58%) preferred to wait for the weapons inspectors to finish their work. In the national Pew poll conducted in early October, Americans who supported the war were asked whether they would still support it if Saddam cooperated with the UN weapons inspectors. Republican supporters of the war were conflicted: 48% continued to favor war but another 47% opposed it. In line with official US policy in the fall of 2002, many Republicans strongly supported using force against Saddam while at the same time preferring to delay such action until the UN weapons inspectors had completed their report.

In contrast, Democrats had substantial misgivings about unilateral action and much preferred the involvement of the UN, as seen in figure 2.3. Three out of four (75%) Democrats included in the TNSS opposed action without UN support, and eight in ten (80%) believed no decision should be made on the use of military force in Iraq until weapons inspectors had completed their work. It is fair to say that Democrats were not just divided on the war; most had stronger reservations about it than indicated by the standard pro- or antiwar poll question, underscoring the existence of a greater rift between rank-and-file and elite Democrats than has been uncovered in previous public opinion analyses.

Reluctance to proceed without the support of the UN was also evident among independents. In the TNSS, just over 60% opposed using military force against Iraq without UN support and almost 70% wanted to wait for the UN weapons inspectors to complete their work. In synch with rank-and-file Democrats, independents wanted the United States to work with the United Nations to disarm or remove Saddam before launching a military attack.

In essence, in the fall of 2002 many Americans wanted the Bush administration to obtain the support of the United Nations—and to wait for the weapons inspectors to complete their work—before sending troops to Baghdad. Yet the administration began military operations against Iraq in March 2003 without achieving these goals. A preference for UN involvement was not just confined to this moment in time. Many Democrats and

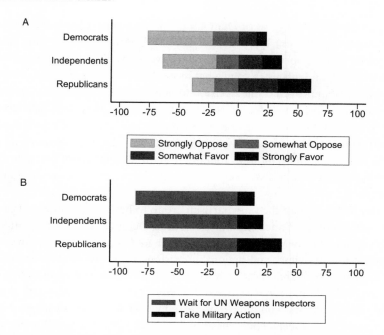

FIGURE 2.3 Partisan differences in support for United Nations involvement: *A*, "How strongly do you favor or oppose U.S. military action against Iraq without the support of the United Nations?" *B*, "Should the U.S. take military action against Iraq sometime soon, or should the U.S. wait for U.N. weapons inspectors to complete their work in Iraq?"

Source: TNSS, October 2002.
Note: Negative numbers indicate the percentage that favors an antiwar position; positive numbers indicate the percentage that favors a pro-war position.

independents continued to support UN involvement even after the war had begun, suggesting further misgivings about the Bush administration's strategy in Iraq. To demonstrate this, we shift focus away from public opinion in the fall of 2002 and look ahead to opinion in the TNSS panel after the war had begun, between March and June 2003. A randomly selected half of the TNSS sample was reinterviewed in the days and weeks immediately following the onset of military action in March 2003. Respondents were asked two questions designed to assess any regrets about the US strategy to go it alone in Iraq: "Should the U.S. have attacked Iraq without the support of the United Nations Security Council, or should it only have attacked Iraq with the support of the U.N. Security Council?" and "Should the U.S. have attacked Iraq now, or should the U.S. have given the U.N. weapons inspectors more time?"

A bare majority (53%) of Democrats said they supported the war (up from 43% in October), but a majority also wished the administration had obtained UN support (55%) and given the weapons inspectors more time (55%). Independents were somewhat more divided: in March 2003, a majority (52%) approved of the decision to begin military operations before the weapons inspectors had finished their work, but only 37% said that the United States should have gone ahead without Security Council support. Another 37% would have preferred to wait for that support, and 26% expressed no opinion. In reality, substantial numbers of Democrats and independents expressed regret about the administration's go-it-alone approach.

Republicans were the only partisan group to have no regret about the lack of UN support once the war started. In October, a majority wanted UN support but by March that preference had dissipated in line with the administration's views and actions, consistent with a motivated defense of the party. In March of 2003, almost 80% of Republicans said that the United States should have attacked *without* UN Security Council support, and only 10% would have preferred giving the weapons inspectors more time. Republican concerns about the need for UN support, evident in October 2002, vanished as the administration backed away from this requirement. It is interesting to note that Democrats and independents, despite a modest rally around the president once the war began in March, still held significant reservations about the decision to go to war without UN support.

Antiwar sentiment among rank-and-file Democrats and many independents persisted even as the Bush administration pushed for a war in Iraq, congressional Democratic leaders failed to vigorously oppose the war, and Democratic members of Congress were split on the Iraq War Resolution. It is important to recognize, however, that Democratic public opinion was not uniformly antiwar. In reality, Democrats remained divided with a significant minority in support of some type of military action. Overwhelming support from rank-and-file Republicans, modest support from political independents, and minority support from Democrats allowed the administration to take the democratic high ground and claim public support for the war, just as it did in interpreting the congressional vote on the Iraq War Resolution as majority support for war.

To gauge American public opinion overall, we created a single measure of war support from four of the five war questions in the TNSS: overall war support, support for the war if it involved large numbers of ground troops, support for the war if it involved substantial casualties, and support for the war if it was not supported by the UN (see figs. 2.1 and 2.2). By combining these questions, we gain a more accurate picture of war support than relying on any one question alone. We did not include the question on weapons inspectors in the scale because it stood somewhat to the side of the main question concerning military action in Iraq.[5] Clearly some Americans thought it might be better to wait for the weapons inspectors to complete their work but backed military action nonetheless. The four war support questions were very highly correlated, and we created a scale that ranged from −1 (strongest opposition to military intervention) to 1 (highest support for military intervention), which we analyze in greater detail.[6] To obtain a score of −1 on the pro-war scale, a respondent had to oppose the war strongly in response to all four questions, and to obtain a score of 1, a respondent had to select the most pro-war option on all four. Numbers between −1 and 1 reflected a more complex or ambivalent position, including mixed positions such as support for military action in Iraq but not if it involved large numbers of troop casualties. With a mean score of −.02, Americans were almost evenly divided on the wisdom of military intervention in Iraq in October 2002. It is not too far-fetched to assume that if the war's reality in terms of cost, casualties, and time span had been forcefully presented to the public in the fall of 2002, the average score for Americans as a whole would have dipped well below 0.

This scale allows us to portray in more detail levels of support for the war among Republicans, Democrats, and independents. In figure 2.4 we show the distribution of the war support scale for the three partisan groups. The strong divergence between Republicans and Democrats is evident in this figure. While Republicans varied in their degree of support for the war, only about two in ten (22%) had a score on the scale that was below zero—reflecting consistent opposition to the war. As we have seen, most of the concerns expressed by Republicans in the fall of 2002 revolved around the need for UN support. And a significant number of Republicans were almost fully supportive of military action against Iraq under any circumstances. The picture was very different for Democrats. Fully 65% were opposed to the war and only 30% joined Republicans in consistently supporting it. Moreover, a large number of Democrats were completely against any military effort in Iraq. In contrast to reasonably opposed Democrats and largely supportive Republicans, independents were quite divided. Barely more than a half (52%) was consistently opposed to the war whereas 42% consistently supported it. Once we make

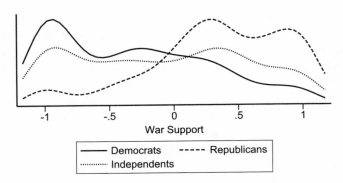

FIGURE 2.4 Distribution of war support by partisanship, TNSS, October 2002

use of more finely grained questions on support for military action, we see that a substantial fraction of independents also had serious concerns about going to war.

Perceived Threat Posed by Saddam Hussein

Bush administration personnel argued for a war in Iraq in part because they claimed Saddam Hussein was in cahoots with terrorists and in possession of weapons of mass destruction that he was willing to deploy in the Middle East and beyond. Did Americans believe these claims? The Pew poll from early October indicates that most Americans regarded Saddam's possession of nuclear weapons as a definite possibility. A few (14%) thought Saddam already had nuclear weapons, most thought he was close (66%), and almost no one thought his acquisition of nuclear weapons was a long way off. There were few differences among Democrats, Republicans, and independents in this assessment. Americans thus believed Saddam had the tools to wreak havoc in the region, but did they think he would employ them?

The TNSS included a series of questions tapping agreement with several statements put forward by the administration concerning the threat posed by Saddam to the United States and his regional neighbors—a key part of the Bush administration's argument for military action in Iraq. Three TNSS questions assessed how much threat the public assigned to Saddam Hussein: "How likely is it that Saddam Hussein is actively supporting anti-U.S. terrorist groups at present?"; "If the U.S. does not take military action in Iraq, how likely is it that Saddam Hussein would attack the U.S. with biological, chemical, or nuclear weapons in the near future?"; and "If the U.S. does not take military action in Iraq, how likely is it that Saddam Hussein would use biological, chemical, or nuclear weapons against countries in the Middle-East including Israel, in the near future?" The responses to these three questions among Democrats, independents, and Republicans are shown in figure 2.5.

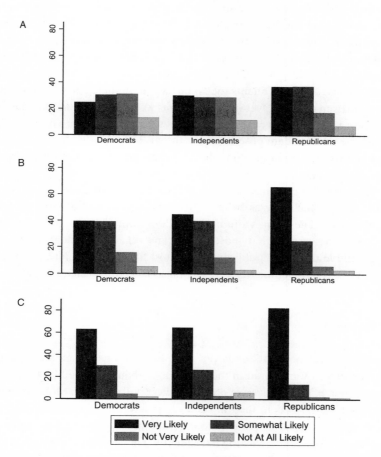

FIGURE 2.5 Perceptions of the threat posed by Saddam Hussein: *A*, "If the U.S. does not take military action in Iraq, how likely is it that Saddam Hussein would attack the U.S. with biological, chemical, or nuclear weapons in the near future?" *B*, "If the U.S. does not take military action in Iraq, how likely is it that Saddam Hussein would use biological, chemical, or nuclear weapons against countries in the Middle-East including Israel, in the near future?" *C*, "How likely is it that Saddam Hussein is actively supporting anti-U.S. terrorist groups at present?"

Source: TNSS, October 2002.
Note: Entries are the percentages that perceived each event as likely or unlikely.

In the months before the war began, Americans of all political stripes believed that Saddam was a major threat to the United States and his neighbors. A bare majority of Democrats and independents and a larger majority of Republicans thought that Saddam might use weapons of mass destruction against the United States; almost everyone, especially Republicans, believed he was likely to use them against other Middle Eastern countries (including Israel); and a large majority of Americans thought it was very likely he was actively supporting anti-US terrorist groups. A majority of Americans in the early October Pew poll also believed that Saddam had helped the terrorists in the 9/11 attacks on the United States. This view was held by a greater number of Republicans (78%) than Democrats (56%) or independents (66%) but was nonetheless a majority view in all partisan groups. Overall, Republicans were more certain than Democrats or independents of Iraq-sponsored terrorism and were more likely to believe that Saddam posed a direct threat to the United States and his Middle Eastern neighbors, though Democrats and independents also saw him as a threat.

We combined the three TNSS questions into a scale of perceived Saddam threat, which ranges from 0 (Saddam is not a threat) to 1 (maximum threat). The mean score in the TNSS sample is .75, well above the midpoint, suggesting that most Americans regarded Saddam Hussein as a credible threat. Republicans were most likely to see him as a threat (mean = .82) but Democrats were not far behind them (mean = .71).[7]

Conclusion

Democrats, independents, and even some Republicans had greater qualms about going to war in Iraq in the fall of 2002 than suggested by trends in war opinion based on a simple pro- or antiwar poll question. Moreover, the public's misgivings about the war occurred in a setting in which Americans were highly engaged in the debate over military action in Iraq—actively thinking about it and discussing it frequently. This strong public motivation to think about the war left many Americans unsatisfied with the amount and quality of information originating with the Bush administration. The debate over military action in Iraq was occurring in the shadow of 9/11, and the threat of terrorism continued to loom large in the public mind, lending weight and gravity to the discussion. Something was afoot among the public, forcing them to consider, digest, discuss, and mull over events in the Middle East to an unusual degree.

When poked and prodded in surveys, Americans displayed a far weaker appetite for war than apparent at first blush. Opinions about large numbers of ground troops in Iraq, large numbers of casualties, or going into Iraq without the backing of the UN provide evidence of substantially less public support for war than was generally believed to exist at the time. More detailed and in-depth poll questions on the war also revealed widespread consternation at the administration's weak rationale and insufficient discussion of alternatives to military action.

Republicans faced a less complex information environment than Democrats. The Republican administration made a singular and powerful argument for war whereas Democrats received muted and mixed signals from their partisan elites. Independents were placed somewhere in between, exposed to a strong pro-war message from the administration but no clear-cut opposition from Democratic politicians, leaving them to either trust the administration or puzzle through the debate on their own. Overall, Republicans supported the war, albeit with some modest concerns; Democrats were remarkably skittish, with many opposed once different facets of military action were taken into consideration; and independents were all over the map, a complete mix of war support and opposition. The public was very far from a unified entity on the matter of the war.

Republicans were the most staunchly supportive of the war but their support was not a simple case of reflexive partisanship. A sizeable minority of Republicans, upward of 40%, wanted more information and thought there had been too little discussion of alternatives to military action in Iraq. They would also have preferred to wait for the UN weapons inspectors to complete their work, and when Republican war supporters were presented with the possibility that Saddam might cooperate with the weapons inspectors, roughly a half rescinded their support. Ultimately, the Bush administration managed to sway Republicans to its side, and in that sense partisan cues ultimately prevailed. But even here, among its most ardent supporters, the Bush administration could not rely on reflexive partisanship to carry the day.

When taken together, these trends reinforce and strengthen our initial conundrums concerning public opinion on the war. If Democrats lacked strong partisan cues one way or another and independents declined to simply follow the Bush administration's lead, where did they obtain information that persuaded them to oppose the war? Not every Democrat or independent opposed the war, as we have noted. But when placed on our war support scale, the majority of Democrats were opposed and independents were squarely in the middle.

These findings also bear directly on the psychology of political judgment, which we discussed in chapter 1. When motivated to think carefully, Americans should employ the more thoughtful and effortful pathway to political decision making. As we've now seen, many Americans were thinking and talking about a possible war with Iraq in the fall of 2002. Many Democrats and independents (and some Republicans) also reported that they were not completely satisfied with the arguments offered by the Bush administration for going to war. Given the magnitude of this decision—committing US military forces to an invasion of Iraq—it is likely that many Americans were motivated to go beyond heuristic processing and think carefully concerning the available facts, arguments, and assertions.

We consider in the next two chapters the role played by the main purveyor of public affairs information to Americans: the news media. The news media has been repeatedly vilified for its prewar coverage, but such condemnations exaggerate and simplify the information environment in the fall of 2002.

CHAPTER THREE

Political Leaders Set the Stage for War

"The performance of the American press leading up to the second Gulf War or the invasion of Iraq was *méprisable* [despicable]. It was just pathetic. It was the worst it's been since before Vietnam. The American press swallowed and regurgitated and amplified just about every lie the Bush Administration put forward." —John MacArthur, president and publisher, *Harper's Magazine*, quoted in Borjesson (2005, 93)

The elite influence model assigns the American electorate a straight-forward role to play when elites announce new initiatives: the public will simply look to their party leaders. In the period under consideration, Republicans would have taken their lead from the Bush administration. Democrats would have turned to their congressional leadership. Each would have obtained the necessary cues to guide them on how to think about a possible war. For September and October of 2002, when the administration shifted its focus from Afghanistan to Iraq, the elite influence model predicts that the public should have done what elite leaders proposed. The Bush administration had ably secured support from many congressional leaders. Indeed, virtually all Republicans and many Democrats, including party leaders in both houses, endorsed the administration's push for military action in Iraq. As a result, the "information flow" directed to the public was dominated by the Bush administration and clearly lopsided in a pro-war direction. In such circumstances, the public should have passively endorsed a pro-war position. Had Democratic leaders fully challenged the administration's facts and arguments, the public would have faced a far more balanced two-message flow of information characterized by opposing partisan stances on the war. And had the news media presented both sides, including the views of skeptical experts, the public would have experienced a richer news environment replete with the claims and evidence for and against war.

The conventional wisdom is that Democratic partisan leaders simply followed the Bush administration's lead, for the most part choosing *not* to make a compelling case against the war. As Frank Rich (2006, 63) puts it, the lack of Democratic opposition to the war was due to "the president's poll numbers, their [Democrats'] fear of being branded unpatriotic, and their eagerness to clear the decks (whatever the price) so as to focus their fire on the supposedly winning issue of the economy before Election Day" (see also Rosenbaum 2002). However, Democratic support for the war was not as uniform as this quote suggests. Twenty-nine Democratic senators voted for the Iraq War Resolution but that left a sizable minority (21) who did not. On the other hand, such Democratic opposition to the war as did arise did not come from congressional Democratic leaders such as Senate majority leader Tom Daschle or House minority leader Richard Gephardt, who both voted for the resolution. In the crucial six-week period between the public revelation of the Bush administration's plans and the congressional war authorization vote in mid-October, the only time period in which citizens had an opportunity to influence the votes of their elected representatives, the news was driven and dominated by the Bush administration and accompanied by muted Democratic opposition at best.

There were antiwar voices in the news during this six-week period. But war opposition was far less prevalent than war support. In terms of influential partisan elites, opposition to the war arose from Democrats in the Senate and the House who lacked leadership positions within the party, but this opposition was far outstripped in the news by the presence of pro-war administration officials, including the president. Antiwar voices in the news were also less singularly partisan and far more diverse than the voices of war support. As we show in chapter 4, opposition arose from some Democratic senators, foreign leaders, intelligence officials, energy scientists, and members of the military (see also Hayes and Guardino 2013; Howell and Pevehouse 2007).

Overall, it is fair to characterize the information environment in the fall of 2002 as dominated by pro-war messages arising almost completely from the Bush administration, with opposition to the war being voiced by a diverse chorus. In this chapter, we briefly review the shifting information environment over the course of 2002, highlighting periods of partisan elite consensus and disagreement on the war to provide an accurate portrayal

of the elite "information flow" directed at the public. Our review reinforces the conventional portrait of a dominant pro-war information environment. We also review the role played by the news media in shaping
public opinion on matters of foreign policy and consider several competing models of the relationship between media and elite opinion. Following Piers Robinson and his colleagues (2010), we focus on journalistic
habits and production constraints imposed by different media platforms
to consider when journalists are willing and able to undertake investigative journalism that allows them to take an independent stance on an administration's claims and arguments.

We believe that differences between newspapers and television in their
prewar coverage help to explain why Democrats and independents became less supportive of war in the fall of 2002. In chapter 4, we present
a more fine-grained content analysis of news stories. Here, we offer an
overview of the general prewar information environment.

Elite Consensus (and Occasional Dissent) on the Iraq War

On the basis of our close reading of news from major electronic and print
sources, the 2002 prewar information environment—consisting of news
content; the views of elites expressed in briefings, speeches, published
op-eds; and other sources of information such as experts domestic and
foreign—can be broken into four phases. The first phase began with
President Bush's State of the Union speech in late January 2002 when he
first referred to Iraq as a member of the "axis of evil," a designation that
attracted initial bipartisan support. By March 2002, roughly two months
later, some Democratic leaders had begun to express increasing unease
at the administration's failure to consult with Congress on its war plans.
This marks the beginning of the second phase of prewar media coverage.
Coverage of Iraq was light, however, in these first two phases, and Democratic and Republican public opinion remained relatively supportive of
war (as seen in chapter 1). The third phase began in late July of 2002 when
clear concern about a looming war became evident among both Republican and Democratic elites, although this concern was largely hidden from
public view. Finally, in September 2002, the administration launched its
information campaign to win favor for a war against Iraq.

In this chapter, we briefly review events in all four periods, although
our main research interest is with the last period, September through

October, a period defined by the administration's initial effort to demonize Saddam Hussein and gain formal congressional approval for the war.[1] The Bush administration dominated the conversation throughout this time period when Congress debated and then voted in support of the Iraq War Resolution.

Phase 1, January–February 2002: The Birth of the Axis of Evil

President Bush hinted at a possible war with Iraq in his State of the Union speech presented to Congress on January 29, 2002. It was then that he identified Iraq as one of three countries composing an axis of evil. Bush's speech was characterized by Michael Gordon, writing for the *New York Times* on January 30, 2002, as the "strongest oratory that the president has used to date to describe Iraq's pursuit of weapons of mass destruction and the United States' determination to neutralize that threat." The speech drew considerable consternation from various European allies, as well as from the countries making up the so-called axis of evil (Daley 2002; Knowlton 2002).

Congressional Republican and Democratic leadership initially supported the president's position on Iraq. Tom Daschle, the Democratic Senate majority leader, was quoted on ABC-TV as saying "if it takes preemptive strikes and preventive action" to stop new terrorist attacks, "I think Congress is prepared to support it" (Knowlton 2002). On February 12, former Democratic vice president Al Gore gave a speech to the Council on Foreign Relations and said the time had come for a "final reckoning" with Iraq, describing the country as a "virulent threat in a class by itself" (Balz 2002b; Nagourney 2002). The speech was covered by the *New York Times*, the *Washington Post*, and *USA Today* along with several other newspapers and CNN's *American Morning with Paula Zahn*. By mid-February, Todd Purdum (2002), writing for the *New York Times*, described the emergence of "a bipartisan consensus . . . in the Bush Administration and Congress alike that the United States can no longer tolerate an Iraqi regime led by Saddam Hussein." Articles appeared in other major publications around this time underscoring bipartisan support for a war in Iraq (Lancaster 2002; Shapiro 2002).

In the coming months, partisan contention centered not so much on whether the United States should remove Hussein but rather the administration's willingness to consult sufficiently with Congress, whether congressional hearings and a vote were needed to authorize war, the role of the UN weapons inspectors, and ultimately the need for a UN resolution in support of US military action. In sum, in the month following Bush's State of the Union speech, partisan elite opinion was characterized by a pervasive bipartisan consensus that Iraq posed a major threat to the United States. This view is encapsulated in a comment made in February by Senator Joe Biden who said, "It would be unrealistic, if not downright foolish, to believe we can claim victory in the war on terrorism if Saddam is still in power" (Shapiro 2002).

Phase 2, March–June 2002: Democratic Disgruntlement

Congressional Democrats' support for President Bush's effort to expand military action beyond Afghanistan was relatively short-lived, however. Democratic senator Bob Graham, then chairman of the Senate Intelligence Committee who ultimately voted against authorization of the war, appeared on CNN in late February raising doubts about Saddam Hussein's possession of WMD.[2] By early March, Democrats increasingly criticized possible US military action in Iraq. Senate majority leader Tom Daschle characterized the war on terrorism as "expansion without at least a clear direction." These comments attracted a spirited response from senior Republicans who questioned Daschle's patriotism. Republican Senate minority leader Trent Lott asked scathingly, "How dare Senator Daschle criticize President Bush while we are fighting our war on terrorism, especially when we have troops in the field?" (Purdum 2002).

Nonetheless, Democrats continued to question the Bush strategy toward Iraq in the following months. A number of key Democratic senators such as Robert Byrd, who later in the year voted against war authorization, and Joe Biden, who voted for it, asked for greater consultation between the administration and Congress. Dick Gephardt, the Democratic House minority leader, captured congressional Democratic sentiment when he said in early March: "If we're going to fight this thing effectively, we got to stay together, we got to collaborate, we got to communicate. It hasn't been happening to the extent in the last few days that it should. I hope it will get back on track" (Purdum 2002). Some Democrats were even more pointed in their criticism of the administration. In a *USA Today* article by Kathy Kiely published on May 14, Senator Bob Graham raised concerns that a war with Iraq would lead to high casualties and fracture the international antiterrorism coalition, and expressed doubts that Saddam Hussein was developing WMD.

While Democratic leaders raised questions about the expanded war on terror, they continued to hint that they would ultimately muster Democratic support for US military action in Iraq.[3] Even Democratic senator Bob Graham, a war critic, urged Bush to try diplomacy before resorting to force, implying that force remained a viable outcome. In sum, bipartisan consensus concerning the war had begun to fray by early spring of 2002, although Democratic disgruntlement stemmed more from feeling excluded from the administration's decision-making process than outright opposition to a war with Iraq.

Phase 3, July–August 2002: The Summer of Discontent

The information environment changed markedly in the summer of 2002 with increased news coverage of a possible war in Iraq.[4] Congressional Democratic and Republican elites began to publicly voice concern about an expansion of the war on terror. Bipartisan doubts began to surface in the news as early as late June. Kathy Kiely, writing in *USA Today* on June 24, noted growing support among Democratic and Republican leaders in the House and Senate for congressional approval of any action undertaken by the Bush administration in Iraq. By late July, various Democrats were pointedly questioning the administration's strategy. Senator John Kerry emerged as one of the administration's key critics during the summer, charging that the administration was planning for a war in Iraq in the absence of any diplomatic plan for what to do after Hussein was removed from power (Balz 2002a). Senator Bob Graham raised doubts in late July about the existence of biological weapons labs in Iraq. And Senator Carl Levin, then chairman of the Senate Armed Services Committee, vocally urged for congressional hearings in July and August and raised concerns about the outcome of a US military invasion in Iraq.[5]

In late July, Democratic consternation culminated in Senators Dianne Feinstein and Patrick Leahy (chairman of the Senate Judiciary Committee) introducing legislation against an attack on Iraq in the absence of specific congressional authorization or an outright declaration of war.[6] At roughly the same time, in early August, the Senate Foreign Relations Committee headed by Democrat Joe Biden held two days of hearings on the threat posed by Iraq. By the end of August, there was an even more concerted effort to demand a full congressional hearing and vote on a possible war with Iraq, spearheaded by Senators Leahy and Feingold. Nonetheless, it still seemed as if congressional Democrats would come around to supporting a war with Iraq, since congressional leaders, such as Richard Gephardt, continued to characterize Iraq as a threat to the United States.[7]

The summer was not solely a continuation of Democratic disgruntlement. Republican dissent also began to filter out to the public. Brent Scowcroft, former national security advisor in George H. W. Bush's administration, published an opinion piece in the *Wall Street Journal* on August 15, 2002. In that article he raised doubts about Saddam Hussein's cooperation with anti-American terrorists and warned that an attack on Iraq "would seriously jeopardize, if not destroy, the global counterterrorist campaign we have undertaken." This editorial followed Scowcroft's appearance ten days earlier on CBS's *Face the Nation* in which he expressed similar concerns. Other high-profile Republicans such as Henry Kissinger, House majority leader Dick Armey, and Lawrence Eagleburger, former Secretary of State under President George H. W. Bush, also expressed concern about the legality, goals, preparedness, and consequences of a war with Iraq (Purdum and Patrick 2002). This culminated in a *New York Times* op-ed article published on August 25 by James Baker III, who had served in various capacities in the senior Bush's administration, in which he argued that a US military invasion lacked unified internal Iraqi support, would be very expensive, would result in a large number of casualties, and would jeopardize US relations with Arab allies in the region. Rather than pursuing unilateral US military action, Baker advocated further UN weapons inspections and subsequent multilateral (not unilateral) action only if necessary (Baker 2002).

There were also signs of division within the administration, led chiefly by Colin Powell. Powell expressed concerns about a military campaign in Iraq and urged for the full involvement of UN weapons inspectors, echoing the position of Scowcroft, Baker, and other high-profile Republicans opposed to unilateral action in Iraq (Dao 2002a).

Some congressional Republicans also raised concern about a war with Iraq, urging administration officials to make their case in hearings and bring the issue to a congressional vote. In mid-July, Senator Chuck Hagel, a Republican from Nebraska, said, "If the United States decides to take action against Iraq, Americans need to understand the risks and objectives" (Dao 2002b). During the Senate Foreign Relations Committee hearings in August, Senator Richard G. Lugar of Indiana, the ranking Republican on the committee, said, "The president and the administration will have to make the case to the American people regarding the threat posed to United States security by Saddam Hussein and the weapons of mass destruction he appears intent on producing," and added, "But the president will also have to make a persuasive case to our friends and allies, particularly those in the region." Lugar also noted that the administration had not done the "military and diplomatic spadework" to justify an invasion of Iraq.[8] Indeed Lugar and Biden published a joint op-ed article in the *New York Times* on July 31, 2002, outlining the questions that would be addressed in the August Senate Foreign Relations Committee hearings on Iraq, including questions about American responsibilities once Saddam was deposed. In late August, Senator John W. Warner, senior Republican on the Senate Armed Services Committee, urged President Bush to gain congressional approval to go to war.[9] Speaking with Wolf Blitzer on CNN on August 4, 2002, Republican senator Arlen Specter discussed the need for a congressional vote on the war, adding that the administration needed to address a number of unanswered questions, including "What will it cost us in terms of casualties to go to war with Iraq? What will we do after we topple Saddam?"[10]

The collapse over the summer of earlier bipartisan support for a war with Iraq was perhaps best explained by Senator Joe Lieberman who said in late August, "I do feel that generally the administration has not handled this well in recent months. . . . They've been stuck in a gray area, a vacuum, in which opponents of military action and people who are just plain puzzled or anxious have begun to dominate the debate" (Bumiller and Dao 2002).

Overall, the news media attended to those voicing concern about a possible war, although Republican dissent received greater coverage than dissent voiced by Democrats. In August 2002, there were 130 CNN segments that referred to one of the key Republican figures expressing dissent on Iraq. In the same period there were 44 similar stories in the *New York Times*, and 63 comparable stories in the *Washington Post*. This was roughly twice the amount of coverage devoted to Democratic dissent: CNN aired 66 segments that referred to Iraq and one of the major Democratic dissenters, there were 11 stories in the *New York Times*, and 30 in the *Washington Post*.[11] This is consistent with research evidence that the news media devotes greater attention to criticism from within the president's party than from the opposing party (Baum and Groeling 2010).

By late August, the case for war had not been made. Nonetheless, few argued forcefully against it either. Democratic senator Evan Bayh said in a CNN interview, "I'm inclined to support going in there [Iraq] and dealing with Saddam. But I think that case needs to be made on a separate basis—his possession of biological and chemical weapons, his desire to get nuclear weapons, his proven track record of attacking his neighbors and others."[12] His comments captured the prevailing view of many Democrats at the time. The administration, recognizing the lack of sufficient congressional support, hinted in late August that it would seek to build a convincing case so as to obtain congressional approval for military action in Iraq (Lewis with Sanger 2002; Oppel with Preston 2002). It began to do so, and quite loudly, in September.

Phase 4, September 2002–March 2003: Making the Case for War

The Senate Foreign Relations Committee hearings on Iraq held in early August 2002 presaged many of the questions that would dominate the discussion of military action in Iraq in the ensuing months. How close was Saddam to having weapons of mass destruction? How likely was he to cooperate with terrorists? And what would happen to Iraq in the aftermath of a US military invasion and the removal of Saddam Hussein? The Bush administration tackled these issues with vigor in the fall. Andrew Card, the White House chief of staff, laid bare the logic of the administration's timing with startling insouciance, and uncharacteristic candor, saying "From a marketing point of view, you don't introduce new products in August" (Bumiller 2002). From the onset of the Bush administration's PR campaign, administration officials spoke largely in a single voice, arguing in support of military action against the Iraqi regime. The administration's push for war generated an unsurprising uptick in news coverage, creating a far more saturated information environment than had existed earlier in the year (Hayes and Guardino 2011).

Elite dissent melted away among Republicans in this period. The unease of the summer simply vanished. Some Democrats continued to voice concerns about the war, but analysis of the *Congressional Record* suggests that Democratic opposition was short-lived, dominating debate on the Iraq War Resolution in late September then shifting to war support in October. After October 16, when President Bush signed the Iraq War Resolution, members of Congress from both political parties essentially vanished from local television news (Howell and Pevehouse 2007). During this time period, both Tom Daschle and Dick Gephardt—the top-ranking Democrats in the Senate and House—announced their support for the administration's position (Rosenbaum 2002). On October 10, a

majority of Democratic senators voted to authorize war (29 out of 50) as
did a substantial minority in the House (81 out of 209). High-profile Democratic senators who voted against the war, including Byrd (WV), Durbin
(IL), Feingold (WI), Graham (FL), and Kennedy (MA), constituted a
major source of domestic opposition to the war. Members of Congress
(mostly Democrats) appeared in roughly 20% of all stories aired on local
and national television and in the *New York Times* from mid-September
until the end of October 2002 (Howell and Pevehouse 2007). These Democratic members of Congress did not include Democratic congressional
leaders, however, and as a vote on the Iraq War Resolution approached in
October, Democratic opposition to the war was effectively drowned out
by Democratic support in congressional debate.

By early February 2003, there was almost no evidence on network
news of elite Democratic or Republican opposition to the war (Entman
2004). Congressional support for the Iraq War Resolution was not unanimous, but it was sufficiently bipartisan nonetheless to produce the following continuation headline in the *New York Times* the day after the vote in
the House: "Congress Authorizes Bush to Use Force against Iraq, Creating a Broad Mandate."[13]

There was continued opposition to the war in early 2003, but it came
from nonpartisan overseas sources, energy scientists, former government
officials, midlevel intelligence officials, and State Department civil ser-
vants, sources that lacked the political clout needed to ensure prominent
news coverage. Robert Entman (2004) believes that once Congress voted
for the war resolution, there was little incentive for the media to report on
dissension among domestic elites. The war simply lacked opposition from
the power brokers who had the ability to change the course of events in
the United States and whose views are typically given prominence in the
media (Bennett, Lawrence, and Livingston 2007). We review the nature
and content of news media coverage of this opposition in greater detail in
chapter 4.

A Puzzle: Declining Democratic Support for the
Iraq War in the Fall of 2002

If the elite influence model is valid, there should have been growing public
opposition to a war in Iraq in the summer of 2002, in what we refer to as
phase 3 of the emerging prewar information environment. This was a time
when both Republican and Democratic leaders publicly raised questions

and some voiced outright opposition to the administration's position. But as we saw in chapter 1, public opinion polls showed continuing popular support for military action in Iraq throughout the summer of 2002. Bipartisan elite grumbling about the war and congressional Democrats' repeated complaints that they were insufficiently consulted on the administration's war plans did little to alter public opinion, perhaps because it was summer vacation, a time when Americans pay less attention to the news. Republican support for the war persisted at high levels in public opinion polls throughout the summer with roughly 80% expressing support for the war against Iraq in August, despite internal dissent among Republican elites. War support did decline slightly among Democrats over the first six months of 2002. In January, roughly 67% of Democrats supported a war in Iraq, whereas by May, support had declined slightly to 62%, a decline that occurred in phase 2 in conjunction with complaints from congressional Democrats about the administration's case. But during the summer (phase 3)—when dissent was most marked—there was little further decline. In August 2002, 60% of Democrats continued to support a war against Iraq. Thus, a majority of Democrats supported the war at summer's end as did an even larger proportion of Republicans.

A far more precipitous decline in Democratic support for war occurred after the Bush administration began its concerted information campaign to increase public and congressional support. Despite meager opposition to the war from Democratic elite leadership during that period, there was a notable drop in Democratic public support for military action in Iraq, from roughly 60% in August to 50% in October. This is the first conundrum that we introduced in chapter 1. There was also a more modest decline of several percentage points in independents' support for the war, introduced as conundrum 2 in chapter 1. War support declined despite the administration's full-throttled, one-sided information campaign, despite a lack of a unified high-profile Democratic opposition to the war, and well ahead of large-scale international antiwar protests (Jacobson 2007; Shapiro and Bloch-Elkon 2008).

How then to resolve conundrums 1 and 2? How can we explain the decline in Democratic support for a war in Iraq in the fall of 2002? And how can we resolve a more modest decline in support for the war among political independents? Even if Democratic senators effectively conveyed doubts about the war to the Democratic public, there is no reason to expect this muted opposition to have influenced the views of political independents. This brings us back to our psychological model. When there is a major issue looming, as in the case of an impending war, especially when elites fail to provide sufficient or trustworthy cues on such weighty matters, the public can become engaged and, on its own, sift through complex information to arrive at its own reasoned position. This is what we believe some Americans did in September and October of 2002.

But even an increased motivation to look beyond the administration and political elites in search of additional information about Iraq would do little to change public opinion in the absence of freely available, high-quality information. Was such information available? Where could it be obtained? How reliable was it? To answer these questions, we return to news media coverage of Iraq in the fall of 2002. Perhaps critical evidence was present in the news even if it did not arise from Democratic elites. A focus on the news may seem difficult to reconcile with the conventional wisdom that the news media failed the public by conveying uncritically the administration's case for war. In MacArthur's words, quoted at the chapter's outset, news coverage in the lead-up to the war was "pathetic" and "despicable." There is no doubt that the press failed the public in numerous ways in the year prior to the war's onset. But in the absence of a strong unified antiwar message from Democratic congressional leaders, the news media is the most logical place to look for information that may have provoked Democrats and independents to increase their opposition to the war in the fall of 2002.

The News Media and War Coverage

Social scientists have generally concluded that the news is dominated by the voices and positions of powerful elites who are drawn from the ranks of the administration and congressional partisan leadership. In Lance Bennett's popular indexing model, elite influence is thought to shape public opinion through the media's tendency to relay elite opinion in an unbiased fashion, fairly conveying the views of key political decision makers (Bennett 1990). Even when news is driven by events and originates from the site of an ongoing natural disaster or war zone far removed from American power centers, it is still dominated by official sources (Bennett and Livingston 2003; Livingston and Bennett 2003). The indexing hypothesis is not without its critics but they do not dispute the dominance of political elites in the news. Rather, the debate over the indexing hypothesis focuses on the degree of elite domination, the extent to which journalistic practices enhance, diminish, or distort elite representation, and the vigor with which journalists challenge and investigate elite claims (Baum and Groeling 2010; Entman 2003; Wolfsfeld 2004).

In the following section we examine several models of news influence. Each of these models acknowledges the influence of political elites on public opinion. However, they also identify different ways in which the news media can inform the public through its representation of elite positions. After we review these theoretical accounts, we next turn to the empirical record and examine the ways in which the news media covered the administration's case for war in the fall of 2002. We seek an answer there: Was there actual news coverage that enabled Democrats and independents to form antiwar judgments?

News Media Conveys Elite Influence

At first glance, news organizations are an unlikely source of antiwar information because of their heavy reliance on official voices and viewpoints. Reliance on elite sources is especially pronounced on matters of foreign policy in which the views of the administration and, to a lesser extent, partisan congressional leaders receive the lion's share of media attention. For example, Donald Jordan and Benjamin Page (1992) found that members of the president's party made up almost half of all the sources in TV news broadcasts for some thirty-two specific foreign policy incidents that occurred between 1969 and the early 1980s. In contrast, only one in seven sources came from members of the opposition party. Bennett and his colleagues (2007) report that only one in twelve (34 out of 414) major TV network stories on the buildup to the Iraq War came from outside the White House between September 2002 and February 2003. Other researchers report similar news media dependence on powerful elites who are in a position to shape policy in the United States and elsewhere (Gans 1979; Sigal 1973; Wolfsfeld and Sheafer 2006). Normal news media practices thus serve to amplify elite influence on public opinion, especially concerning foreign policy. Indeed, as Gadi Wolfsfeld and Tamir Sheafer (2006) found in Israel, government officials are the most common initiators of an ongoing news story.

Bennett's (1990) indexing model has provided a useful framework in which to analyze how the news media conveys elite views to the public (see also Bennett, Lawrence, and Livingston 2006). As noted in chapter 1, from the standpoint of democratic theory, the public is well served when government officials actively and publicly weigh diverse policy options and elite deliberations to reflect a range of viewpoints. It is not so well served when government and other official sources present a unified position. As Bennett and his colleagues (2007, 14) note, "Unfortunately, quite a different press often show up when policy decisions of dubious wisdom go unchallenged within government arenas." The existence of elite discord is thus critical to the balanced coverage of foreign affairs because of the media's tendency to attend most closely to the views of influential policy makers (Bennett, Lawrence, and Livingston 2007; Entman 2004; Entman and Page 1994). If elites of all partisan persuasions agree, if a bipartisan consensus prevails, the public is exposed to a single uncontested view. And when one political party is unified and the other is divided, when one emits a high volume signal while the other is muted, the political impact is likely to favor the more vocal than the more muted.

In their study of news content in the run-up to the Iraq War in September and October of 2002, Bennett and his colleagues (2007) find that information was available to contradict the administration's case, but it came from nonofficial or lower profile news sources that are not typically given prominent coverage in the news. This view is further supported by Danny Hayes and Matt Guardino's (2011) evidence that foreign voices, especially those of Iraqis, dominated opposition to the war on evening network television news between August 2002 and March 2003. Bennett and his colleagues conclude that the Bush administration effectively monopolized the news by controlling the release of information that news organizations felt compelled to cover. The dominance of the Bush administration and members of the international coalition in news coverage of Iraq prior to the war has been confirmed in every analysis of news from this time period conducted in the United States and elsewhere (Bennett, Lawrence, and Livingston 2007; Hayes and Guardino 2011; Howell and Pevehouse 2007; Robinson et al. 2010).

Bennett and his colleagues (2007) find that some officials critical of the administration received coverage in the news, but they were often former officials who lacked access to insider information about ongoing events and so could not drive the news or hold frequent press briefings that would sustain news media interest. They believe that because of the way in which the news media operates, the "absence of credible and potentially divisive opposition from inside government leaves the mainstream press generally unable to build and sustain counterstories" (36). Overall, they fault members of the news media for failing to adequately cover challenges to the administration's factual case for war because of their attentiveness to "powerful officials whose communication experts manage them so well." This assessment reinforces the indexing hypothesis but provides a deeply pessimistic assessment of the ways in which the news media functions.

Bennett's research found that during the September–October period, the index of news coverage was clearly one-sided. Scott Althaus and Devon Largio (2004) provide further evidence that the Bush administration dominated news accounts during the prewar period. They document the shift in President Bush's rhetoric away from Osama bin Laden toward Saddam Hussein beginning in the early months of 2002, a trend, with a slight time lag, that also appeared in Associated Press (AP) stories. Both AP stories and presidential pronouncements show a sharp increase in references to Saddam in September 2002 as the administration launched its case for war. In this instance, news coverage simply followed the administration's lead in moving away from questions about Osama bin Laden to focus on the president's concerns about Saddam.

However, there is something inherently unsatisfying about an account of a docile and compliant press in part because it does little to explain Democratic and independent disaffection with the war in the fall of 2002. We next turn to an alternative model of elite influence, a model that contends that the media relies on the views of elites but elevates the voices of some and downplays the voices of others in ways that serve the news industry's own needs and practices. Typically, this bias errs in the direction of privileging conflict and novelty in the conveyance of elite viewpoints.

News Media Actively Constructs Elite Influence

STOKING CONFLICT. A number of media researchers no longer fully subscribe to the elite indexing model or the notion that the American press simply follows the lead of Democratic and Republican political elites on foreign policy. They believe, instead, that the media plays a far more active role in deciding which elite voices are heard (Althaus 2003; Baum and Groeling 2010; Lawrence 2000; Wolfsfeld 2004). Gadi Wolfsfeld (2004) has developed a broad model, which he describes as the political-media-political cycle, to underscore the influence of political factors on news media coverage and the media's influence in turn on subsequent political events. Wolfsfeld argues that a diverse array of political factors influence news creation and determine which elite voices are heard in the news. Within his model, two factors stand out as relevant to news coverage of the Iraq War. First, he contends that conflict is often exaggerated by the news media because it attracts attention and audiences. When it comes to news coverage of a peace process, for example, a breakdown in talks is likely to be embellished by the news media to emphasize conflict whereas smooth ongoing talks are largely ignored. In this way the media can worsen a peace process by drawing excessive attention to minor problems. As Wolfsfeld and Sheafer (2006, 334) note, "Journalists exercise a good deal of discretion in deciding how to cover events and which voices should be heard."

Baum and Groeling (2010; Groeling and Baum 2008) further develop and test the media's penchant for elite conflict in news coverage of foreign policy. They argue that the press distorts the balance and weight of elite positions on a given issue by giving disproportionate attention to the views of party renegades—for example, Republican elites who criticize or Democrats who support the position of a Republican administration. This is exactly what Hayes and Guardino found in analysis of evening network news in the lead-up to the Iraq War, which gave excessive attention to Republican opposition, even though congressional Republicans were a very minor presence in war-related news. As we note, there was also ample and, perhaps, exaggerated airing of Republican opposition to the war in the summer of 2002, in phase 3 of the prewar information environment.

RIDING THE NEWS WAVE.   A second factor within Wolfsfeld's model concerns the existence of political waves, "sudden and significant changes in the political environment" (Wolfsfeld 2004, 32), which are associated with a dramatic increase in media attention (Wolfsfeld and Sheafer 2006). This may be a good way to describe media coverage of the impending Iraq war in the fall of 2002. The Bush administration initiated the "Iraq War news wave" with a barrage of pro-war facts and arguments delivered by high-level administration figures, including the president, throughout September 2002. Waves typically have a direction and momentum, which further skews news coverage, leading contrary facts and arguments to be swept aside and dismissed (Wolfsfeld and Sheafer 2006).

But the media's tendency to bias coverage in the direction of a powerful news wave does little to resolve our two conundrums concerning growing Democratic and independent opposition to war in the fall of 2002. A biased wave of news that privileged the president's position and provided momentum for a pro-war stance fits with the popular conception of news coverage in the fall of 2002 but does little to help solve the contrary antiwar trends in Democratic and independent opinion. Perhaps the most promising notion to emerge from this line of research is that the media, in its preference for conflict, exaggerated elite Democratic opposition to the war and shaped Democratic public opinion in an antiwar direction. However, evidence on this point is weak. William Howell and Jon Pevehouse report that Democratic members of Congress made 353 speeches concerning Iraq in the last two weeks of September, with opponents outweighing supporters by three to one.[14] But these speeches were not well represented in the news. Members of Congress, most of whom were Democrats, made up only one in five sources in local television news coverage of Iraq between mid-September and the end of October 2002 (Howell and Pevehouse 2007). Democratic members of Congress were also a minor source of war opposition in national network news (Hayes and Guardino 2011).

News Media Challenges Administration Elites

Finally, in a further twist on the elite influence model, some researchers have suggested that news coverage of foreign policy changed in the aftermath of the Cold War to become more critical, independent, and less reliant on American elite opinion. Robinson and his colleagues (2010) consider the possibility that new technology has empowered the news media to challenge elites, although they find scant evidence of this in British news coverage of the 2003 Iraq invasion. Entman (2003, 2004) argues—in support of his cascading activation model—that when conflicts are ideologically ambiguous, the news media is emboldened to present contrary points of view and argue against an administration's position. Focusing specifically on US military involvement in Somalia (in 1993), Haiti (in 1994), and the Balkans (1993–1999), he found ample critical news coverage in the American media of conflicts that occurred during the Clinton administration. He also argues that the news media's growing independence intensifies journalists' reliance on diverse sources, including non-US sources, to criticize an administration's foreign policy.[15]

Others echo Entman's position that the news media has grown increasingly reliant on foreign dissent as a way to "balance" coverage of US foreign policy. For example, Althaus (2003) found that foreign sources drove negative TV news coverage of the 1991 Gulf War. Hayes and Guardino (2010, 2011) explored the presence of diverse voices in the news in the months before the Iraq War and argue that journalists are most likely to rely on foreign sources when there is an absence of domestic political dissent among Democratic and Republican elites. In their analysis of all sources—a total of over six thousand—that appeared in 1,434 TV network news segments aired in the seven to eight months prior to the Iraq War's onset (from August 1, 2002, onward), Hayes and Guardino found that pro- and antiwar sources were remarkably balanced. Roughly a third of all sources in the analyzed stories supported the war, 29% opposed it, and 37% were neutral. This balance masks, however, tremendous variability in the credibility of those who favored versus those who opposed the war. Not surprisingly, the Bush administration dominated the views of those who supported the war, comprising 28% of sources overall and 66% of those who supported the war. Very little opposition emanated from highly credible Democratic elites (4% of all source comments, and 40% of these were pro-war). Antiwar groups received even less attention. Most published war opposition came from foreign sources: Iraqis including Saddam made up 13% of all sources; other international sources, including British prime minister Tony Blair, French president Jacques Chirac, and other French, German, and Russian officials, made up 11%. Blair supported the Iraq invasion but most other foreign sources opposed it. Overall, Iraqis, an especially unreliable and noncredible source for Americans, made up 40% of those opposed to the war in Hayes and Guardino's analysis of network TV.

Hayes and Guardino (2011) also assessed the influence of foreign TV news sources on American public opinion by combining the media data with data from nine public opinion polls conducted by Pew between August 2002 and March 2003. They found that opposition to the war from foreign (non-Iraqi) sources led to increased opposition to the war among well-educated Democrats and political independents, and they conclude that opposition to the war from French president Chirac, German political elites, and UN leaders explains increasing Democratic opposition to the war in the fall of 2002. This is an intriguing solution to conundrum 1, but we remain skeptical of Hayes and Guardino's analysis for several reasons.

First, it is not entirely clear what the count of foreign (non-Iraqi) antiwar sources actually measures. Hayes and Guardino (2011, 837n11) note that the number of pro- and antiwar statements from foreign (non-Iraqi) sources was almost completely coterminous ($r = .97$) in their media data. In other words, when foreign sources appeared in stories about an impending war, they included sources both for and against. This suggests that the appearance of foreign sources in the news, regardless of their position, may be driven by a third unexamined factor—perhaps an international event such as a UN weapons inspectors' report. This complicates the attributions of antiwar Democratic opinion to foreign antiwar sources since Hayes and Guardino's measure may confound a foreign antiwar source with a specific type of event or piece of information that could ultimately be responsible for the decline in war support among well-educated Democrats and independents. We are sympathetic to the difficulties in identifying causality with cross-sectional data but remain troubled nonetheless by the difficulty in clearly attributing Democratic war opposition to foreign sources in this case.

Second, it is difficult to know whether respondents in Hayes and Guardino's analyses were actually exposed to the antiwar positions of foreign sources in TV news. In their analysis, Pew polls measuring public attitudes are combined with research on network news content from the time period prior to each Pew poll. Hayes and Guardino document stronger effects of foreign antiwar views on well-educated Democrats and Republicans, but education level remains a weak proxy for news exposure, and there is no measure in their data of how regularly people watch TV news. As we show in chapter 5, employing data from two different national surveys conducted in the fall of 2002, we were unable to find any evidence of elevated war opposition among Democrats who were well informed about Iraq and regularly obtained their news from television. This adds to our concern about both the robustness and underlying causality of Hayes and Guardino's findings.[16] We thus continue our search for a resolution to the two conundrums posed in chapter 1.

Overall, Hayes and Guardino's research leaves us with the intriguing possibility that support for a war in Iraq declined among Democrats and independents in the fall of 2002 because they were exposed to persuasive opposition from foreign leaders. We remain open-minded but somewhat skeptical for the reasons we have just outlined and continue our search for an answer to the questions with which we began: Why did support for the war decline among political Democrats and independents in the fall of 2002?

News Media Disparities: Television versus Print

There is a tendency to treat the news media as a single entity. Certainly many observers have come to view news media coverage in the lead-up to the Iraq War as a singular failure. But news media organizations are diverse and that diversity has clear consequences for the quality of foreign policy news coverage. As Robinson and his colleagues (2010, 173) note, "News media performance is, at the very least, more nuanced and varied than . . . in the prevailing elite-driven orthodoxy that exists among scholars." They document challenging and independent media coverage of the 2003 Iraq War in the British press by "disaggregating data according to both subject area and a wide range of news outlets" (174). In their study, three of the four selected TV news programs and four of the seven newspapers provided elite-driven pro-war news whereas one of the TV programs and three of the seven newspapers provided news that was independent of, or actually challenged, political elites. In Britain, newspapers provided more independent coverage of the war than did TV. They concluded that greater research attention should also be paid to a broad range of news outlets in the United States to determine whether media independence is also a feature of the American media landscape.

Howell and Pevehouse (2007) provide considerable nuance to the study of media coverage of the prewar period by focusing on local television news, an understudied news medium. They argue that members of Congress hold a check on the president's ability to wage war by making critical appearances on local television within their state or district in the lead-up to war, asking questions and raising concerns about military engagement. This is especially likely to occur when the president's party does not have a majority in Congress. Howell and Pevehouse examined the influence of such negative, antiwar local TV content on public opinion concerning the impending Iraq war in October 2002, focusing on the top fifty US media markets. They find that antiwar coverage on local TV lowered support for the war among Democrats and independents within a specific media market. This is an important claim, which bolsters the elite influence model and suggests a solution to our two conundrums— Democratic members of Congress, mostly senators, opposed to the war appeared on local television and swayed their fellow Democrats toward war opposition. This is an appealing solution to the puzzle but one that does not jibe with our own analysis of public opinion to which we will return in chapters 5 and 6. We found no evidence of greater antiwar opinion among Democratic residents of states with a senator who voted against the Iraq War Resolution.

Howell and Pevehouse's (2007) efforts to dig more deeply into the media environment concerning the war provide a welcome addition to research in this area, but we remain concerned that the tone of war coverage in local television news in a specific media market is strongly linked to prevailing opinion in that area, making it more difficult to disentangle what comes first. The researchers report that the strongest antiwar coverage on local TV occurred in politically liberal locations and the most positive, pro-war coverage existed in conservative locales. Howell and Pevehouse (2007) deal with the conflation of local opinion and tone of media coverage through the inclusion of county-wide demographic factors, such as the percentage of Democratic or college-educated residents, as controls within their analyses. But this may be insufficient to fully unravel the complex interplay of prevailing public opinion and tone of media coverage, especially in the absence of a multilevel model that accounts for place. In addition, we do not know which respondents in Howell and Pevehouse's analysis watched local TV news, and we do not know if they had been exposed to or acquired any information about Iraq. We find their solution to our conundrums interesting but remain unconvinced by their analysis. We find no evidence in our analyses that Democrats and independents exposed to television news were more inclined to oppose war.

There is evidence to suggest that newspaper coverage of the war may have been more balanced than that offered by the TV networks. It is fair to say that if anyone is going to dig below the surface and challenge an administration's arguments, print journalists will be at the forefront of that enterprise. As Alex Jones (2009) notes in his heartfelt paean to newspapers, they are responsible for at least 85% of all core news and are far more likely than TV to support and undertake investigative journalism. So perhaps it is critical newspaper coverage that explains declining Democratic war support in the fall of 2002.

To examine the role of newspapers, we dug more deeply into the news environment in the lead-up to the Iraq War. We included both newspapers and television in our analysis. Prior research has found that newspapers are more likely than TV to criticize an administration's foreign policy. Robert Entman and Benjamin Page (1994) documented greater opposition to the 1991 Gulf War in elite newspapers such as the *New York Times* and *Washington Post* than on the ABC nightly news. Entman (2004) also found fault with TV coverage in the aftermath of the 2001 terrorist attacks, noting that newspapers published several prominent stories critical of the administration's position on Saudi Arabia but that such coverage was absent from television. In a similar vein, Brent Cunningham (2003) documented a narrow sampling of elite views concerning a war with Iraq in television news. He reports that out of 414 stories on the buildup to the

Iraq War aired on ABC, CBS, and NBC from September 2002 to February 2003, only 34 came from a source other than the White House.

Television coverage of the Iraq War has certainly come in for its fair share of criticism. The failure of Fox News to convey the absence of WMD in Iraq after the onset of the war is well known (Kull, Ramsey, and Lewis 2003). Hayes and Guardino (2010) report a clear pro-war bias in TV network news coverage of the war in the eight months before it began, a bias that was especially evident on NBC and CBS. They found that when the tone of TV network news was analyzed on a daily basis between August 1, 2002, and March 19, 2003, coverage of the war was positive on 80% of all days. Network TV coverage was negative at several time points in September and October of 2002. But it was also at its highest pro-war levels in those months as well. On balance, it is clear that television network news supported and amplified the administration's case for war.

The suggestion that newspapers challenged the Bush administration on the war may seem ludicrous in light of the now well-known failure of war coverage in major newspapers such as the *New York Times* and the *Washington Post*. The *New York Times'* prewar stories were seriously flawed, with reporter Judith Miller as the target of much criticism (Massing 2004). War stories in the *New York Times* were faulted for including the use of unattributed sources and failing to verify or reveal sources' motivations. The *New York Times'* mea culpa, published on May 26, 2004, notes that the newspaper contained "information that was controversial then, and seems questionable now, was insufficiently qualified or allowed to stand unchallenged." In addition, the apology acknowledges that "the problematic articles" relied on "people whose credibility has come under increasing public debate in recent weeks," adding that "the accounts of these exiles were often eagerly confirmed by United States officials." On June 20, 2004, the *Washington Post's* ombudsman faulted the paper for failing to publish more critical material about the war on the front page and not providing more complete coverage of critical viewpoints in the lead-up to the war. The paper published a similarly critical article on August 12 of the same year, lamenting its failure to publish antiwar stories on the front page (Getler 2004; Kurtz 2004).

But not all stories in the *New York Times, Washington Post*, or other major newspapers were flawed or unbalanced. As Michael Massing (2004) notes, the *New York Times'* journalists Michael Gordon and Judith Miller wrote two stories, one on October 10 and another on October 24, 2002, on divisions within the administration and concerns within the intelligence community that were critical of the Bush administration's case for war.

In September, the *Washington Post* published two stories critical of the administration's claims concerning Iraq's nuclear program, and later, just days before the war began, on March 16 and March 18, it published several highly critical articles by Walter Pincus (Massing 2004). Massing also underscores the role of the Knight Ridder Washington Bureau reporters Jonathan Landay and Warren Strobel who wrote a searing article in early October on rampant dissent among career officers in the State Department, the military, and the intelligence community. Their story may not have received as much attention as it deserved, but Massing notes that it was eventually picked up by major newspapers such as the *Wall Street Journal*, *USA Today*, and the *LA Times*. Others have also lauded the Knight Ridder team for its maverick coverage in the lead-up to the war (Rendall 2006; Ricchiardi 2008; Ritea 2004).

The distinction between coverage emanating from the Knight Ridder Washington Bureau and content in the *Washington Post* and *New York Times* raises a further distinction between elite (also referred to as prestige, influential, or leading) and nonelite newspapers (Rojecki 2005, 2008). According to Serena Carpenter (2007, 763), "Elite news publications define the news agenda for other publications. Elite newspapers are likely to produce higher-quality content because they have greater resources to hire specialized and freelance reporters." In contrast, "nonelite publications concentrate their efforts on statewide geographic coverage," although there are some exceptions such as *USA Today*, which has a national focus but does not drive the news agenda (761). It is fair to describe Knight Ridder's newspapers as nonelite publications that cover areas outside the power centers of New York and Washington, DC. In 2002, they were broadly distributed nationally and included newspapers such as the *Philadelphia Inquirer*, the *Miami Herald*, the *San Jose Mercury News*, and the *Detroit Free Press*. We apply the term "nonelite" to include all regional and local papers including *USA Today*, and the term "elite" to include papers that influence the national news agenda such as the *New York Times*, the *Washington Post*, and the *Wall Street Journal*.

There is some reason to believe that nonelite papers diverged from elite publications in their coverage of the Iraq War. Conventional wisdom says elite papers set the agenda for nonelite sources. But that may not have been the case when it comes to coverage of the Iraq War. As Carpenter (2007) notes, nonelite media sources are more likely to focus on local aspects of foreign policy and are less likely than elite publications to have direct access to administration, military, and other powerful news sources. Normally, limited access to official sources would be considered an impediment to accurate reporting. But during the months prior to the onset of the Iraq War, when elite news sources were faulted for their undue reliance on administration sources, nonelite newspapers may have been granted a rare advantage. In this instance, lower level officials in the intelligence community, the Pentagon, the State Department, and the Department of Energy provided a more balanced and critical view of the administration's factual basis for going to war in Iraq.

News Media Failures and Accomplishments in the Lead-Up to the Iraq War

In general, news media organizations have been resoundingly condemned for their coverage of the Iraq War. In the popular press, critics such as Frank Rich painstakingly deconstructed the media's poor performance. Elite newspapers such as the *New York Times* and *Washington Post* subsequently apologized for lapses in their coverage. At the time, faux journalists Jon Stewart of *The Daily Show* and Stephen Colbert used the media's poor performance as grist for their hard-edged humor. One of the central critiques of the news media's performance was the willful exclusion of dissenting viewpoints. In his insightful analysis of news coverage leading up to the Iraq War, Michael Massing, writing in the *New York Review of Books* on February 26, 2004, notes that journalists were well aware of dissent within the intelligence community over the administration's factual case for war. But as he writes, "Few chose to write about it." Almost uniformly, critics fault the media for an overreliance on administration sources. Massing notes that "in the period before the war, US journalists were far too reliant on sources sympathetic to the administration. . . . Reflecting this, the coverage was highly deferential to the White House. This was especially apparent on the issue of Iraq's weapons of mass destruction—the heart of the President's case for war."

The exemplary performance of the Knight Ridder newspaper group and evidence from Britain of the superior war coverage in newspapers rather than on television (Robinson et al. 2010) suggest the need to differentiate among news sources and examine coverage more closely in the months before the war. TV news coverage may have failed to critically evaluate the administration's case for a war with Iraq in the latter part of 2002 and early 2003. But it may be erroneous to tarnish all news organizations with the same brush. To date, analysis of American news content before and during the Iraq War has focused almost exclusively on television coverage, making it difficult to assess the overall quality of coverage in newspapers. We know something about TV network news and local TV coverage in the months before the war from the research of Hayes and Guardino (2010, 2011) and Howell and Pevehouse (2007). Groeling and Baum (2008) also analyzed TV network coverage of a series of US military deployments, including sending troops to Iraq in 2003.

Research on newspaper coverage is far less evident (see Glazier and Boydstun [2012] for an exception). Entman (2004) provides a rare glimpse of the nature of war coverage both on TV and in newspapers. Drawing on research by the conservative-leaning Center for Media and Public Affairs, he reports that over 70% of sources on network TV and in the *New York Times* were antiwar in the summer of 2002. Yet this research did not examine the period covering the Bush administration's campaign in favor of a war in Iraq. Anecdotally, the print media, for whatever its failings, seems to have been far more likely than TV to report critically on the war's rationale and factual case.

News Media and the Psychology of Public Opinion

We return finally to the psychological model of public opinion that frames our analysis of public opinion throughout this book, outlined in some detail in the previous chapter. As we note there, the news media plays an important role in providing the public with information. This information often centers on the views of recognizable political elites from the two major parties. But it might also include information that challenges elites or provides alternative viewpoints when elites fail to take a stance on an issue. The news media can facilitate public deliberation, especially when the public is motivated to think hard about an important issue, by relaying a broad set of opinions, reaching out to experts, international leaders, and other "outsiders," and providing new facts and information. In other words, at its best, when the public needs high-quality nonpartisan information, the news media can serve the public interest by engaging in good investigative journalism. This does not preclude partisans from arriving at a biased stance even when exposed to high-quality information, but it does increase the chance that their policy positions will be well reasoned and well informed.

Our position differs from that of Hayes and Guardino (2011), who argue that foreign leaders are an added source of elite influence. Within our model, there is a major difference between elite influence in which partisan cues serve as a form of decisional heuristic or shortcut and systematic information processing in which opinions are formed through the careful consideration of facts, greater adherence to the views of credible sources, and persuasion via high-quality arguments. Unlike partisan elites, foreign sources are more difficult to classify, their motives are harder to discern, and their loyalties less obvious than those of domestic partisan elites. For that reason, they are unlikely to trigger the kind of effortless partisan heuristic that guides so much political decision making within the American public. Once the public shifts to a more systematic form of information processing, foreign leaders are simply one more source of information along with many others. They will be believed to the extent to which they are credible and advance strong factual and well-reasoned arguments.

In the next chapter, we examine the information environment as reflected in news coverage on TV and in newspapers in the critical months of September and October of 2002. This was the period when the administration made its most concerted public case for war. In order to trace news coverage across different media, we focus on two stories that were central to the administration's case. We focus on these two stories to better compare how they were handled by print and electronic media and evaluate the media's performance. We focus carefully on news coverage of these two stories in search of good investigative journalism that may have led Democrats and independents to rethink their support for a war in Iraq.

The News Media Reacts

Channeling and Challenging the Administration

"Unlike a lot of our competitors who write for the people who send other people to war, we write for the people who get sent to war, we write for their mothers and fathers and their sisters and brothers and their sons and daughters."—John Walcott, Knight Ridder Washington Bureau chief, quoted in Borjesson (2005, 337)

Kristina Borjesson, in her 2005 book *Feet to the Fire*, says, "More often than any other journalist or news organization, Knight Ridder was mentioned by those in this book as the best source for post-9/11 reporting" (336). As Paul Krugman put the matter: "Actually, with respect to the war, when all these supposed revelations about everything from aluminum tubes to mobile biological weapons vans came out, I said, 'I knew all that beforehand, why did I know all that? It was because I'd been reading Knight Ridder all along, and the guys at Knight Ridder had been reporting on the doubts among the midlevel people in the intelligence community'" (Borejesson 2005, 187).

The Knight Ridder team's reporting reflected its mission in serving readers in "Columbus, Georgia, Fort Campbell, Kentucky and Fort Hood, Texas, and Shaw Air Force base, South Carolina," as noted by John Walcott at the beginning of this chapter. In addition to providing news for military families, the Knight Ridder papers also lacked the high-level access to policy makers enjoyed by elite news organizations. This may normally be a disadvantage but in this instance it may have proved advantageous. As noted by Walter Strobel, a reporter at the Knight Ridder Washington Bureau: "Knight Ridder is not, in some people's eyes, seen as playing in the same ball field as the New York Times and some major networks. . . . People at the Times were mainly talking to senior administration officials, who were mostly pushing the administration line. We were mostly talking to the lower-level people or dissidents, who didn't necessarily repeat the party line" (Ritea 2004, 16).

Knight Ridder reporting was exemplary but it was not entirely unique.[1] As we will show in this chapter, newspapers were generally more persistent and challenging than TV of the administration's central claims concerning Iraq. Similar trends have been documented in British newspapers such as the *Mirror*, *Independent*, and *Guardian*, which provided more critical coverage of the war than did television. In the United States, Knight Ridder's stories had broader reach beyond its own papers, influencing the content of newspapers such as the *Los Angeles Times* and *USA Today* (Massing 2004). We believe that many American newspapers, including those owned by Knight Ridder, smaller newspapers that carried news from the Associated Press (AP) wire service, and the large-circulation national newspaper *USA Today*, contained sufficient information to cause Americans to think twice about the wisdom of a war against Iraq. This possibility deserves careful research consideration as an explanation for the decline in Democratic and independent war support in September and October of 2002. To date, the lion's share of research attention has focused on TV news coverage of the impending Iraq war (Baum and Groeling 2010; Hayes and Guardino 2010; Howell and Pevehouse 2007). But as we show in this chapter, there were clear differences between TV and newspapers in the tone, content, and timing of news coverage of Iraq in the lead-up to the war.

In this chapter, we evaluate the news information environment that existed in the fall of 2002. We do so by examining in some detail news stories focused on two central claims made by the Bush administration. We look closely at pro- and antiwar information and the sources from which such information emanated. Without doubt, the news media conveyed—and prominently featured—the administration's pro-war position. But did they also convey the views of those with doubts and concerns about the war? And who were such critics? Our hypothesis is that newspapers were more likely than television to air a full range of opinion, including the views of administration skeptics, on a possible war against Iraq, a supposition we put to the test in this chapter.

In the months before the looming war, there were a large number of news stories on many different facets of a possible military intervention in Iraq. We confine our analysis of news content to two key Bush administration claims that appeared in numerous stories in the months of September and October 2002. The two claims were intertwined with critical aspects of the administration's case for war. Moreover, each claim relied on facts that were highly questionable. And both stories were readily refutable on factual grounds at the time they were advanced (Bennett, Lawrence, and Livingston 2007).

We first examine news coverage of the alleged existence of ties between Iraq and al Qaeda. We then turn to the second claim, the purported attempts by Iraq to purchase aluminum tubes for use in the production of enriched uranium to fuel nuclear weapons. This focus on just two administration claims out of the many issues covered by the press in the months before the Iraq War is far from a complete account of prewar news content. But a focus on these two claims allows us to do two things that would otherwise be very difficult. First, we can evaluate the press's performance in handling specious facts put forward by the administration, providing an unambiguous indicator of media performance. As we will show, the administration's claims asserting an Iraq–al Qaeda connection or Iraq's use of aluminum tubes to build a nuclear weapon were supported by weak evidence at best. Yet only a minority of news stories acknowledged the weaknesses that undermined each of the two claims. Second, a focus on two specific administration claims allows us to compare how well different news outlets performed in handling the same facts and allegations. We compare television and newspaper coverage, but go further to distinguish among national elite newspapers (*New York Times*, *Wall Street Journal*, and *Washington Post*), more locally focused nonelite newspapers (including *USA Today*), and the AP wire service, a common source of news for smaller local papers. By focusing on two specific claims, we can directly compare coverage across news outlets, a strategy also pursued by Piers Robinson and his colleagues (2010) in the United Kingdom. We compare the pro- or antiwar tone of news coverage, the degree to which journalists relied on Democratic and Republican leaders as a source of news, the inclusion of other sources such as experts, and the degree to which specific sources provided pro- or antiwar information and arguments. Our analysis of news stories on the Iraq–al Qaeda connection and the aluminum tubes confirms conventional wisdom: in the lead-up to the Iraq War, the administration dominated news in all outlets, including national television and newspapers. But we also find that newspapers did a better job than television in providing the public with a careful and skeptical examination of these claims. Good journalism was present in some newspapers and the AP wire service but was far less sustained or prominent on television. Our analysis of news media coverage hints at why some Americans, many Democrats and independents, began to doubt the case for war and remained skeptical of the administration's facts in the fall of 2002. They obtained information from newspapers, a finding that is confirmed in chapters 5 and 6.

We begin by analyzing news media coverage of the claim that Saddam Hussein's regime was implicated in the activities of al Qaeda.

The Claim That Saddam Was Linked to al Qaeda

Reviving Accusations of a Prague Meeting

To justify military action in Iraq, the Bush administration decided to publicly connect Saddam with al Qaeda. According to former White House press secretary Scott McLellan (2008), President Bush supported a war in Iraq to generate dramatic change in the Middle East. To justify the impending confrontation, the administration decided to emphasize "the threat of WMD, and the possible link between Iraq and terrorism" (130), even as administration officials such as former US deputy secretary of defense Paul Wolfowitz later acknowledged disagreement among officials concerning the validity of the claim.[2] A story had been circulating for some time of a secret Prague meeting between Mohammed Atta, one of the 9/11 hijackers, and Iraqi officials. The claim, attributed to an unnamed source, first surfaced on September 18, 2001, in a Reuters story and was published in the *Washington Post*.[3] This story was followed by many claims and counterclaims from the Czechs about the existence of such a meeting. Czech president Vaclav Havel denied it and then refuted his denial, and then other Czech officials backed away from the claim.[4] Perhaps more importantly, US intelligence found no evidence of such a meeting, a fact that was known and widely reported by the news media well before September 2002 (Suskind 2006; Swoger 2002).[5]

To track news coverage of the Iraq–al Qaeda link, we searched Lexis-Nexis for relevant television transcripts and several different databases for relevant newspaper stories.[6] Our analysis includes all news stories published from mid-September to late October 2002 that referred to a link between Iraq and al Qaeda. This period begins with the story's emergence as part of the Bush administration's case for war and ends just after the passage of the Iraq War Resolution. The period included the congressional debate on the war resolution and coincides with a period in which

Democratic and independent war support declined. We included all news stories that discussed the Iraq–al Qaeda connection on evening television news on any of the three major networks (ABC, CBS, NBC) or either of the two major cable TV news channels (CNN, Fox News), or were printed in one of the top thirty newspapers (for a complete list of newspapers, see the appendix).[7] A further distinction was drawn between the three influential elite papers (the *Wall Street Journal*, the *New York Times*, and the *Washington Post*) and twenty-seven nonelite or local newspapers. We also coded AP wire service stories (Lacy, Chang, and Lau 1989).

We searched for the terms "Iraq" and "al Qaeda" (including alternative spellings such as "al Qaida"). The search yielded a total of 226 stories (22 on TV news, 161 in the top thirty newspapers, and 43 AP stories; all stories are listed in the online appendix at http://press.uchicago.edu/sites/Feldman/index.html). We omitted opinion stories, interviews, transcripts of speeches, and talk shows from the coding so that we could focus on the news, both televised and in newspapers. The Iraq–al Qaeda link was not the primary focus in all stories, but the connection was mentioned in each one.

The claim of a connection between Iraq and al Qaeda was forcefully revived by Secretary of Defense Donald Rumsfeld on September 24 when he reported that NATO defense ministers had discussed a link between Iraq and al Qaeda at a CIA meeting in Warsaw. On September 26, President Bush amplified the claim, saying in a Rose Garden speech that "the [Iraqi] regime has long-standing and continuing ties to terrorist organizations, and there are al Qaeda terrorists inside Iraq."[8] That evening, Condoleezza Rice, then national security advisor, said on ABC's *World News Tonight*, "Several of the [al Qaeda] detainees, in particular, some high-ranking detainees, have said that Iraq provided some training to al Qaeda in chemical weapons development." Also, that same day, Secretary Rumsfeld stated that "Iraq and al Qaeda have discussed safe haven opportunities in Iraq, reciprocal non-aggression discussions,"[9] and then later in the evening of September 26 on ABC's *Nightline*, he said, "We have what we consider to be credible evidence that al Qaeda leaders have sought contacts in Iraq who could help them acquire weapons of mass destruction capabilities." CNN reporter Suzanne Malveaux described the news unleashed on September 26 as "a Bush administration blitz."[10]

The story was carried widely on September 26 and discussed on numerous television news talk shows. The only voice of dissent from within the administration, such as it was, came from CIA director George Tenet who gave tepid support to the administration, saying on *ABC World News Tonight*, "Their ties [Iraq and al Qaeda] may be limited by divergent ideologies, but the two sides' mutual antipathies toward the United States and the Saudi royal family suggests that tactical cooperation between them is possible." The one qualifying administration statement was given by an unnamed CIA source on CBS the following evening (September 27), who when asked about the claim replied, "Is there conclusive proof that they are working together? No."[11]

Some outside the administration, including several congressional Democrats, challenged the validity of this claim. The night after the president's speech, on September 27, Senator Ted Kennedy said on *CBS Evening News*, "A case has not been made to connect al-Qaida and Iraq. To the contrary, there is no clear and convincing pattern of Iraqi relations with either al-Qaida or the Taliban." Several other high-profile Democrats expressed surprise at the administration's announcement of a newly discovered connection between Iraq and al Qaeda. A report on the previous evening's *NBC Nightly News* noted that "leading Democrats who get classified briefings said this evidence was news to them." On the same day, Fox News' *Special Report with Brit Hume* included quotes from Senators Joe Biden and Tom Daschle, with majority leader Daschle saying that it was a "reversal of information the administration shared with us earlier this year." This skepticism was echoed by a number of reporters who raised questions about the lack of conclusive evidence supporting the administration's case.

A few Republican officials also questioned the credibility of the administration's claim. For example, Lawrence Eagleburger, former secretary of state in the first Bush administration, appeared on CNN's *Crossfire* on September 26 to cast doubt on the link, saying "I think that it is tenuous to argue that the al Qaeda connection and Saddam Hussein is so intense that it merits invading Iraq." Added opposition to the administration's claim came from murky, unnamed sources such as "a senior intelligence official" on that day's *ABC World News Tonight*, a Scottish academic on ABC's *Nightline*, and "some U.S. allies" on *NBC Nightly News*. None of this opposition definitively refuted the existence of a connection between Saddam and al Qaeda.

For the most part, opponents simply argued that the administration had not made an iron-clad case. Statements and arguments for and against the Iraq–al Qaeda link in major national media sources make clear that the fight was not an even match. Powerful administration officials such as

Rumsfeld, Rice, and Bush were pitted against former Republican secretary of state Eagleburger, Democratic Senate majority leader Daschle, and Senator Ted Kennedy, along with a collection of unnamed intelligence officials, analysts, and US allies.

Coverage Declines, Questions Linger in Newspapers

After the initial flurry of news coverage of the Bush administration's claims concerning an Iraq–al Qaeda connection, the story declined in prominence both in print, elite and nonelite newspapers alike, and on TV. As shown in figure 4.1, the decline was far more precipitous on TV than in newspapers. In the week in which the claim of an Iraq–al Qaeda link was resurrected (September 23–29), the five TV outlets aired a combined total of fifteen evening stories on the connection. This resulted in a weekly average of three evening news segments per outlet. In the same week, the top thirty newspapers published a total of 72 stories, or a weekly average of 2.4 stories per newspaper, that mentioned the link. The three elite newspapers published a total of 10 stories that week and the remaining top thirty newspapers published 62. This resulted in a somewhat higher weekly average of 3.3 stories in each elite newspaper compared to a weekly average of 2.3 stories in each local newspaper. There was a short-lived spike in the number of stories on the Iraq–al Qaeda connection both on TV and in newspapers around October 8, a day after a major speech on the war by President Bush and coinciding with the publication of an influential and highly critical Knight Ridder news story on doubts about the war within the intelligence community. Overall, there was greater continued attention to the Iraq–al Qaeda link in newspapers than on TV, with the average top thirty newspapers printing roughly two to three times as many stories each week as aired on the average TV outlet in the three weeks following the story's launch.

Of course, the looming war (but not necessarily the Iraq–al Qaeda link) continued to be covered on television. Hayes and Guardino report that each of the three major networks aired between one and two stories a night on Iraq in September and October 2002, but few of these discussed the existence of a link between Iraq and al Qaeda.

The stories sourced to the AP are not included in figure 4.1. But not surprisingly, of any single news organization, the AP issued the greatest number of stories referring to the Iraq–al Qaeda connection. Moreover, its coverage was more persistent over time than that observed for

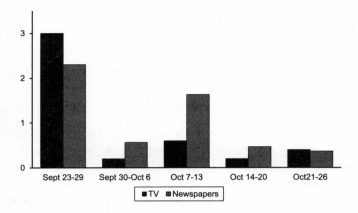

FIGURE 4.1 Iraq–al Qaeda link: Average weekly number of stories per TV channel/newspaper

Note: Weekly averages are calculated for news on five TV channels (ABC, CBS, NBC, CNN, Fox News) and the top thirty newspapers.

television. The AP released eighteen stories beginning in late September. A further six stories appeared in the week beginning on September 30, followed by ten the week of October 7, six the week of October 14, and three in the final week included in the study (October 21). The AP's sustained attention on the Iraq–al Qaeda link is crucial because its stories were likely picked up by many smaller-circulation newspapers around the country.

The administration continued to assert the existence of an Iraq–al Qaeda connection well into late October. Vice President Dick Cheney repeated the claim on NBC's *Meet the Press* on October 21, 2002, saying "We have reporting that place [*sic*] him [Atta] in Prague with a senior Iraqi intelligence official a few months before the attack on the World Trade Center." In addition to this claim, *CBS Evening News* included a segment on October 1, 2002, that claimed Khalid al-Mihdhar, one of the 9/11 hijackers, had met an Iraqi contact at an al Qaeda summit in Malaysia in late 2000. And President Bush in a speech to the nation on October 7, 2002, included the claim that the terrorist leader al-Zarqawi had spent time in a Baghdad hospital.[12]

In general, TV stories tended to support the administration's case to a greater extent than did newspapers. For example, in the October 1 *CBS Evening News* segment, anchor Dan Rather announced that "CBS News national security correspondent David Martin has done some digging into

this alleged [Iraq–al Qaeda] connection and found new evidence, which is at least enough to keep suspicions alive." Rather unveiled evidence that claimed a meeting was held in 2000 between 9/11 hijacker Khalid al-Mihdhar and an Iraqi official and that Mohammed Atta had visited Prague at least four times between 1993 and 2001. Fox News ran a story on October 24 on the Department of Defense's creation of an alternative intelligence unit that had supposedly confirmed some of the administration's claims.[13]

During this period Fox News conducted interviews with former CIA director James Woolsey, Republican senators Kay Bailey Hutchinson and Richard Shelby, and Democratic senator Bill Nelson, who were broadly supportive of the administration's factual claims.[14] And when the Bush administration's claims were challenged on TV, such challenges were part of long segments in which the administration's case was amply aired.[15] Indeed, after the revival of the supposed Iraq–al Qaeda connection on September 26, only one of the major networks (NBC) aired a long story that consistently challenged the administration's position.[16]

In this period, while TV conveyed and amplified the administration's claims, the same claims were being challenged in newspapers. Local papers published stories with headlines such as "Iraq No Friend of al-Qaida, Experts Say" (*Cleveland Plain Dealer*), "Experts Skeptical of al-Qaeda–Iraq Tie" (*USA Today*), "On Its Streets, Iraq Seems Unlikely Enemy" (*Philadelphia Inquirer*), "Bush's Evidence of Threat Disputed"(*San Francisco Chronicle*) (see the online appendix). Elite newspapers also expressed doubts. The *New York Times* ran an editorial on September 30 titled "Saddam Hussein and Al Qaeda Are Not Allies" and published stories on October 20 and 21 and an editorial on the twenty-third refuting the existence of a meeting between Atta and Iraqi officials. Even the typically conservative *Wall Street Journal* published a story on October 23 titled "Missing Links: Bush Efforts to Tie Hussein to al Qaeda Lack Clear Evidence—U.S. Intelligence Can't Affirm Claims Despite His History with Other Terror Groups."

In the days following the alleged link between Iraq and al Qaeda, skepticism was voiced in diverse newspapers. Of course, newspapers also published stories favorable to the administration. But overall there were many more biting headlines on the alleged Iraq–al Qaeda connection in newspapers than on TV. Newspaper stories critical of the administration's claims conveyed the views of skeptics that came from among congressional Democrats, members of the intelligence community, and numerous international leaders. These were published in diverse locations around the country including Cleveland, Columbus, Dallas, Grand Rapids, Houston, Long Island, Milwaukee, Miami, Philadelphia, San Jose, St. Louis, and Sarasota.

News coverage critical of the administration's claim appeared in both elite national and local newspapers. Criticism also surfaced in *USA Today*, the most widely read newspaper in the nation (with a weekday circulation of over two million households) at that time. *USA Today* ran a story on October 8, 2002, about President Bush's little-noticed and poorly watched October 7 speech on Iraq, noting that "by every sign, the president already has the bipartisan support he seeks for a war resolution." However, the article also noted that "the speech's relatively limited reach could shortchange the public, which has pushed for clearer explanations of why a confrontation now, how high the risks and what comes next." *USA Today* also ran other highly critical articles with titles such as "Experts Skeptical of al-Qaeda–Iraq Tie" (September 27, 2002), "Maintain CIA's Independence" (October 24, 2002), and "Rush to War Could Sabotage Rumsfeld Plan for Success" (October 16, 2002).

The Knight Ridder Washington Bureau, which disseminated stories to its own and other local newspapers, was actively challenging the administration's claims of an al Qaeda–Iraq connection. In late September and early October, the three Knight Ridder newspapers included in our quantitative analysis—the *Philadelphia Inquirer*, the *Detroit Free Press*, and the *Miami Herald*, ranked 19, 20, and 27 by circulation—published a number of stories that raised serious questions about the connection. Other non–Knight Ridder newspapers picked up this content, and Knight Ridder stories were published in various newspapers including the *Dallas Morning News*, the *Bergen County (NJ) Record*, the *Monterey County (CA) Herald*, the *Saint Paul (MN) Pioneer Press*, and the *Albany (NY) Times Union*. Knight Ridder Washington Bureau reporter Walter Strobel issued a highly influential story on October 8, which revealed considerable dissent within the intelligence community. The story begins with the following sentence: "While President Bush marshals congressional and international support for invading Iraq, a growing number of military officers, intelligence professionals and diplomats in his own government privately have deep misgivings about the administration's double-time march toward war." This story was printed in numerous Knight Ridder newspapers on that day including the *San Jose Mercury News* (Knight Ridder's flagship paper), the *Philadelphia Inquirer*, the *Miami Herald*, and the *Contra*

Costa Times. In addition, the story also appeared in the *Houston Chronicle*, the *Milwaukee Journal Sentinel*, and the *Pittsburgh Post-Gazette*. An editorial published in the *St. Louis Post Dispatch* on September 29 explicitly mentioned information obtained by Knight Ridder as raising doubts about a connection between Iraq and al Qaeda.

AP stories, a common source for print news, also contained extensive criticism of the Bush administration's claims of an Iraq–al Qaeda link. Critical headlines issued in late September and early October included "U.S. Is on the Edge of Available Evidence, Maybe Over, in Making the Case for Iraq War," "U.S. Lawmakers in Iraq Say They Oppose War; Russia Not Convinced of Terror Links," and "Chirac: France Has No Proof of a Link between Iraq and al-Qaida" (see online appendix). An AP story written by Calvin Woodward on September 28 begins with the following sentence: "In making the case for war, the Bush administration has delivered a bill of particulars against Saddam Hussein that includes al-Qaida terrorist links yet to be demonstrated and weapons he may or may not have within reach." This is followed by an equally damning statement: "Publicly, President Bush's officials are touting reports that al-Qaida operatives have found refuge in Baghdad and that Iraq once helped them develop chemical weapons. Privately, government intelligence sources are hedging on that subject, suggesting there might be less than meets the eye." The story was published in the *St. Louis Post Dispatch*, a large-circulation newspaper, and in a number of smaller newspapers including the *Lewiston (ME) Sun-Journal*, the *Ukiah (CA) Daily Journal*, and the *Topeka (KS) Capital-Journal*.

Differences in Newspaper and TV Coverage Tone

To assess the differences between newspapers and television in their coverage of the administration's claim of an Iraq–al Qaeda link, five coders read and coded news stories that referred to the connection. Table 4.1 provides a summary of the number of stories and sentences coded for each type of media outlet.

The overall gist of a story was coded on a five-point scale: strongly antiwar, antiwar, neutral, pro-war, strongly pro-war. Further, the coders were directed to evaluate each sentence of every story. Every nonneutral sentence within a story was coded on a four-point scale: strongly antiwar, antiwar, pro-war, strongly pro-war.[17] Antiwar sentences, for example, included explicit doubts about a link between Iraq and al Qaeda, raised

TABLE 4.1 **News stories coded on Iraq–al Qaeda link**

September 24– October 25, 2002	TV	Elite newspapers	Nonelite, within top thirty newspapers	Wire service
Media organizations	ABC, CBS, CNN, FOX, NBC	*New York Times,* *Washington Post,* *Wall Street Journal*	*USA Today,* local papers	AP
Total number of stories (225)	22	35	126	43
Total number of pro- and antiwar sentences (2,842)	257	542	1,693	350

questions about the quality or existence of the administration's evidence, showed a preference for diplomacy over war, presented reservations about going to war, or made reference to the possible negative outcomes of war (see the appendix for more information on comments coded as pro- and antiwar).

Negative statements about Saddam, a reference to the existence of an Iraq–al Qaeda link, doubts about the ability of the UN to monitor the situation, a reference to the war's positive consequences, and any reference to the negative consequences of not going to war were all coded as pro-war and supportive of the administration. Our coding regime is similar to those employed by other scholars (Hayes and Guardino 2010).

Overall, 2,842 nonneutral sentences were coded from articles that made reference to the Iraq–al Qaeda link. In general, coders erred on the side of caution in coding the thrust of sentences, resulting in liberal use of the neutral category (there were an additional 4,700 neutral sentences that were not coded any further).[18]

Systematic coding of the news stories demonstrates that the administration's claim of an Iraq–al Qaeda link received far less critical coverage on TV than in newspapers. News stories on TV were skewed toward support of the administration's position, containing more pro- than antiwar content. This arose, in part, because TV coverage was heavily concentrated around the time in which the administration launched its claims of the Iraq–al Qaeda connection when news segments were dominated by administration officials. Over 50% of TV stories supported the administration's position whereas less than a third of newspaper or AP stories did so, as seen in figure 4.2. Newspaper stories, in both elite and local papers, were fairly evenly balanced between stories that supported and opposed the administration, whereas the wire service tilted more toward opposition, with almost half of all stories adopting an antiwar thrust. A pro-war position was evident in 55% of TV segments but substantially less so in elite (31%) or local (29%) newspapers or AP stories (28%). Examining the balance of pro- and antiwar sentences in each story reflects a similar pattern, with a higher ratio of pro- to antiwar content on TV than in newspapers or AP stories, as seen in figure 4.3. By every measure, television news coverage was more favorable to the administration's claims than were newspapers or the AP wire service.

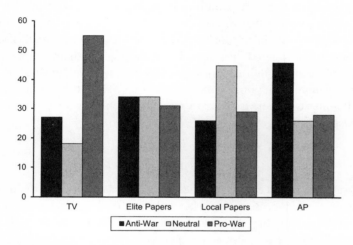

FIGURE 4.2 Tone of Iraq–al Qaeda stories: Percentage of pro-war, antiwar, and neutral articles

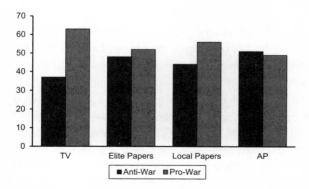

FIGURE 4.3 Percentage of pro- and antiwar sentences in Iraq–al Qaeda stories

Consistent with the administration's strong push for war and the absence of a strong opposition, pro-war news was more vehement in nature than antiwar content. Antiwar sentences within a news story conveyed relatively mild opposition whereas sentences that supported the administration's position were strongly supportive. This trend held across all media outlets, although it was somewhat greater for TV than newspaper stories. On TV, 64% of pro-war sentences were strongly pro-war whereas only 38% of antiwar sentences were strongly antiwar. The imbalance was somewhat less stark in newspapers in which 54% of pro-war sentences were strongly pro-war and 34% of antiwar sentences were strongly antiwar.

In sum, coverage that referred to the Iraq–al Qaeda link was more favorable to the administration's position on TV than in newspapers. Elite and local papers tended toward balanced coverage, with an equal mix of stories and content that supported and opposed the administration, although, as noted, support for the war was more ardent than war opposition. If Americans were exposed to antiwar content, it was more prevalent in newspapers than on TV.

Numerous and Diverse Critics Emerge in Newspaper Coverage

One way that media coverage varies across news outlets is in the degree to which stories represent voices beyond those of the administration. We next examine whether there were systematic differences between TV news, on the one hand, and newspaper coverage, on the other hand. We turn first to the partisan voices and focus on congressional Democrats as the most obvious source to challenge the credibility of the administration's claims.

KEY PLAYERS: THE ADMINISTRATION VERSUS DEMOCRATS.   As the Iraq–al Qaeda story unfolded over time, members of the Bush administration, prominent Republicans, and Defense Department officials dominated the news with their claim of a link between Saddam and al Qaeda. In the current project, coders identified the specific individuals or types of people who were most likely to support and oppose the administration on the war. Our initial interest lies in the degree to which the debate over going to war in Iraq was structured along typical partisan lines, with Republicans on one side and Democrats on the other.

In figure 4.4, we show that Bush administration officials dominated the news in all media outlets. Over 80% of all stories on TV and in newspapers

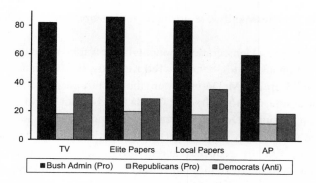

FIGURE 4.4 Partisan sources in Iraq–al Qaeda stories: Percentage of articles in which source made a pro- or antiwar comment

included quotes or comments from Bush administration figures. But the administration's dominance was weakest in AP stories, of which only 61% contained a position advanced by an administration official (details on the coding of news sources can be found in the appendix). The ubiquitous presence of administration officials in the news is hardly surprising given their powerful influence on foreign policy, but it is striking nonetheless. The administration was out in front, breaking news about Iraq in September and October of 2002. This activity consigned congressional Republicans to the sidelines. They were mentioned in roughly 20% of stories on TV and in newspapers and in even fewer AP stories.

We noted earlier that congressional Democrats expressed muted opposition to the war in the fall of 2002, a fact reinforced by their far weaker presence than Republican administration officials in news stories on the Iraq–al Qaeda connection (fig. 4.4). Hayes and Guardino (2013) found that the modest presence of Democrats in news at this time understated their actual activity in Congress as some, such as Democratic senator Robert Byrd, spoke at length about Iraq on the floor of the Senate. But the prevalence of such congressional speeches was not reflected in the news. Democrats were not entirely absent from news stories and were far more visible than congressional Republicans. Between 19% (AP) and 36% (nonelite newspapers) of stories referring to the Iraq–al Qaeda link featured a Democratic political figure, including current members of Congress and former Clinton administration officials, who made a nonneutral statement on the war. Nonetheless, Democrats remained a minor presence in stories on the Iraq–al Qaeda link, were underrepresented when compared to their activity in Congress, and were nowhere near as ubiquitous as administration officials.

In addition, few Democratic opponents of the war matched the stature of administration advocates. Senators Ted Kennedy, Bob Graham, and Dick Durban and Rep. Jim McDermott were the most frequent Democratic critics in stories referring to an Iraq–al Qaeda link. But not one of them represented congressional Democratic leadership. Tom Daschle, Senate majority leader, was the only congressional Democratic leader who appeared in news stories with any frequency, and he was mentioned many fewer times than Senators Kennedy or Graham. Other Democratic administration critics who appeared in stories on the Iraq–al Qaeda link included Senators Biden, Bonior, Feingold, and Kerry, Rep. Lewis, and former secretary of state Madeleine Albright. These Democrats varied in national stature but only Daschle was a member of the congressional Democratic leadership and Democratic critics could not match the Republican firepower of the president, Secretaries Rumsfeld and Powell, and National Security Advisor Rice.

It is important to note that Democratic critics seemed to have been treated less positively on TV than in newspapers. The case of Rep. Jim McDermott is instructive. On a visit to Iraq, he questioned President Bush's veracity and received considerable TV coverage. He was interviewed on both CNN and ABC on September 29, facing questions about his patriotism in both interviews, and his comments attracted particular ridicule on Fox News.[19] In contrast, the *New York Times*, *Boston Globe*, and *Los Angeles Times* ran stories on McDermott's comments that resulted in articles with a strong antiwar thrust.

The administration dominated the news across all media outlets. There were few differences between TV and newspapers in this respect. The average TV and newspaper story almost always referred to a member of the administration but conveyed the views of Democrats far less frequently. Interestingly, the AP was the least partisan news outlet, conveying the views of administration officials, congressional Republicans, and congressional Democrats less frequently than others. Lesser attention to the views of the administration may help to explain why, of all news outlets, the AP issued stories that were the least pro-war. But overall, news outlets differed little in their portrayal of the partisan divide or the degree to which they conveyed the views of a Democratic opposition.

Partisan debate most commonly structures public opinion by articulating Democrats' and Republicans' competing claims and counterclaims.

This is the essence of the elite influence model in which party leaders powerfully cue the "correct" party position to their followers. But partisans are not the sole voices within political debate. We turn next to the presence of nonpartisan sources in news on the administration's claim of an Iraq–al Qaeda connection. Nonpartisan experts or foreign voices can influence public opinion but only after the public has carefully evaluated their comments in the absence of simple partisan cues. In that sense, their influence is contingent on close public attention to the news in ways not needed for partisan leaders.

BEYOND PARTISAN ELITES: DIVERSE ADMINISTRATION CRITICS. We coded the source for each pro- and antiwar statement in news stories on the Iraq–al Qaeda link and arrayed them from the most antiwar to the most pro-war in order to identify the administration's strongest supporters and detractors. Figure 4.5 shows the major sources in Iraq–al Qaeda news stories and their pro- or anti-administration stance with scores ranging from 0 (strongly opposed to the administration's position) to 1 (strongly supportive). The results are hardly surprising. Administration officials and British leaders were the most consistently pro-war whereas Iraqis anchored the antiwar end of the scale. Other somewhat less strident administration detractors included UN officials, Democrats, experts, members of the public, foreign leaders such as the French president and the German chancellor, and the intelligence community.

The diverse nonpartisan collection of administration critics in the news raises an interesting question about whether the nature of administration opposition differed across news media. We examined the presence of four nonpartisan domestic sources—experts, members of the public, members of the intelligence community, and former military and Defense Department officials—sources that were, on balance, more anti- than pro-war. We then compared the prevalence of partisan and nonpartisan war critics across news media. In newspapers and the wire service, domestic criticism of the administration was more likely to arise from nonpartisan than partisan sources. For example, in elite papers 49% of stories on the Iraq–al Qaeda link included an antiwar comment from one of the four nonpartisan domestic sources compared to 29% that contained an antiwar comment from a Democrat. A comparable difference is found in local papers and the AP; 45% of newspaper and 35% of AP stories contained an antiwar comment from a nonpartisan domestic source compared to 36% of newspaper and 19% of AP stories with an antiwar comment from a

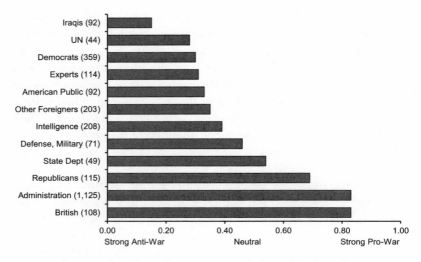

FIGURE 4.5 Pro- or antiwar thrust of source comments in Iraq–al Qaeda stories

Note: Entries are the average valences of sentences containing each source (from strongly antiwar [0] to strongly pro-war [1]). The number of pro- or antiwar comments made by each source is in parentheses.

Democrat. In contrast, antiwar comments on TV were more likely to arise from Democrats (32%) than nonpartisan domestic sources (27%). These differences can be seen in figure 4.6.

One of the striking differences across news media concerns the presence of experts; 21% of stories in local papers included an antiwar comment from an expert compared to but 9% of TV stories. With no one individual dominating in this category, references to experts tended to be just that: a comment attributed to a Middle East expert, a terrorism or counterterrorism expert, or simply an expert. It is important to underscore that experts or intelligence officials are not often counted as key elements of the political elites thought to normally influence the public.

Foreign critics of the administration also appeared with frequency in news stories on the Iraq–al Qaeda link. International figures including French president Jacques Chirac and Iraqi deputy prime minister Tariq Aziz voiced their opposition to the administration's claims about an Iraq–al Qaeda link. Such foreign criticism was more common in local newspaper stories (39%) and the AP (40%) than in TV segments (27%). Hayes and Guardino (2013) report that foreign sources were quite common administration critics on network TV in the months before the war and argue that such individuals helped to undermine support for the war among Democrats and political independents, a claim to which we will return below. For the moment, it is worth noting that at this critical time in the fall of 2002, when public support for the war dropped dramatically among Democrats, foreign voices were only one of several sources of administration criticism. They appeared on TV only slightly less often than Democrats and were more prevalent than Democrats as critics of the administration in newspaper and AP stories, but they were outnumbered by nonpartisan domestic critics such as experts and intelligence personnel in newspapers.

Our analysis of news stories on the Iraq–al Qaeda link, a key facet of the administration's argument for a war with Iraq, underscores the importance of nonpartisan critics of the administration as a source of antiwar information. The elite influence model of American public opinion assumes that partisan sources are the key filter through which pro- and antiwar arguments most successfully drive public opinion on war. But on the specific point concerning the Iraq–al Qaeda connection, antiwar views were more likely to emanate from nonpartisan sources, especially in print media. Democratic administration critics were present and equally common in all news sources, appearing in roughly 30% of all stories (with the exception of AP stories where they appeared in less than 20%). In contrast, nonpartisan domestic critics such as weapons experts, intelligence officials, and members of the public were more common overall and more apparent in newspapers than on TV. International critics were also

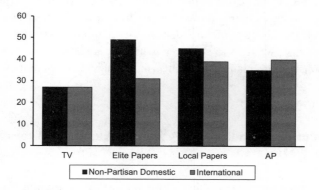

FIGURE 4.6 Presence of administration critics in Iraq–al Qaeda stories: Percentage of articles in which source took an antiwar position

Note: Nonpartisan domestic critics include experts and members of the intelligence community, the defense establishment, and the American public. International critics include the Iraqis, UN officials (including weapons inspectors), and foreigners.

more common in local newspapers and the AP than on TV. All in all, this suggests that Americans who read newspapers were exposed to greater critical antiwar content from diverse nonpartisan sources than those who relied on TV news, at least in stories dealing with the alleged Iraq–al Qaeda connection. It is possible that Democratic critics were responsible for declining war support among Democrats and independents at this time. But our later analysis, demonstrating that Democratic and independent support was most likely to decline among newspaper readers, suggests that nonpartisan administration critics played a role in shaping public opinion.

Summary of News Coverage of an Iraq–al Qaeda Link

The Bush administration's claim of a connection between Saddam and al Qaeda was least likely to be challenged on TV and most likely to be challenged in stories published by newspapers and the AP wire service. Newspapers followed claims of an Iraq–al Qaeda link more doggedly than did TV. And in television news, the administration's claims were at best lightly challenged by critical voices and these offered generally muted criticism (Gershkoff and Kushner 2005; Hayes and Guardino 2010). Newspapers, however, were actively evaluating the administration's claims and featured a wide variety of critical voices, including those of credible nonpartisan experts.

The difference in coverage between televised and print news raises the question that we examine in the chapters to follow. Did this difference in news coverage affect public opinion and later the direction of war support? But first, we turn to consider news media coverage of another of the administration's claims, that concerning Iraq's development of nuclear weapons.

The Claim That Saddam Was Acquiring Aluminum Tubes for Nuclear WMD

In addition to terrorist ties, the administration's case for military action in Iraq rested on Saddam's supposed access to and development of weapons of mass destruction (WMD), including, most fearfully, nuclear weapons. The United Nations weapons inspectors had been ejected from Iraq in 1998, leaving considerable uncertainty about the existence of weapons of mass destruction in Iraq. In September 2002, the Bush administration launched a series of claims concerning the escalation of Iraq's nuclear weapons program that were difficult to directly disprove, although certain specific claims were shown to be specious. Two days after the release of an important British intelligence dossier, President Bush said on September 26, 2002 (reported in the *New York Times* on September 27): "The danger to our country is grave. The danger to our country is growing. The Iraqi regime possesses biological and chemical weapons. The Iraqi regime is building the facilities necessary to make more biological and chemical weapons. And according to the British government, the Iraqi regime could launch a biological or chemical attack in as little as 45 minutes after the order was given."

The Bush administration's claims concerning Iraq's possession of WMD were central to its effort to marshal elite and public support for confronting Iraq. To evaluate how well the news media handled such claims, we examine in depth stories about Iraq's alleged attempts to purchase aluminum tubes for use in the production of nuclear weapons, a factual claim that was ultimately determined to be false. As the *New York Times* noted in its mea culpa, published on May 26, 2004, there were indications that the tubes could not be used for nuclear fuel production at the very time that the claims were first advanced. The administration's assertion that the tubes were destined for use in nuclear centrifuges was immediately greeted with considerable suspicion by energy scientists and other experts. This should have made it easy for journalists to investigate and refute the administration's claims at that time.

News Coverage of Iraq's Attempt to Purchase Aluminum Tubes

The first major story to surface in the administration's PR campaign concerning a possible war with Iraq was built around the startling news that Saddam Hussein was importing aluminum tubes to build the centrifuges necessary to extract and enrich uranium that would, in turn, fuel nuclear weapons. The story of the aluminum tubes broke on September 8, 2002, in the *New York Times* and was amplified by Vice President Dick Cheney on that day's *Meet the Press*. Reporters Michael Gordon and Judith Miller, authors of the now discredited *New York Times* article, began their story with the following claim: "In the last 14 months, Iraq has sought to buy thousands of specially designed aluminum tubes, which American officials believe were intended as components of centrifuges to enrich uranium." They went on to write that "Mr. Hussein's dogged insistence on pursuing his nuclear ambitions, along with what defectors described in interviews as Iraq's push to improve and expand Baghdad's chemical and biological arsenals, have brought Iraq and the United States to the brink of war."

To bolster claims concerning use of the tubes for nuclear purposes, Gordon and Miller wrote, "Officials say the aluminum tubes were intended as casing for rotors in centrifuges, which are one means of producing highly enriched uranium. The *Washington Times* reported in July that Iraq sought to acquire stainless steel for centrifuges on one occasion. Officials say that the material sought was special aluminum tubes and that Iraq sought to acquire it over 14 months." Gordon and Miller's story appeared in the *New York Times* and was reprinted in part in various other newspapers including the *Long-Beach Press Telegram*, the *St. Petersburg Times*, the *Deseret News*, and the *Boston Herald*.[20]

The *New York Times* story broke on a Sunday and administration officials were ready to discuss it, dominating that day's morning talk shows.[21] Dick Cheney referenced the *New York Times* article on that day's *Meet the Press* and asserted that "we do know, with absolute certainty, that he [Hussein] is using his procurement system to acquire the equipment he needs in order to enrich uranium to build a nuclear weapon."

There was some initial Democratic opposition to the claim. Democratic senators Schumer and Graham made skeptical comments on morning talk shows that same day. But other critics were met with considerable ridicule. The night before (September 7, 2002) the *New York Times* published the story, former UN weapons inspector Scott Ritter appeared on CNN speaking from Baghdad and was asked during the interview about the next day's aluminum tubes story. He responded, "With all due respect to the *New York Times*, they've been wrong in the past and, you know, I wouldn't jump immediately out and say, gosh, they're right." In time, his circumspection would prove prescient, but it did not garner much respect from other journalists. The day after the *New York Times'* revelations (September 9, 2002), CNN anchor Paula Zahn interviewed Gary Samore, an expert from the British think tank the International Institute of Strategic Studies (IISS), who rejected Ritter's suggestion that the tubes had purely civilian purposes. Ritter faced a belligerent line of questioning on September 9 from Jane Clayton, cohost of the early morning CBS show, who suggested that Ritter was out of the "American intelligence chain." Paula Zahn conducted a similarly skeptical interview with Ritter that day on CNN, asking him to respond to personal attacks directed at him by Senator Richard Shelby. Not surprisingly, Ritter was treated with even greater vitriol on the September 9 Bill O'Reilly show on Fox News.[22]

TABLE 4.2 **News stories coded on Iraq and aluminum tubes**

September 24–October 25, 2002	TV	Elite newspapers	Nonelite top thirty newspapers	Wire service
Media organizations	ABC, CBS, CNN, FOX, NBC	*New York Times, Washington Post, Wall Street Journal*	*USA Today,* local papers	AP
Total number of stories (72)	17	11	31	13
Total number of pro- and antiwar sentences (1,213)	223	279	556	155

Over the next few days, the major networks and national newspapers continued to uncritically amplify the administration's claims, quoting from Dick Cheney and the *New York Times*. CNN's Paula Zahn asked Republican senator Richard Shelby whether he had previously heard Cheney's claims about the tubes, and he said, "I have and I believe the Vice President's description of that is very accurate." On the September 9 edition of ABC's *Nightline*, Gary Milhollin, a weapons expert, raised tepid concern about the need for more information on the tubes but concluded by saying that it was difficult to gauge whether the United States faced greater risk through action or inaction against Iraq. Other sources of dissent, such as Iraqi officials, presumably had limited credibility with the American public.[23]

To assess how well different news outlets covered the story, we conducted a search similar to that carried out for stories on the Iraq–al Qaeda link. We searched Lexis-Nexis for TV transcripts and several additional databases for newspaper stories to uncover all relevant stories that appeared on TV, in newspapers, and on the AP wire.[24] We once again eliminated editorials, interviews, and op-ed articles, and analyzed the stories qualitatively and quantitatively (all articles are listed in the online appendix). We analyzed stories published beginning on September 8, 2002, the day the story broke, and ending on October 24, coinciding with the end of our survey data collection period.

We focused on stories that mentioned the aluminum tubes on one of the major networks (ABC, CBS, NBC), on cable TV (CNN, Fox News), in elite and nonelite newspapers, and on the AP wire service. Overall, the search yielded a total of seventy-two stories (seventeen TV news segments, forty-two newspaper stories, and thirteen AP stories; see table 4.2).[25]

News stories were coded in the same way as those on the Iraq–al Qaeda link (using the codes shown in the appendix). Codes reflect assessment of the article as a whole, such as whether the story supported or opposed the administration's case for war. Additionally, each sentence was scored as for, against, or neutral toward the war, and each pro- or antiwar source was recorded. Overall, 1,213 nonneutral sentences were coded in articles mentioning the aluminum tubes, although not every coded sentence dealt specifically with the tubes. The neutral content of an additional 1,378 neutral sentences was noted but no further content was coded in these sentences.

The number of newspaper and TV stories referring to the tubes peaked on September 8, the day the story broke; the greatest number of stories was aired on television on the first two days of news coverage. In total, the five TV outlets aired fifteen stories in those two days. But this was followed by a marked decline over time in TV coverage of the story; only two more stories were aired on the tubes on TV and both occurred within the week in which the story broke. No segment on the tubes was aired on evening TV after September 12. The tubes story was never high profile but once again print media followed the story somewhat more doggedly than did TV. Newspapers provided modest coverage of the story on September 8 and 9, with the top thirty newspapers printing a total of twelve stories and the AP issuing two. Newspapers continued to follow the story, albeit at a low level. From September 13 to October 25, a period during which there was no reference to the tubes on nightly news, the top thirty newspapers printed a total of forty-seven stories and the AP issued a total of ten. A number of newspapers printed stories making reference to the tubes after President Bush's speech to the UN on September 12, and several additional stories were published around September 24 with the release of a British intelligence dossier concerning Iraq.

News outlets continued to cover other aspects of Iraq's possession of WMD. Hayes and Guardino (2010) report that roughly one in five stories on the three major TV networks focused on WMD in the eight months before the war. This translates into roughly one story every third night on the networks beginning in September and continuing through October of 2002. Few of these stories, however, dealt with the readily refuted evidence that the aluminum tubes were destined for a nuclear centrifuge.

The news media provided less criticism of Iraq's alleged purchase of aluminum tubes than of the ostensible Iraq–al Qaeda link, but critical coverage was still present. Unlike news coverage of a possible Iraq–al

Qaeda linkage, the tone of elite and local newspapers differed on the aluminum tubes story. In their coverage of this story, elite newspapers were more likely to follow the administration's lead and in that sense their coverage is more similar to that found on TV than in local papers. Out of eleven stories in elite papers referring to the tubes (four in the *New York Times*, five in the *Washington Post*, and two in the *Wall Street Journal*), only one story in the *Washington Post*[26] raised concerns about the accuracy of the administration's claims. For the most part, it was left to others, particularly to less lofty print sources to scrutinize the administration's factual case.

News Coverage Supports the Administration's Claims

The administration's claim that Iraq was attempting to purchase aluminum tubes was repeated with regularity in news reports, including in nonelite newspapers, and such stories often began by repeating the administration's claims. Administration officials dominated the news in all media outlets. Despite skeptical elite newspaper coverage of a possible link between al Qaeda and Iraq, elite papers were far more willing to endorse the administration's claim that Iraq had or was seeking possession of WMD. Judith Miller, the *New York Times* reporter, broke the news about the tubes and helped to make the administration's case for war. In no instance did the *New York Times* publish stories with headlines that suggested anything but support for the administration's argument about the existence of Iraq's nuclear program (see headlines listed in the online appendix).

Overall, we found that news coverage of the aluminum tubes story was more favorable to the administration than was news coverage of the claimed link between Iraq and al Qaeda. This is amply clear in figure 4.7, which shows the preponderance of pro-administration stories across all news media outlets. The administration's position was touted in headlines such as "Administration Lays Out Evidence against Hussein" (*CNN Talkback Live*, September 9, 2002), "Bush Administration Cites Evidence That Iraq Is Trying to Build Nuclear Weapon" (*NBC Nightly News*, September 9, 2002), and "C.I.A. Says Iraq Revived Forbidden Weapons Programs after the U.N. Inspectors Left" (*New York Times*, September 30, 2002). Local newspapers were most critical of the administration, yet even their stories contained more pro- than antiwar content, with only an occasional critical headline such as "U.S. Conclusion on Iraq Acquisition Questioned" (*Chicago Tribune*, September 20, 2002), "Iraq Has Failed in Quest for

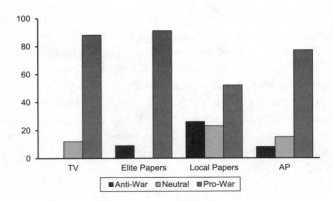

FIGURE 4.7 Tone of aluminum tubes stories: Percentage of pro-war, antiwar, and neutral stories

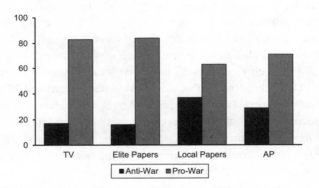

FIGURE 4.8 Percentage of pro- and antiwar sentences in aluminum tubes stories

Bomb Ingredients" (*Philadelphia Inquirer*, September 13, 2002), and "Experts Dispute CIA Appraisal of Hussein Arsenal" (*Miami Herald*, October 5, 2002).

Nonelite newspapers were more likely than other news outlets to challenge the administration's facts concerning the tubes. Roughly 80% of TV and AP stories and 90% of elite newspaper stories mentioning the tubes were coded as pro-war, compared to a bare majority (54%) of local newspaper stories. The pro-war slant of AP stories on the tubes differs from their antiwar coverage of the Iraq–al Qaeda link, although their coverage was only moderately pro-war. Of all pro-war stories aired or printed by a news outlet, there were fewer strongly pro-war stories in the AP (36%)

than on TV (58%) or in elite papers (70%). Actual sentence counts, seen in figure 4.8, demonstrate the unusually long articles printed in elite newspapers on the aluminum tubes and related WMD issue. The original *New York Times* story about the tubes published on September 8 is a prime example of this lengthy, pro-war news, containing fifty-one pro-war but a mere five antiwar (along with eighty neutral) sentences. Overall, local papers provided the greatest balance on the tubes story, even though these stories retained a pro-war thrust.

Partisan Sources and Administration Dominance

Bush administration figures featured prominently in media coverage of the tubes story. Regardless of media outlet, administration officials broke the story and dominated the news. With respect to the aluminum tubes story, congressional Democrats were even harder to find in news stories on this subject than in stories on the Iraq–al Qaeda link. Vice President Cheney played a key initial role in advancing the tubes story and promoting the administration's claims. He was an especially prominent source in TV segments on the tubes, appearing in 47% of all TV stories, but was present in only 27% of stories in local newspapers. Indeed, in TV segments mentioning the tubes, Cheney was referred to more frequently than was President Bush (who was referred to in 37% of all TV stories). In addition to Cheney's comments, President Bush made several speeches outlining the administration's case, and other administration officials, including Rice, Rumsfeld, and Powell, amplified the story concerning Iraq's growing nuclear capabilities.

As shown in figure 4.9, Democrats were a minor presence on TV, in the AP, or in elite newspapers. They appeared in only 12% of TV segments, 18% of stories in elite newspapers, and 23% of AP stories. They were more visible, however, in local papers. For the most part, Democratic criticism of the administration came from US senators, including Senators Bayh, Biden, Durbin, Feinstein, Graham, and Levin. For example, AP reporter John Lumpkin released a story on October 4 on a CIA briefing to the Senate Intelligence Committee concerning Iraq's possession of WMD. The story included a comment from a frustrated Senator Durbin who said in reaction to information presented at the meeting, "It is maddening to have classified information which contradicts classified information leaked by the administration." This story, including Durbin's comment, was reprinted in a number of local newspapers including the

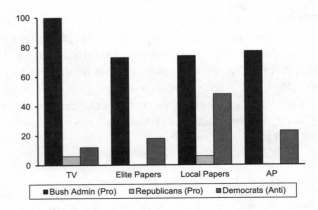

FIGURE 4.9 Partisan sources in aluminum tubes stories: Percentage of articles in which source made a pro- or antiwar comment

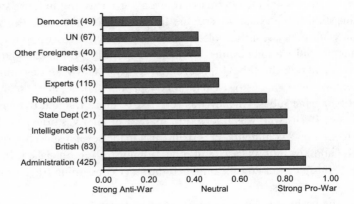

FIGURE 4.10 Pro- or antiwar thrust of source comments in aluminum tubes stories

Note: The number of coded comments for each source is listed in parentheses.

Chicago Tribune, the *Chicago Sun-Times*, the *St. Louis Post-Dispatch*, and the *Newark Star-Ledger*. Durbin's comment did not outright condemn the administration but hinted at conflicting intelligence on Iraq's possession of WMD.

Not surprisingly, Democrats' comments were largely antiwar across all news outlets. In stories on the tubes, Democrats were one of only four broad classifications of sources who consistently voiced criticism of the administration. As shown in figure 4.10, additional sources of consistent criticism included Iraqis, other non-British foreigners, and UN personnel, and all three sources were weakly anti-administration on average. Overall, coverage of the tubes issue was dominated by the administration and only secondarily included the views of critical sources such as congressional Democrats or foreign leaders.

Local Newspapers Convey the Doubts of the Scientific and Intelligence Communities

The depth of opposition to the administration's claims concerning the tubes is masked by striking differences across news outlets in the position of experts and intelligence officials. Unlike the Iraq–al Qaeda story in which members of the intelligence community and experts raised consistent questions about the veracity of the administration's facts, the WMD and aluminum tubes story involved dueling experts and intelligence officials on both sides of the debate. The pattern shown in figure 4.10 suggests that experts adopted a neutral stance on the tubes issue, but in fact this graph masks considerable heterogeneity in their views.

Technical expertise played an important role in evaluating the administration's claims concerning the tubes, which were allegedly purchased for use in centrifuges designed to generate nuclear fuel. In this instance, technical expertise may have mattered just as much or more than the political claims concerning the tubes. Did television and print news make equal and effective use of technical experts in their coverage of the aluminum tubes story? We turn to that issue next.

WEAPONS EXPERTS.   Quantitative coding of the news stories on the tubes confirms the greater presence of experts in nonelite newspapers than in other media outlets. Experts appeared in a meager 21% of TV stories compared to 47% of nonelite and 50% of elite newspaper stories. And experts were far more visible in the aluminum tubes than the al Qaeda story. For example, experts were featured in only 21% of stories on the Iraq–al Qaeda link in local newspapers, 14% of stories in elite papers, and 9% of stories on TV. The greater presence of experts in news stories on the tubes is consistent with the notion that journalists regarded it as a different kind of news story than the Iraq–al Qaeda link, one that required sources with differing background and expertise (Wolfsfeld 2004). Moreover, as seen in figure 4.11, experts who appeared in newspapers held differing views compared to those who were quoted or interviewed for TV segments. When we calculated the pro- or anti-administration stance of

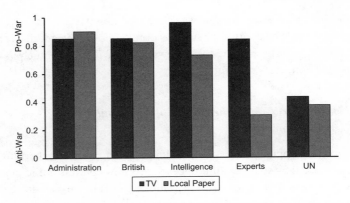

FIGURE 4.11 Thrust of source comments in aluminum tubes stories: TV versus local newspapers

experts on stories mentioning the tubes, experts were almost uniformly pro-administration on TV, scoring .84 on the 0–1 scale; neutral in elite papers, with an average score of .49; and antiwar in local newspapers, with an average score of .3.

A closer reading of news stories on the tubes makes clear that TV journalists and newspaper reporters were drawing from a different roster of experts. For example, Gary Samore, director of studies at the British International Institute for Strategic Studies (IISS), was the key weapons expert on TV. His organization had just published a dossier on WMD in Iraq, suggesting that Iraq could produce a nuclear weapon within months if it acquired sufficient raw material. Samore was featured in eighteen of the twenty-five sentences in TV segments that quoted or mentioned an expert in connection to the tubes story, and these references were predominantly pro-war in flavor. In contrast, newspapers featured experts such as David Albright, a former weapons inspector and head of the Institute for Science and International Security (ISIS), and Anthony Cordesman, a national security expert at the Center for Strategic and International Studies (CSIS). Both Albright and Cordesman raised serious questions about whether the tubes could really be used within a nuclear centrifuge, views that did not make it on TV.

The Knight Ridder Washington Bureau was out in front on the WMD issue. It released a story on September 9, which stated that even Vice President Cheney "conceded that the evidence against Iraq remains sketchy and largely circumstantial." This story was reproduced in its entirety in the *Phil-*

adelphia Inquirer, the *Milwaukee Journal Sentinel,* and the *New Jersey Star-Ledger.* Knight Ridder journalist Jonathan Landay wrote a story on September 13, which was printed in the *Philadelphia Inquirer,* in which he questioned Iraq's success in acquiring material for a nuclear weapon. Landay also cowrote (with Dan Stober) a story that appeared in the *San Jose Mercury News* that same day quoting Mark Gwozdecky, an International Atomic Energy Agency official in Vienna, who noted that the aluminum tubes could be used for various purposes not just the production of a nuclear weapon. Another weapons inspector noted in the story that the same kinds of tubes had been found previously in Iraq and would need to be considerably altered before they could be used in a centrifuge. The article also quoted David Albright, who said, "There's nothing distinct about this material," adding that "it's a weak indicator of a centrifuge program."

Other newspapers joined the critical chorus. On September 13, Susan Page, writing for *USA Today,* harshly evaluated Bush's claims against Saddam, underscoring that Bush had said only that Iraq "sought to buy the aluminum tubes for possible use in uranium enrichment centrifuges" with no implication that it had succeeded in doing so or that the tubes would be used to enrich uranium. In the same article, Anthony Cordesman, commenting on a recent speech by Bush, said: "We need to make the case as to why, after 11 years, we need to act now," adding "We probably could make that case, but we didn't make it (in this speech). We rounded up the usual suspects and provided their history, but we didn't spell out the indictment, and we certainly didn't indicate why we needed to arrest them." In the *Pittsburgh Post-Gazette* on the same day, Gary Milhollin, the Iraq arms expert, said, "Given the high priority for knowing what is going on in Iraq, I'm stunned by the lack of evidence of fresh intelligence."

On September 24, the Blair government (United Kingdom) released an intelligence dossier on Iraq that contained reference to the aluminum tubes. In that document, the Iraqi government's attempt to procure aluminum tubes is noted as possible evidence of an attempt to build centrifuges to enrich uranium. Dan Stober published a story the next day in the Knight Ridder *San Jose Mercury News* reporting that the dossier undermined rather than supported the Bush administration's claims. In the same story, David Albright made reference to the views of "scientists working in the intelligence operations at the Energy Department and Lawrence Livermore National Laboratory" who "raised the possibility that Iraq may intend to use the aluminum tubes as launchers for small artillery rockets."

Stober also reveals startling evidence in this article of a memo issued on September 13 by Michael Anastasio, director of the Lawrence Livermore Labs, who cited national security concerns and forbade scientists at the Livermore Labs and Energy Department from speaking to the news media about Iraq. Information about the memo was posted in mid-October 2002 on the Federation of American Scientists' Secrecy News site but was not referred to explicitly elsewhere in the mainstream news media.[27] The administration's ban was obliquely noted in several other newspapers: a *Washington Post* story published on September 19 noted that several Energy Department officials had declined to comment on David Albright's ISIS report which raised doubts about the tubes. Other articles, such as a highly critical piece in the *San Francisco Chronicle* on October 12 and a story in *USA Today* on October 24, noted the political pressure being placed on the intelligence community.

David Albright had authored a report for ISIS, the organization he directed, which challenged the administration's claims that the tubes were intended for centrifuges designed to produce weapons-grade uranium, arguing that the aluminum was the wrong kind and that Iraq had shifted away from the use of aluminum to steel and carbon in its centrifuges. Albright appeared frequently in the print news media in stories touching on the tubes but only occasionally made it on TV. He was interviewed along with several other former weapons inspectors on *CNN Diplomatic License* on September 21. The discussion largely revolved around return of the weapons inspectors to Iraq. As part of the lengthy discussion, Albright noted that the aluminum tubes were not evidence of a nuclear program, but this was a not a central focus of the segment. And as noted, energy scientists provided an important source of dissent but could not be quoted directly or appear on TV because they had been officially muzzled by the administration.

Yet another source contributed to the public debate. Members inside the intelligence branches of the US government were called on to comment on the tubes and Iraq's possession of WMD. We examine whether their views were aired evenly across different news outlets.

INTELLIGENCE COMMUNITY. In addition to dissent from weapons experts and energy scientists, some in the intelligence community raised doubts about the aluminum tubes' purpose. On October 5, the Knight Ridder Washington Bureau published a lengthy story on a recently released CIA report concerning Iraq's WMD program, which cast doubt on use of the

aluminum tubes. The *Miami Herald* printed part of the story and reiterated dissent within the intelligence community on the tubes, going so far
as to suggest that the administration was "pressuring intelligence analysts
to highlight information that supports Bush's policy and to suppress information and analysis that might undercut congressional, public or international support for war." The Knight Ridder story (also reprinted in
the *Salt Lake City Deseret News*) notes that "the CIA report acknowledges that some intelligence analysts believe the tubes were intended for
conventional weapons, not nuclear devices." The *Durham Herald-Sun*,
commenting the same day on the CIA report, noted that a minority of
intelligence analysts were skeptical that the tubes could be used in any
way to build WMD. In contrast, the *Washington Post* and the *New York
Times* covered the CIA report without reference to dissent from within
the intelligence community.

On October 8, the Knight Ridder Washington Bureau followed with its
key story on skepticism about the Bush administration's case from within
the intelligence community, which we mentioned earlier in connection to
coverage of the Iraq–al Qaeda link. In defense of George Tenet and the
CIA, the article included comments from a senior administration official
who said: "Tenet made sure that a State Department official told Congress
that the Energy and State departments disagreed with an intelligence assessment that said hundreds of aluminum tubes Iraq tried to purchase
were intended for Baghdad's secret nuclear-weapons program. Analysts
in both departments concluded that the Iraqis probably wanted the tubes
to make conventional artillery pieces." As noted earlier, the Knight Ridder story was reprinted widely and continued to influence print journalism over time. On October 24, *USA Today* ran a long story on the political
pressure being exerted on the intelligence community and prominently
included a series of quotes from the October 8 Knight Ridder story on
"deep misgivings" about "the administration's double-time march toward
war" (Bamford 2002).

For the most part, intelligence officials supported the administration's
views on the tubes, as shown in figure 4.11 (with an overall score of .82
on the 0–1 pro-war scale). They appeared in over a third of TV segments,
and a half or more of all newspaper stories on the tubes. But the position
espoused by intelligence officials varied across news outlets. Intelligence
officials always adopted a pro-war position on TV and in elite newspapers.
But in local newspapers they took an antiwar position in roughly a quarter
of all stories on the aluminum tubes. Elite newspapers referred largely to

the views of the CIA and other agencies as singular entities. Stories published in nonelite papers contained a more complete mix of references to the CIA and individual intelligence and military officers. This difference may reflect the Knight Ridder reporting in which journalists reached out to skeptical midlevel intelligence officials. These experts were unlikely to appear in more prominent news outlets given their low political status.

Overall, nonelite newspapers were far more likely than TV to include the perspective of experts and relay their critical stance on Iraq's use of aluminum tubes for the construction of a nuclear weapon. They were also more likely than other news outlets to represent a broad range of views from within the intelligence community. Newspapers conveyed skepticism about the tubes. Such criticism was largely absent from TV.

Confusing and Conflicting Claims from UN Personnel and Foreign Sources

Domestic critics of the administration were present in local papers but scarce in TV segments on the tubes. In contrast, foreign administration critics were far more common on TV than in newspapers. On television, over three-quarters of the segments on the tubes included Iraqis, other non-British foreigners, or UN personnel critical of the administration. Foreign criticism was equally common in AP stories on the tubes (occurring in 85% of all stories). In contrast, foreign criticism occurred in fewer elite (27%) or local (58%) newspaper stories. The predominance on TV of foreign criticism of the administration's claims concerning the tubes is apparent in figure 4.12. There was far greater balance between foreign and domestic criticism in local newspapers, especially when coupled with the stronger presence of antiwar congressional Democrats in these stories (as seen earlier in fig. 4.9). Hayes and Guardino (2013) argue that foreigners led the charge against the administration on the WMD issue and pushed some Americans toward opposition to the war. But our data suggest that domestic opposition from experts and members of the intelligence community may have also played a role, given their prominence in coverage of the tubes issue in local newspapers.

Former UN weapons inspectors appeared often on TV as administration critics. This began with Scott Ritter's opposition to the administration's claims concerning the tubes. But UN personnel did not speak with a unified voice. Their comments were slightly antiwar on average, but over a third of UN personnel made pro-war statements on TV and in local newspaper stories on the tubes. For example, Katie Couric interviewed

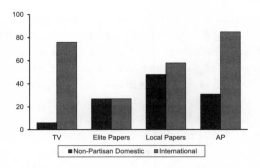

FIGURE 4.12 Administration critics in stories on aluminum tubes

Note: Entries are the percentages of articles or TV segments featuring each critic. Nonpartisan critics include experts and intelligence personnel who made antiwar comments; international critics include UN personnel, Iraqis, and other non-British foreigners who made antiwar comments.

Richard Butler (the former UNSCOM chief) on September 13, the day after Bush's UN speech. Butler supported the administration's claims and denounced Scott Ritter, his former colleague and a key administration critic. On the same day, CNN aired a contentious and not particularly illuminating debate between former inspectors Butler and Ritter, in which Ritter called Butler a liar, and Butler reiterated the administration's claims about the aluminum tubes.[28] Television stories occasionally included a quote or interview with Scott Ritter but also frequently included others such as David Kay (another weapons inspector) who challenged Ritter's information and claims.[29]

There was also disagreement among foreign leaders and officials in stories on the tubes. Non-British, non-Iraqi political figures, including the French, Germans, and Russians, were moderately critical of the administration's position on balance (with an average score of .43 as shown in fig. 4.10). Foreign critics appeared far more frequently in TV than newspaper stories on the tubes. They were mentioned in over 40% of TV news segments but only 13% of local and 10% of elite newspaper stories. These foreign critics were counterbalanced to some extent by support from Britain, a major US ally. Tony Blair and other British officials played a prominent role in support of the administration's claims concerning the tubes, frequently appearing in stories linked to the British intelligence dossier on Iraq released in late September 2002. The British were mentioned in 26% of TV segments on the tubes and 23% of nonelite newspaper stories and in all instances were rated as taking a moderately to strongly pro-war stance (as shown in fig. 4.10).

It is difficult to know, in the end, how influential foreign voices were on the aluminum tubes issue or WMD more generally. In television coverage of the tubes, foreign voices were largely critical although counterbalanced to some degree by support for the administration from the British. But foreigners were less prominent in newspapers and countered there by vigorous opposition from credible domestic experts and intelligence personnel. Hayes and Guardino (2010, 2013) suggest that foreign voices of dissent influenced US opinion in an antiwar direction. But foreigners did not speak with a singular voice, and there were other sources of opposition to the administration's claims concerning the tubes, especially in local newspapers, that deserve attention as a possible influence on American public opinion at that time.

Summary of News Coverage of Iraq's Nuclear Use of Aluminum Tubes

Right from the outset, there was good reason to doubt that Iraq's aluminum tubes could be used in the production of nuclear weapons. Nonetheless, different news sources varied considerably in how persistently and critically they pursued the story. Local, nonelite newspapers provided far more critical coverage of the story than did other news media outlets. In contrast, TV and elite newspapers were far more accepting than local newspapers of the Bush administration's claims. Nonelite newspapers, spearheaded by the efforts of the Knight Ridder Washington Bureau, brought to light severe doubts within the intelligence community on the Bush administration's claims. Other local newspapers reported on the views of energy scientists and weapons experts who simply did not believe the administration's intelligence concerning use of the tubes. Local newspapers also captured more fully than other media the critical views of congressional Democrats.

As the story developed over time, there was a notable absence of discussion of the aluminum tubes on television. Rep. Evan Bayh made passing reference to the tubes on *Fox News Sunday* in early October; President Bush mentioned aluminum tubes in a speech on October 7 and his words appeared in several television segments. But that was about it. In essence, doubts about the use of the aluminum tubes raised by weapons experts such as David Albright, the administration's media ban on scientists in the Energy Department, and skepticism from within the intelligence community only rarely made it on network or cable TV news. The divergence between newspaper and TV coverage of the tubes reinforces the conclusion that television failed to convey well-known problems with the administration's case for going to war with Iraq.

Our fine-grained analysis of news coverage of Iraq's alleged use of aluminum tubes in the production of nuclear weapons underscores the pivotal role played by nonelite newspapers in challenging the administration. There is no question that the news media was overly favorable toward the administration in covering the tubes story. But nonelite papers did a far better job than other outlets in conveying serious and credible sources of opposition. We observed a similar pattern in media coverage of a claimed Iraq–al Qaeda linkage.

Conclusion

We will show in the following chapters that newspaper coverage appears to have had resonance with the American public, helping to explain why some independents and Democrats turned against the war just as the administration made a concerted pitch for a war in Iraq. In our examination of two of the administration's justifications for war, we found that newspaper coverage was more critical of the administration, on balance, than nightly television news coverage. This suggests that differences in the degree to which TV and newspapers challenged the administration might have influenced public opinion. Those who relied on newspapers would have found themselves in a different informational environment than those who regularly watched the nightly television news. In the chapters that follow, we trace the effects of this differing news content on the public. And we ask whether and in what ways it mattered.

The Deliberative Citizen Emerges

Democratic and Independent Opposition to the Iraq War

"A sect or party is an elegant incognito devised to save a man from the vexation of thinking."
—Ralph Waldo Emerson (Andrews 1993, 703)

In the fall of 2002, some months before the onset of the Iraq War, Democrats and independents faced confusing signals concerning the wisdom of a war in Iraq. Republican officials were unified in their support of war, whereas Democratic officials were weakly supportive, at best, and a sizeable minority were opposed. Political support for and opposition to the war were present in the news media, but support far outweighed opposition as administration officials provided a steady flow of information about various transgressions committed by Saddam Hussein's regime.

Administration officials dominated the news and trumped skeptical congressional Democrats who were present in the news with far less frequency. Administration officials also outranked congressional Democrats in stature. The most prominent Democrats in the news did not represent Democratic leadership and were not always in a position to challenge the administration's facts. In sum, rank-and file Democrats were exposed to a moderately pro-war message from their partisan leaders, a largely antiwar message from Democrats in the news, and other confusing and mixed signals from their elected Democratic representatives. In total, Democratic elites were not strongly pro-war but nor were they especially antiwar either. Independents faced an equally unclear landscape in which Republicans and Democrats neither completely agreed nor completely disagreed on the war.

This brings us back to our fundamental question: Why did Democrats and independents increasingly oppose the war at the same time the administration intensified its pro-war campaign? The longstanding conventional wisdom, backed by considerable empirical research, is that publics follow where elites lead, especially in times of war, external threat, and patriotic appeal. In the presence of a strong pro-war signal from the administration and many Democratic leaders, rank-and-file Democrats and independents should have increased their support for the Iraq war project. Yet Democrats and independents did not just resist the administration's pro-war message; they increasingly opposed the war in the fall of 2002.

News Source and Elite Influence

If powerful war opposition did not emanate from partisan elites, perhaps then the news media, the third key player within a well-functioning democracy, played a role. Where did Democrats get news about the war? In the fall of 2002, Americans were most likely to rely on TV as their major source of news, followed by newspapers, which had not yet experienced the full brunt of economic woes that subsequently dominated and decimated the industry. At that time, few people obtained their news from the Internet (Rainie, Fox, and Fallows 2003). We showed in chapter 4 that newspapers—nonelite and, to some extent, elite—and the AP wire service provided more critical coverage than did TV of the administration's key facts on two readily refutable stories. Newspapers were also more likely than TV news to convey the views of administration critics and cover the views of a more diverse group of anti-administration domestic sources when reporting on two of the administration's key factual claims. Americans who relied singularly on newspapers for information about the war were exposed to a very different news environment than those who relied solely on television.

As we showed in chapter 2, Democratic and independent citizens were much less supportive than Republicans of a possible war in Iraq. They were also more skeptical of the administration's claims that Saddam posed a direct threat to the United States or was supporting terrorists. But from where did this skepticism arise? Congressional Democrats were just one source of opposition to the administration's claims that Saddam had terrorist links or planned to use aluminum tubes for uranium enrichment, and they were less numerous in newspaper stories on the Iraq–al Qaeda link than other nonpartisan critics such as experts, intelligence officials, and members of the defense establishment, as we showed in chapter 4. Moreover, a majority of Democratic senators and a minority of Democrats in the House voted to support the Iraq War Resolution, sending a very mixed message to rank-and-file Democrats. In combination with a unified Republican push for military action in Iraq, the elite influence model predicts that well-informed Democrats and independents should have supported the war given the combined pro-war information flow. That is not what we observe. But before we completely reject an elite influence account of war opinion, we need to add a critical ingredient to our test. Within the elite influence model, citizens need to be exposed to partisan messages before they can be influenced by them. This raises an important and as yet unexamined question: Did exposure to the views of political leaders increase support for going to war in the fall of 2002?

The elite influence model makes clear predictions on how the public will respond to a strongly one-sided information flow—in this instance, the Bush administration's dominant pro-war message, which was amply conveyed by the news media. The model predicts stronger war support among those with the most information on Iraq because they have been most exposed to the administration's arguments for war. Since Republican elites were almost unanimous in their support for war in Iraq, knowledgeable Republicans should have been more supportive than other Americans of military action in Iraq. Democrats confronted a mixed and muted message from their elites. The most-knowledgeable Democrats would have been heavily exposed to the administration's arguments for war in the absence of strong opposition from their party leaders, boosting their support for the war. Even more clearly, the elite influence model predicts that war support among political independents should increase as they learn more about the war because they, too, will have been exposed to a greater flow of pro-war information.

These predictions follow from the view that public opinion is almost entirely driven by messages directed at the public, messages sent by partisan elites. As noted in chapter 4, however, diverse nonpartisan critics questioned the administration's facts in the fall of 2002, especially on issues such as whether Iraq was sponsoring anti-American terrorism. Administration critics included some congressional Democrats, but the voices of intelligence personnel, national security experts, weapons experts, and former military personnel were more numerous. If the public only attended to partisan information, the views of congressional Republicans would have loomed large. But if, as we suspect, public opinion is influenced by a broad chorus of voices when partisan elites are internally divided (as occurred among Democrats), then information, its content, strength of arguments, and the credibility of various news sources, matters.

By information we mean specifically the kind of information about Iraq that would require Americans to mull over competing arguments, scrutinize sources, and evaluate factual claims in the absence of strong partisan cues. In that sense, nonpartisan information about Iraq, if considered carefully, would enable Americans to make their own judgment on whether to support a war in Iraq. If some Democrats and independents based their opinion about war on this kind of independent, nonpartisan information, the best informed may not have simply followed the direction of their partisan elites. Indeed, it is possible that close scrutiny of nonpartisan information provided by intelligence personnel and security experts may have incited the best-informed Democrats to oppose the war.

Acquiring Information about Iraq

Given the contentious nature of many key assertions about Iraq and Saddam—the existence of weapons of mass destruction and connections to anti-US terrorists—we chose to measure information about Iraq and unfolding events with simple factual questions in the Threat and National Security Survey (TNSS) to which there were clearly correct answers. The questions were designed to tap knowledge of facts—some of which were easy and others more difficult to acquire—in order to differentiate between those who were paying more and less attention to news on Iraq. Correct answers to all these questions would have been known to those attending most closely to the news. We present in table 5.1 the specific Iraq knowledge questions included in the TNSS and the percentage who answered each question correctly. Ultimately, when taken together, the five questions provide a good measure of each person's exposure to, and retention of, information about Iraq. The observed range in the number of correct answers indicates substantial variation among Americans in their knowledge of Iraq at that time. Nearly three out of every four (73%) Americans in the TNSS could name one country that bordered on Iraq. But only about one in twenty (6%) could identify the name of the Iraqi ruling political party.

TABLE 5.1 **Iraq information quiz**

	Correct (%)
Can you tell me the name of one country that shares a border with Iraq? [Correct = Iran, Jordan, Kuwait, Saudi Arabia, Syria, or Turkey]	73
What is the capital city of Iraq? [Correct = Baghdad]	51
What is the name of the Middle Eastern TV network that has broadcast statements by Osama bin Laden and Al Qaeda? [Correct = Al Jazeera]	21
What is the name of the ruling political party in Iraq? [Correct = Baath Party]	6
What is the name of the major ethnic group that lives in the north of Iraq? [Correct = Kurds]	31

Source: TNSS, October 2002.

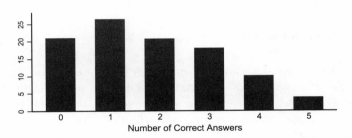

FIGURE 5.1 Percentage correct on the five-item Iraq information scale, TNSS, October 2002

We create a scale of information about Iraq by summing the number of correct answers provided by each participant to the five questions included in the TNSS.[1] As shown in figure 5.1, there is considerable variation in how much Americans knew about Iraq. One in five (21%) could not provide a single correct answer to any of the five questions; another quarter (27%) got only one out of five correct, whereas nearly four in ten (38%) answered at least three of the five questions correctly. While the information scale does not directly tap awareness of key facts about Iraqi capabilities, intentions, or ties to terrorists, a higher score is likely to be strongly associated with knowledge of the general situation, including the existence of strong Republican war support and the absence of strong Democratic opposition to US military action.[2]

Using questions from wave 1 of the TNSS, we are able to compare survey participants' information about Iraq with their knowledge of Afghanistan and Osama bin Laden assessed in the months after the 9/11 terrorist attacks. Four information questions were included in wave 1: the name of one country that shares a border with Afghanistan, whether Afghanistan is an Arab country, the name of bin Laden's home country, and the name of the Muslim holy book. Not surprisingly, information about Afghanistan and Iraq are highly but far from perfectly correlated.[3] Research has shown that general political information is a good predictor of specific information concerning political issues and events, helping to explain why people have a consistent level of political knowledge over time and across situations (Price and Zaller 1993).

Information about Iraq is likely to be highest among those with a good grasp of general political facts acquired through exposure to a broad flow of ongoing news and events. But the Iraq and Afghanistan information scales are also somewhat distinct, indicating the importance of factors beyond education and broad political awareness, which resulted in some Americans knowing more about Afghanistan than Iraq, and vice versa.

The Role of Information

War Support

THE NEGATIVE EFFECTS OF INFORMATION ON WAR SUPPORT IN THE TNSS.   The Iraq information scale enables us to answer the following question: Did Americans with greater information about Iraq evince stronger support for the war across the political spectrum? Or did information lead Democrats, independents, and Republicans to adopt differing positions on the war? If elites led public opinion, the best-informed Americans should have been the most likely to receive the strong pro-war message present in the news, an agenda advanced by Republicans and only weakly rebutted by Democrats, resulting in their acceptance and support for war regardless of partisanship. But if this did not occur, and the effects of information had differing effects on war support among Democrats, Republicans, and independents, we need to dig more deeply to understand why.

The elite influence model predicts that public opinion, in this case support for war in Iraq, depends heavily on both information and party identification (the latter is crucial in a bidirectional information environment). Information signifies exposure to many messages, including those from party leaders, and party identification identifies the source of messages (i.e., Democrats or Republicans) most likely to be accepted or rejected. Information and partisanship are therefore key variables in our analysis of war opinion. In addition, we need to consider several other potential predictors of war support and opposition: age, education, gender, and race/ethnicity. These factors have been linked to war opposition in related analyses (Huddy, Feldman, and Cassese 2007).

To examine the role of information and partisanship on war opinion in the fall of 2002, we estimated a regression model of war support. We measured public opinion with the four-item scale of war support introduced in chapter 2, which varies from +1 (strong support) through 0 (neutral) to −1 (strong opposition). This model included an interaction between information and partisanship to test whether information (and the pro-war information environment) boosted war support to the same degree among Republicans, independents, and Democrats.[4] If information has a uniform pro-war influence on all people, the interaction term should be small. If, however, information affects Democrats and Republicans differently, the interaction term should be quite large. In order to simplify interpretation of the coefficients in this model, we coded the Iraq information measure to range from 0 (no correct answers) to 1 (five correct answers).[5]

For ease of presentation, we include here a series of figures that depict war support at different levels of information, newspaper reading, and television news viewing.[6] The results of the full model are shown in appendix table A5.1, column (1), and largely support past research: younger people, men, and white Americans are more supportive of the war. Moreover, Republicans are more supportive of the war than Democrats, as we demonstrated more simply in chapter 2.

Our first result presents a clear challenge to the elite influence model, which predicts increased war support among Republicans, Democrats, and independents as their levels of information increase in the strong one-way, pro-war information environment that existed in the fall of 2002. Instead, we find a large and significant interaction between information and partisanship, which we portray in figure 5.2. In this figure, war support is plotted as a function of increasing information about Iraq on the basis of the statistical model in the appendix (table A5.1). The three lines in the graph, one each for Democrats, independents, and Republicans, defy expectations of the elite influence model in two respects.

First, Democrats' support for the war declines substantially as they acquire more information about Iraq. This pattern would be expected if

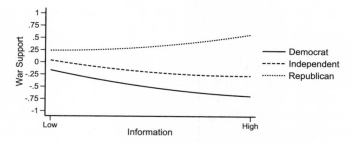

FIGURE 5.2 The effects of information on war support, TNSS, October 2002

Democratic congressional elites had strongly and consistently opposed the war, which they did not. Second, support for the war among independents also declines as they acquire information about Iraq. This is quite puzzling. The Republican administration's unified and vociferous support for the war, in the absence of strong opposition from congressional Democrats, should have resulted in greater support for the war among independents as they learned more about Iraq. The decline in war support between the least- and most-knowledgeable independents is smaller than for comparable Democrats, but its downward slope more powerfully contravenes the predictions of the elite influence model. According to the model, war support should have *increased* as independents grew more knowledgeable about Iraq and were more fully exposed to the prowar news environment. Finally, the results for Republicans conform more closely to the elite influence model. As Republicans became more knowledgeable about Iraq, they grew increasingly supportive of the Bush administration's position on the war.

A Replication: The 2002 American National Election Study (ANES)

A well-accepted theory contradicted by data from a single survey raises the possibility that this finding is simply a fluke. In a case like this it is particularly important to replicate the result. To do so, we turned to the American National Elections Studies (ANES) 2002 election survey. The ANES staff interviewed a national sample of Americans between September 18 and November 4, 2002, overlapping closely with the wave 2 TNSS data collection period.

There are some significant differences between variables in the ANES and the TNSS that we need to consider before we run the same analytic model. Most importantly, the ANES survey contained only one question on support for military intervention in Iraq, which is worded as follows: "As you may know, President Bush and his top advisers are discussing the possibility of taking military action against Iraq to remove Saddam Hussein from power. Do you favor or oppose military action against Iraq—or is this something you haven't thought about?" In other words, we can only analyze war support in the ANES data using a single question with just two response categories. This is a far less reliable and discriminating measure of war opinion than the more robust and detailed four-item scale of war support we used in the TNSS analysis. Thus, we need to caution in advance that we have reduced statistical power in the ANES with which to estimate the effects of knowledge and partisanship on war support. Additionally, as we showed in chapter 2, Americans held greater reservations about undertaking military action in Iraq than reflected in this type of very general summary question. This creates an added hurdle to replication of the TNSS findings, making any supportive evidence that much more impressive.

A second significant difference between the two surveys arises in their measure of information. In the TNSS data, survey participants were asked directly about their knowledge of Iraq. Specific knowledge questions about Iraq were not available in the ANES data, but fortunately, many of the respondents interviewed in 2002 were also interviewed earlier in 2000 and asked a number of general political knowledge questions. The 2000 survey included eight questions: what job or political office was held by Trent Lott, William Rehnquist, Tony Blair, and Janet Reno; and George W. Bush, Al Gore, Dick Cheney, and Joe Lieberman's state of residence. We combined all eight questions into a scale of general political information, which was coded to range from a low of 0 (none correct) to a high of 1 (eight questions answered correctly).[7]

In search of the interaction between partisanship and information depicted in figure 5.2, we ran a similar model to that estimated on the TNSS data.[8] Estimates for this model are in appendix table A5.1, column (5). As shown in figure 5.3, the results are reassuringly similar to those obtained from analysis of the TNSS data. In this graph, the y-axis represents the predicted probability that someone favors taking military action against Iraq. Once again, the findings contradict the elite influence model. Increased information, in this instance general political information, substantially reduced support for the war among Democrats and independents whereas it modestly increased support among Republicans.[9]

Two different national surveys, two different measures of war support, and two different measures of political information yielded strikingly sim-

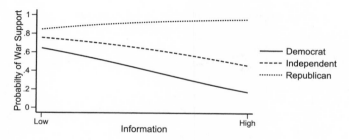

FIGURE 5.3 Information and war support, ANES

ilar results. Information promoted opposition to the war in Iraq among Democrats despite the pervasive pro-war message within the news media. Perhaps even more surprisingly, support for war significantly decreased with information about Iraq among independents, who had no obvious reason to favor a few antiwar Democratic critics over strong unified pro-war Republicans. More consistently in line with the elite influence model, increasing information among Republicans was associated with some-what greater support for war.[10]

In sum, in both sets of data, well-informed Democrats and independents appear to have been exposed to information that increased their opposition to war. But what was this information exactly?

Perceptions of the Threat Posed by Saddam

A key component of the Bush administration's case for sending military forces to Iraq was the threat posed by Saddam Hussein. Bush administration officials and congressional Republicans argued that Saddam was strengthening his weapons arsenal, was collaborating with anti-American terrorists, and needed to be removed. As we have shown in chapter 4, there were also intelligence officials, former military officers, and weapons experts in the news who disputed these claims. It is therefore important to see if the acquisition of information about Iraq led Democrats and independents to also downgrade the threat posed by Saddam.

In chapter 2, we introduced three questions included in the TNSS to measure perceptions of the threat posed by Saddam: "How likely is it that Saddam Hussein is actively supporting anti-U.S. terrorist groups at present?"; "If the U.S. does not take military action in Iraq, how likely is it that Saddam Hussein would attack the U.S. with biological, chemical, or nuclear weapons in the near future?"; and "If the U.S. does not take

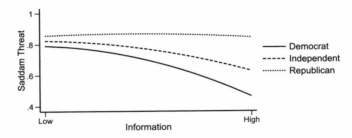

FIGURE 5.4 Information and perceptions of Saddam threat, TNSS, October 2002

military action in Iraq, how likely is it that Saddam Hussein would use biological, chemical, or nuclear weapons against countries in the Middle-East including Israel, in the near future?" We combined these questions into a single scale that ranges from 0 (no threat) to 1 (maximum threat). The mean of this scale is .75, indicating that most Americans saw Saddam as a serious threat, as someone who supported anti-American terrorists and would use weapons of mass destruction in the Middle East (though perhaps not against the United States). How did information about Iraq affect such perceptions? The dominance of a pro-war Republican message in the news should have resulted in the best informed viewing Saddam as an imminent threat. We therefore estimated the same model as for overall war support, but replaced war support with a measure of Saddam threat as the dependent variable. Estimates for this model are in appendix table A5.1, column (3). The key relationships are shown graphically in figure 5.4.

While Americans of all partisan proclivities viewed Saddam as a threat, the perceived threat posed by Saddam did *not* increase with greater information about Iraq. Republicans were most likely to view Saddam as a threat, but this did not increase as they acquired more information.

Instead, Democrats and independents were *less* likely to see Saddam as a threat as they became more informed about Iraq. Increasing levels of information about Iraq are associated with a steep decline among Democrats and a somewhat lesser decline among independents as to how much threat Saddam evoked. Once again, the downward trend among independents is particularly intriguing. Lacking a partisan preference, independents should have agreed with the Bush administration that Saddam posed a looming menace to the United States. The fact that information led independents to question the imminent danger posed by Saddam presents an obvious empirical dilemma for the elite influence model.

We have seen that increasing levels of information about Iraq among both Democrats and independents were associated with less support for military action and lower estimates of the threat posed by Saddam Hussein to the United States and the Middle East. If the administration's prowar message was conveyed more powerfully by the news media than the mixed signals issued by Democrats, as we demonstrated in chapter 4, why does war support decline as Democrats and independents learn more about Iraq?

Not All Information Is Equal: The Importance of News Source

News Source, Information, and War Support

To explore these questions in greater detail, we turn to the diverse news environments occupied by Democrats and independents to better understand why greater information led many to oppose war. Our analysis of news content in chapter 4 revealed a different, and more critical, perspective on the Bush administration's claims concerning Saddam Hussein and the threat he posed to the United States in newspapers than on TV. We therefore shift our attention to examine the diverse news environments in which TNSS and ANES respondents were located.

If the findings reported in chapter 4 accurately reflect the broader tone and content of the news in the fall of 2002, Americans who primarily learned about Iraq from newspapers would have been exposed to a higher proportion of critical stories than those who acquired information from television news. We thus predict that well-informed Democrats and independents who obtained their information from newspapers were primarily responsible for the growing opposition to a war in Iraq that emerged in September and October 2002.

To test this hypothesis, we examine the effects of regular newspaper and TV consumption on support for war among well-informed Democrats and independents. We measured media consumption with two basic questions: "How many days in the past week did you watch the national TV news on ABC, CBS, CNN, FOX, or NBC?" and "How many days in the past week did you read about national events in a daily newspaper?" Questions like this, that ask respondents to report the number of days in the past week in which they obtained news from TV or read a newspaper, have been criticized as giving an inaccurate account of news consumption (Prior 2009). It appears that many people exaggerate the number of days in which they read or watch news. We do not view this as a fundamental problem for our analysis, however, because we use these questions to distinguish between those who read newspapers or watched TV news more or less frequently, and we are less concerned about the absolute number of days in which this occurred. These media questions fall short in yet another way: they provide no information about the specific news organization to which respondents were exposed. We do not know, for example, if regular television news viewers primarily watched Fox News or obtained their news from CNN. Nor do we know which newspaper(s) people read or what stories about Iraq they encountered. All of this adds "noise" to our analysis which should make it more difficult to detect any clear effect of news source on public opinion.[11]

Can opposition to the war in Iraq be attributed in part to the more negative and critical content of newspapers than TV? To test this hypothesis, we examine whether information acquired from regularly reading newspapers had a different effect on war support than information obtained from regular TV news viewing. This test entails the addition of an interaction between information and TV viewing and information and newspaper reading to our basic analytic model. In essence, we test whether the effect of information on war support depends on where it came from: newspapers or TV news.[12] Content analysis of newspaper and TV stories on the Iraq–al Qaeda and aluminum tubes stories in September and October 2002 led us to expect growing opposition to war as Democrats and independents obtained information from newspapers but no such opposition among Democrats and independents who obtained information from TV.

We begin with the effects of information acquired from newspapers on war support in the TNSS data. Estimates for this model are shown in appendix table A5.1, column (2). The key finding of this model is depicted in figure 5.5, which is divided into three panels showing the predicted effect of Iraq information on levels of war support among strong Democrats, independents, and strong Republicans. For each group of partisans, we show the relationship between war support and information among two subgroups: those who said they had not read a newspaper in the last week and those who read a newspaper every day.[13]

Consistent with our predictions, well-informed Democrats who regularly read a newspaper were far more opposed to the war than well-

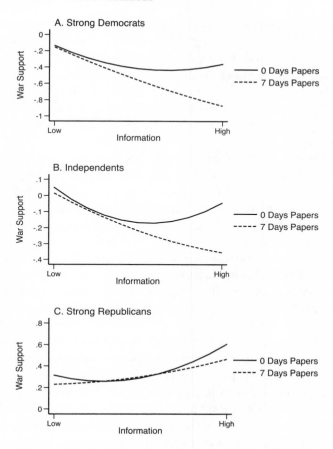

FIGURE 5.5 War support by Iraq information and newspaper reading, TNSS, October 2002

informed Democrats who never read a newspaper. The same trend is
observed among independents. Panel A of figure 5.5 depicts the effect of
increasing levels of Iraq information on war support among strong Democrats. We noted earlier in the chapter that as Democrats learned more
about Iraq their support for the war declined (see fig. 5.2). Panel A of
figure 5.5 demonstrates, however, that this decline is far more precipitous
among Democrats who read a newspaper on a daily basis than among
Democrats who had not read a newspaper in the last week.

The trends portrayed in panel A of figure 5.5 also make clear that opposition to the war among strong Democrats was a joint function of information and newspaper reading. At low levels of information about Iraq,

there is no difference in war support between those who did and did not read newspapers. Poorly informed Democrats are only slightly opposed to war. As information increases, the gap in support across levels of newspaper reading grows larger. At the highest levels of information, Democrats who had not read a newspaper in the last week score a predicted value of −.35 on the (−1 to +1) war support scale. Those who read newspapers daily score a predicted value of −.88, not far from the maximum value of war opposition. This difference is arrestingly large.

Panel B of figure 5.5 shows a similar effect of newspaper reading on war support among political independents (although they are less opposed to the war overall than are strong Democrats). Among political independents, information about Iraq barely depressed war support if they had not read a newspaper in the last week (with support dropping from .05 at the lowest level of information to −.04 at the highest), but information had a far greater effect on war support among those who had read a newspaper every day in the past week (from .02 at the lowest levels of information to −.34 at the highest). Among independents, war opposition mounted with the acquisition of Iraq information but only among frequent newspaper readers.

In contrast, regular newspaper reading had virtually no effect on war support among strong Republicans, as shown in panel C. Republicans who had read a newspaper every day in the last week were slightly less supportive of the war than Republicans who had not read a newspaper, but the difference is too small to be meaningful. As they became better informed about Iraq, Republicans grew somewhat more supportive of the war regardless of how often they read a newspaper.

The negative effect of Iraq information on Democrats' and independents' support for military action is thus highly dependent on news medium. The more avidly Democrats and independents read newspapers and acquired information about Iraq, the more likely they were to reject military action. At the extremes, the differences are substantial. Among Democrats who read a newspaper on a daily basis, learning more about Iraq shifted their position from ambivalence on the war to strong opposition. Democrats who knew a lot about Iraq were *much* less supportive of going to war than those who knew a little about Iraq but *only* if they were regularly exposed to news in newspapers. Learning information about Iraq had significantly less effect on Democrats who acquired their information elsewhere. Newspaper reading also decreased war support among independents, although the effects are somewhat smaller.

Once again, we need to confirm that these findings are not merely a quirk of the TNSS data. To do so, we return to the 2002 ANES data. As we noted earlier, the ANES survey had only a single question on war support and a very different way of measuring information. Fortunately, the ANES data does, however, include the same questions as the TNSS on the number of days in the past week in which someone had watched TV news and read a newspaper. We are thus able to estimate a very similar model among Democrats in the ANES to that tested in the TNSS. In this model, the effects of information on war support depend once again on news medium. Estimates for this model are in appendix table A5.1, column (6).

Figure 5.6 contains three panels in which the effect of Iraq information is plotted against war support among strong Democrats, independents, and strong Republicans. Each panel contains two predicted relationships, the first for those who had not read a newspaper in the last week and the second for those who had read one every day.[14] In this instance, we estimate the predicted probability that a respondent supports military action in Iraq.

ANES findings essentially mirror those observed in the TNSS data. Among strong Democrats who read a newspaper each day, the acquisition of information about Iraq decreased war support dramatically. In panel A, figure 5.6, learning more about Iraq has little or no effect on war support among Democrats who had not read a newspaper in the last week. The predicted probability that a strong Democrat who knew nothing about Iraq supported the war was .42. This predicted probability dropped to .3 among Democrats who had modest levels of information about Iraq, and then increased to .39 among those who knew the most. In essence, there is no systematic relationship between Iraq information and the probability of supporting the war among Democrats who did not read a newspaper.

In contrast, among Democrats who had read a newspaper every day in the last week, acquiring information about Iraq substantially decreased (monotonically) the probability that they supported the war. The probability of supporting the war dropped from a substantial .65 among Democrats who knew nothing about Iraq to a meager .10 at the highest levels of information—a very large decline.[15] As was the case in TNSS data, staunch opposition to the war originated with highly informed Democrats who regularly read a newspaper.

Among independents in the ANES, the effects of regular newspaper reading on war support, depicted in panel B of figure 5.6, are similar to those observed for Democrats and replicate findings for independents

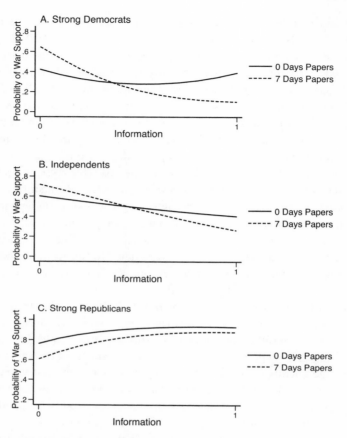

FIGURE 5.6 War support by information and newspaper reading, ANES

observed in the TNSS. There is a small negative effect of information on the probability of war support among independents who did not read a newspaper and a far more dramatic decline in war support with increasing information among those who read a newspaper regularly. Among independents who did not read a newspaper, the predicted probability of war support dropped from .60 among the least informed to .40 among the best informed. Among independents who read a newspaper daily, the negative effect of information is more than twice as large—with the predicted probability of war support dropping from .72 among the least well informed to .26 among the best informed.

In both national samples, information about Iraq had a robust and consistently negative effect on war support among Democrats and independents who regularly read newspapers. Informed Democrats and independents were most likely to oppose military action in Iraq if they were regularly exposed to information in newspapers. Our findings suggest that the critical newspaper coverage of the Bush administration's claims concerning an Iraq–al Qaeda connection and Iraq's possession of WMD presented in chapter 4 may have increased opposition to the war among Democrats and independents.

Newspaper reading had almost no effect on war support among strong Republicans. As Republicans learned more about Iraq, those who had not read a newspaper in the last week and those who had read one daily increased their support for the war at virtually the same rate.

News Source, Information, and Perceived Saddam Threat

As we reported earlier in this chapter, Democrats and independents who acquired greater information about Iraq were less convinced that Saddam Hussein was as menacing a threat as claimed by the Bush administration and congressional Republicans. Our media content analysis, however, uncovered greater skepticism about the threat posed by Saddam in newspaper stories than on television news. This leads to our next question: Did greater Democratic and independent doubts about the threat posed by Saddam arise from exposure to information in newspapers? An affirmative answer strengthens our argument that newspaper coverage accounts, in part, for declining war support among Democrats and independents in the fall of 2002.

To examine this hypothesis, we assess whether the acquisition of greater information from newspapers weakened the perceived threat posed by Saddam. Estimates for this model are in appendix table A5.1, column (4). Using the TNSS data, we estimated the same model for Saddam threat as we did for overall war support. As we did for the two war support analyses, we show the key results among strong Democrats, independents, and strong Republicans in figure 5.7.

Panel A of figure 5.7 illustrates greater skepticism that Saddam posed a direct threat to the United States or the Middle East among well-informed Democrats who read newspapers than among well-informed Democrats who did not read a newspaper. The dampening effect of information on the Saddam threat was twice as large among daily newspaper readers than

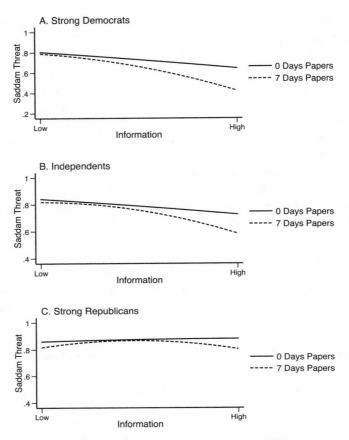

FIGURE 5.7 Saddam threat by information and newspaper reading, TNSS, October 2002

among those who had not read a newspaper in the last week. Thus, knowledgeable Democrats who regularly read a newspaper were far less likely than others to regard Saddam as a threat. This finding suggests that opposition to the war among well-informed Democrats who read newspapers was, in part, grounded in doubt about the imminent threat posed by Saddam, the very issue tackled critically by regional newspapers such as those in the Knight Ridder group.

Although the overall effect of information on the perceived threat that Saddam posed to his region and the United States is somewhat lower for independents than Democrats, newspaper reading had a very similar effect among them as shown in panel B of figure 5.7. The negative effect of information is relatively small for independents who didn't read newspapers and more than twice as large for those who read a newspaper daily.

Consistent with the results for war support, panel C illustrates that regularly reading a newspaper did not affect Republicans' perception that Saddam was a menace. Across all levels of information and newspaper reading, Republicans were quite convinced that Saddam was a threat to his neighbors and the United States.

A comparison of figures 5.5, 5.6, and 5.7 underscores the common antiwar thrust of information obtained from newspapers by Democrats and independents. Better-informed Democrats and independents who read newspapers frequently saw Saddam as less imminently dangerous and were more opposed to the war than those who obtained their information elsewhere. These findings jell with our content analysis of TV and newspaper sources on two key issues connected to the war: Saddam's link to al Qaeda and his use of aluminum tubes to make nuclear weapons. In both instances newspapers provided far more scathing coverage than TV of the administration's claims, conveyed criticism from a broader range of sources, and pursued the stories more doggedly, dampening war support among Democrats and independents who read newspapers.

We should note one other common pattern in our analyses: in each case, knowledgeable Democrats who regularly read newspapers were more opposed to war and less likely to see Saddam as a threat than were equally knowledgeable independents who read newspapers. Information acquired from newspapers dampened war support and raised doubts about Saddam as a looming menace among both Democrats and independents, but the magnitude of this effect was consistently larger among Democrats. Opposition to the war was especially pronounced among Democrats who had considerable knowledge of Iraq and regularly read a newspaper when compared to comparable political independents. In both instances, we believe that Democrats and independents who lacked a strong, uniform signal from Democratic elites, engaged in deeper processing of information, seeking information that was present but not dominant in newspapers (operating under an accuracy motive), and processing it carefully since it was not always easy to obtain. Even so, Democrats could not entirely evade motivated partisan reasoning (Lodge and Taber 2013). Once strong Democrats obtained information that was critical of the Bush administration, they were more than willing to run with it and opposed the war even more strongly than independents in possession of similar information.

The Effect of Television News Viewing

What about the information obtained from television? We have discussed at length the effects of information obtained from newspapers on support for an Iraq war among Democrats and independents but have said little about the effects of news acquired from television. Just as we did for newspaper reading, we also examined the effect of television news viewing on war support and the threat posed by Saddam in the TNSS and war support in the ANES (shown in appendix table A5.1). In two of these three analyses, information about Iraq acquired from television had no significant effect on war support or perceived Saddam threat. In stark contrast to the estimates for newspaper reading, regular TV news viewers— whether they were Democrats, independents, or Republicans—did not significantly differ from nonviewers in their support for war regardless of how much they knew about Iraq. There was one exception to this pattern. In the TNSS, well-informed Americans who frequently watched television were *more* supportive of the war. This finding is intriguing, but we could not replicate that result in the ANES data nor does it appear in the TNSS model predicting Saddam threat, leading us to question its robustness.[16]

Overall, this is a critical nonfinding. One way to understand the newspaper effect is that it shows that Democrats and independents who were more attentive—more highly informed *and* more frequent news consumers—were more opposed to the use of military force in Iraq. If that were true, then the same pattern of results should occur for well-informed Americans who watched TV news nightly. But that does not occur in analysis of either national survey data set. In one case, the opposite arises; the most frequent TV news viewers in the TNSS (Democrats, independents, and Republicans) were the *most* supportive of going to war, and the difference between daily TV news viewers and nonviewers increased as they became better informed about Iraq. The small differences in war support in the ANES and the perceived threat posed by Saddam in the TNSS between regular and non–TV news viewers reveal that regular TV news viewing generated greater support for the war. In these two models the effects are substantively small and well below conventional social science standards for establishing a convincing relationship. We therefore veer toward caution in interpreting these effects. Even if we were to conclude that TV news had no effect on support or opposition to the use of military force in Iraq, that nonfinding must be juxtaposed against the consistently negative effects of regular newspaper reading. It was not simply a matter of Americans attending to news about Iraq in the fall of 2002. The source of that news—newspapers or television—was critically important.

Conclusion

Contrary to much accepted wisdom in political science, we find clear evidence that general political information (ANES) or information specifically about Iraq (TNSS) led Democrats and independents to oppose a war in Iraq despite the absence of a strong antiwar message from political elites. Greater war opposition among the most-knowledgeable Democrats and independents hinges on one other factor, however: the source from which they obtained their news. Well-informed Democrats who regularly read a newspaper turned robustly against the Bush administration's plan to militarily confront Saddam Hussein. They were less likely to view Saddam as a major threat and ultimately opted to oppose the use of military force in Iraq. Independents responded similarly although not quite as strongly. There is no evidence in any of these analyses that attention to television news had negative effects on war support (and in the TNSS data, television viewing actually increased war support). At equal levels of political knowledge, Democrats and independents who regularly read a newspaper were substantially more opposed to war than those who regularly got their news from television.

As we demonstrated in chapter 4, television failed to confront, let alone refute, the administration's claims concerning Saddam, al Qaeda, and the aluminum tubes even when strong contrary evidence was readily available and elsewhere reported. Newspapers, in contrast, were critical of the same claims (to varying degrees), especially Saddam's link to al Qaeda but also his purported use of aluminum tubes for WMD. Our findings suggest that different news content in newspapers and on television, specifically coverage that was more critical of the administration in newspapers, led Democrats who regularly read newspapers to acquire information about Iraq that increased their opposition to war. That was not true for knowledgeable TV viewers.

Of course, the skeptical reader will have generated a number of alternative explanations for our findings, which we have not yet addressed. Perhaps there is something inherently different about Democrats and independents who regularly read newspapers that led them to be more opposed to the use of force: they might be more liberal or more opposed to President Bush. Such selection effects, or preexisting differences between regular newspaper readers and others, would invalidate our proposed causal order in which the content of newspaper stories influenced public opinion. From this skeptical vantage point, causality runs in the other direction, with antiwar Democrats and independents simply being more inclined to read newspapers. The next chapter, which presents the results of numerous analyses designed to rule out this and other alternatives, is for just such a reader. We ultimately remain convinced of our key finding. In sum, after examining various alternative explanations, we find that none alter our conclusion that Democrats and independents who obtained information about Iraq from newspapers learned something that others did not, something that made them question the wisdom of a war in Iraq.

There is one other facet of news content that bolsters our confidence in the findings we report in this chapter. Among news organizations, the administration's claims were scrutinized more critically by regional, nonelite newspapers, which were read widely and reached 50% of US households at that time. As a news source, nonelite papers are often ignored by social science researchers because they are numerous and more time-consuming to code and analyze than national news sources. But they also attract a more diverse audience than the elite national papers and as a consequence may be less subject to selection effects. It is also worth noting that newspapers were still flourishing and far more widely read in 2002 than today. When taken together, these facts remind us that newspaper readers are not as different from others as we might assume.

Finally, we found no effect of newspaper reading on war support or perceptions of the threat posed by Saddam among Republicans. Across our analyses, information slightly increased Republican support for war regardless of news source. The effect of information on Republicans is not large but its direction is consistent with predictions from an elite influence model. Rank-and-file Republicans were confronted with a strong and consistent pro-war drumbeat from Republican elites and responded accordingly. The surprise in our analyses is the very different response of Democrats and independents.

CHAPTER SIX

Newspaper Content or Newspaper Readers?

"Fifty percent of people won't vote, and fifty percent don't read newspapers. I hope it's the same fifty percent." —Gore Vidal[1]

D ecades of political communications research have come to a singular and well-established conclusion about the news media's influence on public opinion: the news media tells people what is important by setting the issue agenda and provides through framing a basis for how to understand a specific policy issue. Moreover, the established view is that it is elite messaging rather than the news media that tells people which side to take or what position to support on a given policy debate (Bennett and Iyengar 2008; Kinder 2003). In the previous chapter, we presented evidence that information gleaned from newspapers by Democrats and independents increased their opposition to an impending Iraq war and led them to doubt the imminence or danger of the threat posed by Saddam to the United States. In this instance, newspaper content appears to have shaped directly public support for the war. This is a highly unusual finding in the context of communications research. As such, it bears closer scrutiny, especially for skeptics who will argue that we erroneously mistake the effects of newspaper reading for the qualities of newspaper readers. This chapter is dedicated to such skeptics.

Let's return to our original conundrum: well-informed Democrats and independents, to a lesser extent, opposed an Iraq war in the fall of 2002, despite an intensely pro-war information environment, because some of them paid close attention to information in newspapers. Well-informed Democrats and independents who regularly read a newspaper were more opposed to going to war than their well-informed politically comparable counterparts who did not read a newspaper. There was no difference of this kind among regular viewers of TV news; they were no more opposed to the war than other Americans.

But what if Democrats and independents who read newspapers were substantially different—more liberal, partisan, anti-Bush, or pacifist? Our results might then be dismissed as selection effects caused by newspaper readers who were simply different from others: those already inclined to oppose the war read newspapers, but their opposition to the war did not originate in newspaper content. From this contrary vantage point, opposition to the war rested on the everyday psychological process of people reading news that flattered and reinforced their existing beliefs. This is an important line of criticism directed against the findings we presented in chapter 5.

If we stretch our skeptics' concerns a little further, they might point to pervasive evidence of selective exposure within the history of communications research as the basis for their doubts. Researchers have failed to find much past evidence of news media persuasion because ordinary people often tune in to simpatico sources in order to read, see, or hear information with which they already agree. Our devoted Democratic and independent newspaper readers may have fallen into that category. The image of the typical reader of the *New York Times* comes readily to mind—urbane, politically left-leaning, possibly cynical, definitely well educated, and very likely opposed to George W. Bush. However, this is an unlikely profile of the typical reader of *USA Today*, Knight Ridder papers, or other local newspapers, which when taken together had far larger combined circulation than elite national newspapers in the fall of 2002. In this chapter, we take a series of deliberate and careful steps to explore the viability of this possibility.

Our initial defense of the role of newspapers in heightening war opposition can be found in the details of multivariate analyses reported in the previous chapter. In those analyses, we observed greater war opposition among well-informed Democrats and independents who obtained information from newspapers even as we held constant a number of the factors that promote newspaper reading or opposition to war. These factors included age, education, gender, race and ethnicity, and partisanship. Perhaps well-informed Democrats who read newspapers were older and more antiwar, better educated and more supportive of diplomacy, or die-hard partisans who disliked George W Bush. In all the analyses on which findings in the previous chapter are based, information obtained

from newspapers increased opposition to the war regardless of these demographic and political factors. In essence, information gathered from
newspapers increased antiwar attitudes among Democrats and independents, those with more and less formal education, young and old, male
and female, black and white. Increased opposition to the war among
knowledgeable newspaper readers is statistically independent of such basic demographic and social factors.

That said, there are other factors that may have influenced attitudes
toward the impending Iraq war. Partisanship is obviously a major factor, as we have already shown. Regardless of media exposure, Republicans largely supported the Bush administration's proposal to attack Iraq
militarily. Political ideology may also have played a role. Perhaps liberal
Democrats were less likely than moderate Democrats to accept the Bush
administration's arguments for going to war. Or opposition to the use of
military force may have been based simply on a raw distrust of George
Bush. We must also take into account the possibility that some Democrats
generally opposed the use of military force, and they may have been more
likely to read newspapers.

In what follows, we examine in considerable detail a number of possible objections to our conclusion that newspapers provided critical information that led Democrats and independents to oppose an Iraq war.
Many if not most of these objections emanate from the notion that rather
than being influenced directly by news content, Americans selectively expose themselves to newspapers and consume information that reinforces
their preexisting views. In addition to examining the robustness of our
newspaper account, the analyses in this chapter also shed light on differences between Democrats and independents in their assimilation of
newspaper content, underscoring the difficulties partisans face in evading
partisan reasoning even when they carefully and systematically process information. We also compare the magnitude of newspaper effects to other
factors that led people to oppose the war and in so doing provide a more
complete account of public opinion on the proposed Iraq war at that time.

Ideology, Partisanship, and News Consumption

The most obvious objection to our conclusion that newspapers drove antiwar sentiment is that well-informed Democrats and independents who
obtain their news from newspapers are simply more liberal, partisan, and

antiwar and would have opposed the war in Iraq regardless of newspaper content. This selective exposure argument, in which like-minded people choose news sources with which they agree, turns our argument on its head. Instead of information in newspapers leading some people to oppose the war, it suggests that antiwar Democrats and independents were more likely to read newspapers. If the results reported in the last chapter can be attributed to selective exposure, our findings say little about the distinct effects of newspaper content on public opinion and undermine the notion that some Americans engaged in an effortful process to obtain reliable information about Iraq.

One indicator of selective exposure to a specific news medium is evidence that particular kinds of people regularly read newspapers whereas others are more reliant on TV news. Therefore, we first examine the correlates of media attention. Are strong Democrats more likely than weak Democrats to obtain their news from newspapers? Are liberals or those who consistently oppose war more likely than others to read newspapers? To answer these and related questions, we compare the profile of regular newspaper readers and TV news viewers. Data are drawn from both the Threat and National Security Survey (TNSS) and American National Election Studies (ANES) and analyzed in several multivariate ordered probit analyses. In these analyses, TV and newspaper consumption is coded as the number of days in the last week that a person reported consuming news from each source (ranging from zero to seven days). A number of factors that might account for antiwar views among newspaper readers are analyzed, including partisanship, liberal/conservative political ideology, and demographic factors such as education and age.

To fully understand the link between news media source and political orientation, we examine whether ideology had differing effects among Democrats, Republicans, and independents, through the inclusion of interaction terms in the statistical model. This allows us to test, for example, whether ideology enhanced newspaper reading to a greater degree among Democrats than Republicans. Estimates for the ANES and TNSS models are shown in appendix table A6.1., columns (1), (3), (5), and (6).

In both data sets older Americans, men, and the better educated are more likely than others to regularly read a newspaper. But these are the only consistent trends in media consumption across both data sets, and two of these demographic factors—age and gender—are more likely to drive support rather than opposition to war (Huddy et al. 2005). TV news viewing increases with age but only in the ANES, and men are a little more likely than women to watch TV news in the TNSS. African Americans are somewhat less likely than others to read newspapers in the ANES but more likely to watch TV in the TNSS and the ANES.

Perhaps political preferences have a more direct influence on the decision to read a newspaper or watch TV news. However, our analyses demonstrate that their influence is quite limited. Overall, we find that there is no consistent relationship between partisanship, ideology, and patterns of news consumption. The effects of partisanship and ideology on newspaper reading are relatively small in both of the data sets and, where significant, they are in opposite directions. In the TNSS data, Republicans are the most likely to read a newspaper seven days a week, followed by Democrats and independents. The differences are quite small (probability of .38 for strong Republicans, .34 for strong Democrats, and .31 for independents).[2] In the ANES, the small partisan differences are reversed with greater newspaper reading among Democrats than Republicans (probability of .41 for strong Democrats, .37 for strong Republicans, and .34 for independents).

The effects of ideology are similarly small and inconsistent across the two data sets. In the TNSS, liberal Democrats and independents are slightly more likely than others to read a newspaper; newspaper reading does not vary by ideology among Republicans. In the ANES data, conservative Democrats are slightly more likely than liberal Democrats to read a newspaper regularly. Among independents and Republicans, there is a small relationship in the opposite direction, with higher levels of newspaper consumption among moderates than conservatives.

Political views also have weak or inconsistent links to regular TV news viewing. There are no significant relationships between partisanship, ideology, and reported frequency of TV news viewing in the ANES data. In the TNSS data, Republicans are more likely than Democrats or independents to regularly watch TV news (probability of .54 for strong Republicans and .45 for independents and strong Democrats). There are also inconsistent links between ideology and TV news viewing: liberal Democrats and Republicans watch somewhat more TV news than others but liberal independents watch less.

Overall, there is little or nothing in these results to suggest that avid newspaper readers (or TV news viewers) are systematically different in terms of their political outlook. Where there are statistically significant effects of partisanship or ideology, the effects are substantively small. And none of those effects replicate across the two national survey data sets.

TABLE 6.1 **Measures of attitudes toward war**

How strongly do you favor or oppose increasing the level of military action (in Afghanistan) even if it means that U.S. armed forces might suffer a substantial number of casualties?

Do you think it will be best for the future of the United States if the country takes an active part in world affairs, or if the country stays out of world affairs?

Do you think the U.S. should limit its military action to Osama bin Laden and the Taliban, or should it broaden its action to include other countries that harbor and support terrorists?

Do you think the United States should or should not take the leading role among all other countries in the world in trying to solve international problems?

Source: TNSS, October 2001–March 2002.

In the main, Democrats and Republicans, liberals and conservatives are equally likely to read a newspaper on a regular basis.

The three-wave structure of the TNSS allows us to extend the search for sources of political bias in patterns of media consumption beyond partisanship and ideology. Specifically, we draw on a series of questions asked shortly after the 9/11 terrorist attacks on support for the use of military force in Afghanistan and aggressive action against terrorists. In this way, we can further check to see if those who opposed aggressive military force after 9/11 were more likely to read newspapers. We examined the link between war views in wave 1 and news consumption in wave 2, by adding war attitudes to the overall model predicting levels of newspaper reading and TV viewing in the TNSS. Estimates for these models are in appendix table A6.1, columns (2) and (4). The wording of all four war-linked questions from wave 1 is included in table 6.1.

None of these variables were, individually or jointly, related to the frequency with which Americans reported reading a newspaper. Favoring an increase in the level of military action in Afghanistan after 9/11 was significantly associated with more frequent TV viewing in the fall of 2002. But even here, the magnitude of the relationship was very small. Those who strongly supported increased military action in Afghanistan were somewhat more likely than those who strongly opposed action to view TV news daily (an estimated 41% vs. 35%).

Across two data sets and several measures of political orientations, we find little evidence of systematic political bias in patterns of news consumption. In particular, there is no evidence that avid newspaper readers are more liberal, antiwar, or Democratic than others. While these analyses are inconsistent with the selective exposure argument, they are not quite sufficient to fully sustain our main conclusions. The antiwar effects of newspaper consumption among Democrats and independents, presented in the preceding chapter, are based on an interaction between newspaper reading, information, and partisanship. This is a complex statistical relationship, which means we need to explore the model in more detail to test whether alternative explanations, such as the possibility that stronger war opposition among well-informed liberal Democrats or well-informed pacifists, could be confounded with newspaper reading in ways we have not yet detected.

How Robust Are the Antiwar Effects of Newspaper Reading?

Since our primary objective in this chapter is to examine whether the effects of newspaper reading on war opposition hold up to very close scrutiny, we need a simple way to summarize their effects and compare the antiwar effects of newspapers to alternative factors. In chapter 5, we graphically presented our analytic results by plotting levels of war support across the range of information about Iraq (least to most) separately for those who never read a daily newspaper and again for those who read one daily (see, e.g., fig. 5.5).

We found that newspaper exposure had its strongest effect among those who knew the most about Iraq, with the graphs showing a far steeper decline in war support across the range of information among regular than non–newspaper readers. This is likely to occur because some newspaper readers, even regular readers, are more attentive than others and better able to absorb information. In that sense, the most knowledgeable obtain the most complete exposure to newspaper content.

We can thus show the effect of reading a newspaper on war opinion by returning to the models discussed in chapter 5 (see appendix table A5.1, columns [1] and [5]) for both nonreaders and daily readers who have the most information about Iraq. These differences are plotted in figure 6.1 for the TNSS data (panel A) and the ANES data (panel B) across the seven categories of party identification ranging from strong Republican through independent to strong Democrat. Although the war support scale differs in these two data sets—the TNSS analysis uses a four-item scale and the ANES depends on a single dichotomous question—the pattern of war support is very similar in the two graphs. There is virtually no effect of newspaper reading among strong Republicans, but as newspaper reading increases among Democrats and independents, they grow increasingly opposed to the war.

We can further simplify the newspaper effect by computing the *difference* in war support between nonreaders and daily readers at each level of partisanship. Consider, for example, the TNSS data. The best-informed independents are slightly antiwar (on a scale that ranges from strong war opposition at −1 to strong support at +1) and this ranges from a very slight antiwar stance (−.05) among those who never read a newspaper to far stronger war opposition (−.36) among daily readers, a difference of −.31. The comparable values of war support for strong Democrats are −.36 among those who never read a newspaper to −.88 among those who read one daily, a difference of −.52. These values are shown in figure 6.2 for the TNSS and ANES data. Each point in figure 6.2 is simply the difference between the predicted values of war support for newspaper nonreaders and regular readers from figure 6.1. These differences in predicted values across the range of newspaper reading provide us with a simple way of comparing the effects of newspaper reading as we introduce other factors into the model of war support.[3] Figure 6.2 shows the greater antiwar effect of regular newspaper consumption among Democrats and independents than Republicans.

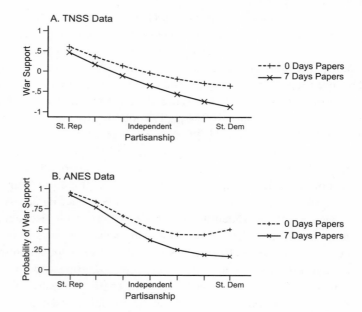

FIGURE 6.1 Difference between daily and non–newspaper readers in war support

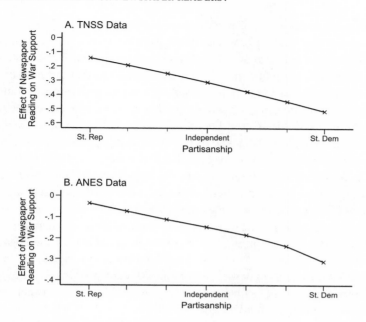

FIGURE 6.2 Effect of newspaper reading on war support

Exploring the Effects of Ideology

The analysis in chapter 5 focused on the joint effects of media use, information, and partisanship on support for military action in Iraq. The focus on partisanship is consistent with a great deal of research in political science showing the importance of partisan cues in the formation of public opinion (Green, Palmquist, and Schickler 2002; Lewis-Beck et al. 2008; Zaller 1991). And with the growing polarization in American politics and the controversies stemming from the 2000 presidential election, it is likely that many Americans used partisan cues to help make sense of the arguments over the justification for using military force in Iraq.

However, partisanship is not the only political predisposition that could have shaped support or opposition to an Iraq war. Another major factor that we need to consider is political ideology. Although ideological conflict has never been as pronounced in the United States as in other Western democracies, there has been an increase in ideological polarization in recent years, and many Americans use ideological labels to distinguish among politicians and their political messages. We assess ideology as liberal/conservative self-identification on the basis of a question that asks people to indicate how they think of themselves on a seven-point scale with strong liberal at one end, moderate in the middle, and strong conservative at the other end. While we acknowledge that this measure is not a perfect indication of policy-based ideology, it does capture an ideological identity that might incline a liberal to be influenced by Senator Ted Kennedy, a self-avowed liberal, or a conservative to be swayed by arguments on Fox News. Some of the Democrats opposed to the war—Kennedy, Feingold, Biden, Byrd, and others—were readily classified as being from the party's liberal wing. In that sense, a liberal or conservative identity may have helped Americans to sort and classify pro- and antiwar sources in the months before the onset of the Iraq War to serve as a useful shortcut to the acceptance or rejection of their various arguments.

We have two goals in mind as we examine the effects of ideology on support for military action in Iraq. Most importantly, we need to demonstrate that the effects of newspaper reading, documented in the preceding chapter, are not simply a function of ideological differences between well-informed newspaper readers and others. We found little evidence that newspaper readers were more liberal than others in the preceding analysis, so there is nothing in those results to suggest that the antiwar effects of newspapers arose because newspaper readers are liberal. However, our conclusions are based on the more complex effects of newspaper content among the best informed, and we need to ensure that well-informed newspaper readers are not excessively liberal. Moreover, adding ideology to the analysis sheds additional light on the origins of support and opposition to the use of military force in Iraq. The inclusion of political ideology in the analysis provides a more complete picture of the determinants of war support and enhances our understanding of the way in which newspapers shaped public opinion on the war.

We thus add ideology to the general model of war support presented in chapter 5 and allow its effects to vary with levels of information and partisanship. In other words, the model tests whether ideology had differing effects among the least and best informed, and among Democrats, Republicans, and independents. We return to our general model and examine the difference in war support among well-informed, non–newspaper readers and well-informed, regular newspaper readers (as we did in fig. 6.2). Estimates for this model are in appendix table A6.2, columns (1) and (3).

Figure 6.3 documents the degree to which newspaper reading affected war support with and without statistical controls for ideology in the TNSS

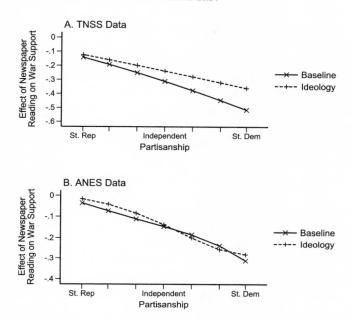

FIGURE 6.3 Effects of newspaper reading on war support, with and without ideology

(panel A) and the ANES data (panel B). In these graphs, the solid line represents the newspaper effect as estimated in chapter 5 (appendix table A5.1, columns [2] and [6]) without ideology (baseline), whereas the dashed line shows the effect when ideology is included in the model. In neither analysis does ideology eliminate the effect of newspaper reading on war support. Ideology modestly reduces the negative effect of newspapers on war support in the TNSS data but has virtually no effect in the ANES data. The decreased effect of newspaper reading in the TNSS data is seen largely among relatively strong Democrats. These analyses underscore that greater war opposition persists among regular newspaper readers regardless of their political ideology.

Ideology does not seriously diminish the effects of newspaper reading on war opposition, but it does have very direct effects on attitudes toward the use of military force in Iraq. We present the impact of ideology on war support for the TNSS data (fig. 6.4) and the ANES data (fig. 6.5), showing the link between war support and information among strong Democrats who are either strong liberals or moderates (panel A), among liberal, moderate, and conservative independents (panel B), and among strong Republicans who are either strong conservatives or moderates (panel C).[4]

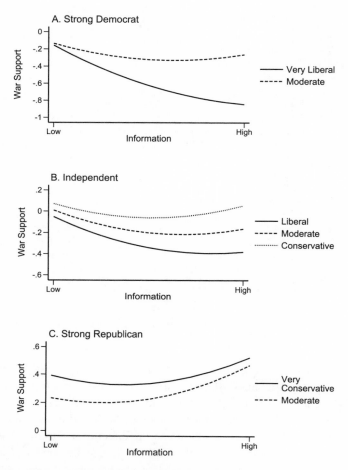

FIGURE 6.4   Effects of ideology on war support, TNSS, October 2002

Two consistent results emerge in analysis of both national surveys. First, ideology has very little effect on war support among Republicans. Very conservative Republicans are slightly more supportive of the war than moderate Republicans in the TNSS data, though there is very little difference in the ANES. Second, ideology matters greatly for Democrats. In both data sets, war support declines rapidly among liberal Democrats as they obtain more information about Iraq. In contrast, there is no significant decline in war support with rising information levels among moderate Democrats. This results in a large gap in war support between the most-informed moderate and liberal Democrats. Ideology also matters among independents, although the findings are slightly different in the two data sets. In both the ANES and TNSS, war support declines most rapidly as information levels increase among liberal independents. In the ANES, war support declines significantly with information among moderate independents, but information has little effect on war support among moderate independents in the TNSS data.

These analyses demonstrate that ideology—identifying as liberal— was a major factor underlying opposition to the use of military force in

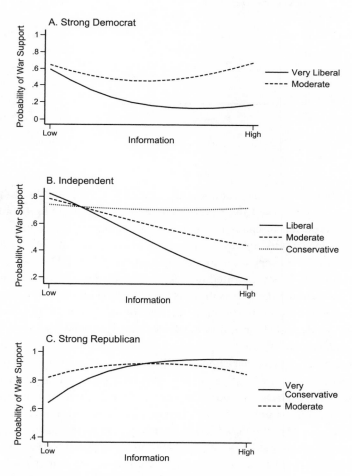

FIGURE 6.5 Effects of ideology on war support, ANES

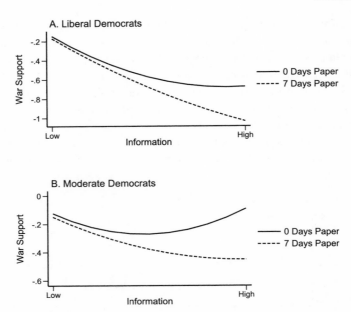

FIGURE 6.6 Effects of regular newspaper reading on war support among Democrats, TNSS, October 2002

Iraq. While these results reinforce the finding that rank-and-file Republicans largely followed their party's cue and supported going to war in Iraq, as reported in chapter 5, they also show that ideology drove war support significantly among Democrats and independents. We now see that the strongest opposition to the war came from liberal Democrats and independents. This elaborated model, which includes ideology, allows us to better examine the effects of newspaper reading on war opposition by differentiating among partisans on the basis of their ideology. Because the results are virtually identical in the TNSS and ANES data, we show only the results for the TNSS.

Figure 6.6 depicts war support by information levels among strong Democrats who were either strong liberals (panel A) or moderates (panel B). In each case we show the effects of information on war support for those who did not read a newspaper and those who read a newspaper daily. For liberal and moderate Democrats, knowledgeable individuals who regularly read a newspaper were more opposed to the war than those who did not read newspapers. The effect of newspaper reading is especially apparent for ideological moderates: moderate Democrats who did not read a newspaper show almost no decrease in war support as they became more informed whereas war support declined significantly among daily newspaper readers. Interestingly, even if they were not reading newspapers, very liberal Democrats became more opposed to the war as they acquired greater information about Iraq. This is consistent with the sharp decline in war support with information among liberals, as seen in figure 6.4. Figure 6.7 depicts similar findings for liberal and moderate independents. In sum, as information levels rose, support for the war declined among Democrats and independents who regularly read a newspaper regardless of whether they were politically liberal or moderate.

When taken together, it is clear that greater opposition to the war among well-informed Democrats and independents who obtained information from newspapers was not due to their ideology, although a liberal ideology did increase opposition to the war. Some of this opposition may have occurred because liberals who attended to the news learned that some liberal senators opposed the war in the fall of 2002. As we noted in chapter 4, antiwar Democratic elites, who were largely senators, appeared equally on TV and in newspaper stories on the Iraq–al Qaeda

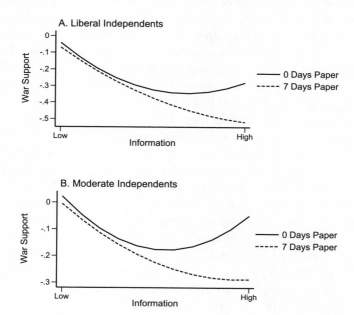

FIGURE 6.7 Effects of regular newspaper reading on war support among independents, TNSS, October 2002

link. Nonetheless, liberal opposition to the war was quite independent of the media source from which Democrats and independents obtained their information about Iraq.

As we will see in the next section, some of the opposition to the war among well-informed liberals also arose because they disliked George W. Bush. But once again, this effect is additional to the antiwar influence of newspapers.

George W. Bush as a Polarizing Figure

The standard political science account of public opinion portrays a deeply partisan world in which citizens look to partisan elites for guidance on policy matters and process political information through a partisan filter. Adam Berinsky (2009) has modified the standard elite influence model to argue that the public does not need especially strong cues from their political leaders in order to take a partisan stance on foreign policy matters. Extending the work of John Zaller (1992), Berinsky notes that in the absence of strong Democratic elite opposition, as occurred in the buildup to the Iraq War, Democrats could have based their opposition to the war on their dislike of President Bush. The president had been broadly unpopular with Democrats following the outcome of the 2000 presidential election, and Berinsky argues that this dislike drove their opposition to the Iraq War. All Democrats needed to know to oppose the war was that Republican president George W. Bush supported military action. According to Berinsky, this effect was further intensified among Democrats who were more attentive and knowledgeable politically. As Berinsky (2009, 109) concludes in summarizing evidence that well-informed Democrats opposed the war and well-informed Republicans supported it, "The identification of the Iraq War with the Bush administration allows partisans who pay attention to politics to quickly ascertain their stance on the war."[5] Berinsky's account provides no reason, however, to expect any greater opposition to the war among well-informed Democrats who read newspapers than among well-informed Democrats who did not. Moreover, his account does little to explain a decline in war support among well-informed independents who regularly read a newspaper.

We therefore take Berinsky's argument one step further to examine whether *anti-Bush Democrats* were especially likely to engage in biased processing of information about the proposed Iraq war. According to Berinsky, Democrats who disliked Bush should have been most skeptical of the administration's case for war in Iraq. Since George W. Bush played a critical role in promoting the war, it is possible that attitudes toward him specifically (rather than general partisanship) lay at the heart of Democratic opposition to military action. Bush was, as Jacobson (2007) has so clearly demonstrated, a polarizing figure in American politics. We test the possibility that Democrats' dislike and mistrust of Bush drove their opposition to the war more powerfully than specific information they obtained from newspapers. We also extend this logic to independents to determine if dislike of Bush also influenced their opposition to the war.

Unfortunately, we cannot use the TNSS to test the effects of anti-Bush sentiment on war support. The first wave of TNSS data was collected in the months immediately following the 9/11 terrorist attacks when Bush was extremely popular, even among Democrats. The second wave was collected when attitudes toward Bush were almost certainly influenced by, if not heavily intertwined with, Americans' views on the Iraq War, making them difficult, if not impossible, to disentangle.

We therefore turn to the ANES data, taking advantage of the fact that many respondents interviewed in the fall of 2002 were previously interviewed in the fall of 2000. We measure attitudes toward Bush in the two months before the 2000 election using a 0 to 100 "feeling thermometer" measure. Respondents were asked to rate Bush on this measure with 100 representing very warm feelings and 0 very cold feelings. We reversed and recoded the variable to represent negative feelings toward Bush, with 1 marking the most negative and 0 marking the most positive, to more clearly assess the effects of prior anti-Bush sentiment on war support. As we did with ideology, we added the Bush feeling thermometer to the ANES model, allowing its effect on war support to vary with information level and partisanship. Ideology remains in the model because it has a large independent effect on war support. Estimates for this model are shown in appendix table A6.2, column (4).

Our first goal is to determine whether the inclusion of attitudes toward Bush decreases the influence of regular newspaper reading on war opposition among the best-informed Democrats and independents. As before, we calculate war support among well-informed individuals who had not read a newspaper in the past week and those who had read one each day and calculate the difference as a measure of newspaper influence. A negative number indicates stronger opposition to the war among regular newspaper readers than among nonreaders. We calculate this effect across all levels of partisanship, ranging from strong Republicans to strong Democrats. Finally, we plot the effect of newspaper reading separately for the

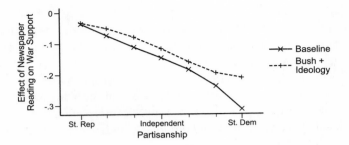

FIGURE 6.8 War support among non–newspaper readers minus support among daily readers, with and without Bush attitudes and ideology, ANES

baseline model from chapter 5 and the new model that included attitudes toward Bush as well as ideology. The findings are shown in figure 6.8.

The greater antiwar influence of newspaper reading among Democrats and independents than Republicans remains largely unaltered by the addition of Bush with one exception. Among strong Republicans, newspaper reading continues to have almost no influence on war support. The antiwar effect of newspapers increases among independents and those who lean toward the Democratic Party. But the inclusion of Bush attitudes reduces somewhat the antiwar effect of newspaper reading among strong Democrats. Newspapers still powerfully drive opposition to the war among well-informed political independents and Democrats, but the magnitude of this effect does not differ greatly between strong and not so strong Democrats once Bush attitudes are included in the model. Overall, this first look at Berinsky's model does little to modify the antiwar effect of newspapers among the well informed, which remains sizeable. It does suggest, however, that the very powerful antiwar effect of newspapers on the strongest Democrats may have been due, in part, to their negative attitudes toward Bush.

Bush attitudes dampen only slightly the effect of newspaper reading on war support. But attitudes toward Bush are strongly related to support for military intervention in Iraq, even after controlling for partisanship and ideology. Figure 6.9 depicts the effects of Bush attitudes on support for the war. Findings are presented in two panels: one for strong Democrats and another for independents. In each panel, the effects of Bush attitudes on war support are shown separately for four ideological groups (very liberal, somewhat liberal, liberal, and moderate). It is clear in this figure that being liberal and strongly disliking George W. Bush virtually guaranteed strong opposition to the use of military force in Iraq (among both

Democrats and independents). Pro-war attitudes among those who liked Bush and antiwar attitudes among those who disliked him are not terribly surprising. Bush was not only president; he was also one of the most vocal and visible supporters of the war. If someone held him in low regard—and mistrusted him—he or she was unlikely to accept his justification for the use of military force in Iraq.

What does this mean, if anything, for the antiwar effect of newspapers? Some inkling of this can be gleaned from figure 6.9. This figure shows that liberals who disliked Bush were extremely opposed to the use of military force (among both strong Democrats and independents), leaving little additional room for newspapers to further intensify war opposition.

We can pinpoint the effects of newspaper reading more precisely by graphing the maximum effect of newspapers on war support—subtracting support among those who read newspapers seven days a week from support among those who had read a newspaper on zero days—for those highest in knowledge. Figure 6.10 shows these effects in two panels: one for ideological moderates (panel A) and another for liberals (panel B). In each panel, we depict the effect of newspaper reading at four levels of partisanship (independent, lean Democrat, Democrat, strong Democrat) as attitudes toward Bush vary from very warm (100 degrees) to very cold (0 degrees).

Looking first at moderates (panel A), we see that newspaper reading has a far more dramatic antiwar effect among Democrats than independents. Among independents (and independents who lean Democratic), the antiwar effect of newspapers is modest and fairly constant across the range of feelings toward Bush. For Democrats, the impact of newspaper reading varies by feelings for Bush. Newspapers have their greatest effect among strong Democrats who are politically moderate and hold negative, but not strongly negative, views of Bush. Newspapers have similar antiwar effects among liberals (panel B). Once again, they have their maximum effect among strong Democrats, but in this instance they have increasingly muted effects among liberals who dislike Bush. As we had surmised, among liberal Democrats, disliking Bush was reason enough to oppose the war and newspapers had little further antiwar influence.

It is important to underscore that newspaper reading consistently increased opposition to the war among everyone (except Republicans) in figures 6.9 and 6.10. The more frequently well-informed Americans read a newspaper, the less likely they were to support the use of military force in Iraq. But newspapers did not affect all people equally. Newspaper reading had greater influence on war opposition among Democrats

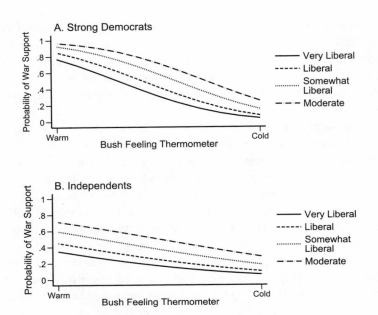

FIGURE 6.9 Effects of ideology and Bush attitudes on war support, ANES

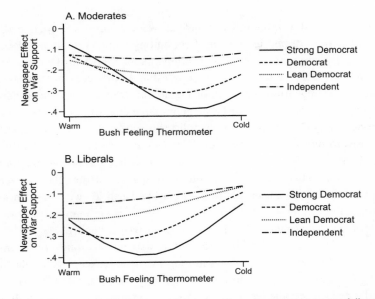

FIGURE 6.10 War support among non–newspaper readers minus support among daily readers, by attitudes toward George W. Bush, ANES

than independents. This suggests that it was not newspaper content alone that promoted opposition to the war. In general, well-informed Democrats seemed more receptive than independents to the antiwar content of newspaper stories, and in that sense, once they had factual ammunition, they may have employed partisan reasoning to amplify its meaning in familiar ways.

Some Democrats (and independents) did not require antiwar information to decide that they opposed the war. Being very liberal and strongly disliking George W. Bush was sufficient. In that sense, newspapers were most influential in increasing opposition to the war among Democrats who did not strongly dislike Bush. Strong Democrats who may have been somewhat predisposed to accept antiwar arguments were the most affected by newspaper content. And those effects are quite large: Among well-informed strong Democrats who were relatively neutral toward Bush, war opposition was substantially greater among those who read a newspaper daily than among nonreaders. We can place a number on this effect. Since the dependent variable in the ANES data is dichotomous, the predicted value shown in figure 6.10 is the probability of supporting the war (which varies from 0 to 1). By that metric well-informed Democrats who held neutral attitudes toward Bush and read a newspaper daily were almost .4 less supportive than nonreaders. In other words, if well-informed Democrats who did not read a newspaper held a neutral position on the war, their newspaper-reading compatriots would have strongly opposed it. This shows the hefty effect of newspaper reading on war opinion.

Were Opponents of the Iraq War Simply Antiwar?

To this point, our analysis has focused on the possibility that the observed effect of newspaper reading on war support might have occurred because it is conflated with the partisanship or ideology of newspaper readers. We can take this one step further to ask if some Democrats and independents who regularly read newspapers were generally antiwar and predisposed to oppose the use of force in international affairs. We know that people vary in their willingness to use military force and, historically, isolationism has been a significant element of the American political culture. Thus, some well-informed newspaper readers may have been strongly predisposed to oppose going to war in Iraq given their preexisting pacifist tendencies.

Wave 1 of the TNSS data included several questions tapping attitudes

toward military conflict assessed in the months after the 9/11 terrorist attacks that can be used to extend our analyses.[6] The survey lacks direct
questions on the general use of force. However, as we discussed earlier in
this chapter (see table 6.1), there are four questions in wave 1 that assess
a range of attitudes on the use of military force post-9/11. The questions
and responses are shown in figure 6.11 broken down by partisanship.

Two of these questions tap reactions to military action in Afghanistan, assessing the adequacy of US military action and the strength of

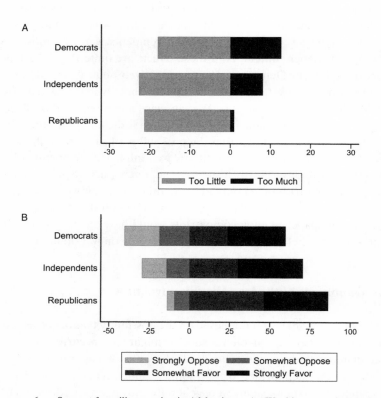

FIGURE 6.11 Support for military action in Afghanistan: A, "Would you say that the level of
U.S. military action in response to the terrorist attacks is too little or too much?" B, "How
strongly do you favor or oppose increasing the level of military action even if it means that
U.S. armed forces might suffer a substantial number of casualties?" C, "Do you think the
U.S. should limit its military action to Osama bin Laden and the Taliban, or should it broaden
its action to include other countries that harbor and support terrorists?" D, "In your view,
how important is it that any U.S. military action be supported by an international coalition
against terrorism?"

Source: TNSS, October 2001–March 2002.

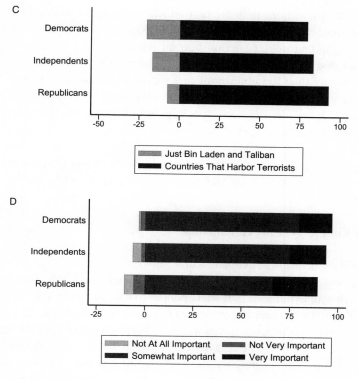

FIGURE 6.11 *continued*

support for greater use of military force even with substantial US military casualties. Democrats were slightly more likely than Republicans to view military action as excessive (12% vs. 1%), but it is clear that Democrats overwhelmingly endorsed military action. Support for war was somewhat less widespread if it meant that "U.S. armed forces might suffer a substantial number of casualties." Overall, 73% of Americans in the survey favored increased military action even in the face of greater casualties. These numbers differed by partisanship (as seen in fig. 6.11), with 40% of Democrats opposed to increasing the level of military activity under these conditions, compared to 30% of independents and 14% of Republicans. In the aftermath of 9/11, Democrats and independents were overwhelmingly supportive of military action against the Taliban but somewhat more reluctant than Republicans to risk greater levels of casualties. There is only slight evidence of stronger antiwar sentiment among Democrats than Republicans in the aftermath of 9/11 in these data.

Two other questions in figure 6.11 anticipate elements of possible future military action against Iraq. Overall, 86% of survey respondents supported expanding military action beyond Afghanistan to include other countries that might support terrorism; Democrats were only somewhat less supportive than Republicans of such extended action (79% vs. 93%). Democrats and Republicans also strongly supported international cooperation in the war on terrorism; few Republicans or Democrats thought the United States should act alone.[7]

Overall, there is little here to suggest that Democrats and independents opposed military action to fight terrorism in the months after 9/11, or did so to a substantially greater degree than Republicans.

Opposition to War in Afghanistan

The military invasion of Afghanistan a full year before the onset of vigorous public debate about a war in Iraq allows us to delve further into the alternative hypothesis that some people (particularly Democrats and independents) were simply opposed to war. On the heels of the 9/11 terrorist attacks, Afghanistan was quickly identified by the US government as the geographic home of al Qaeda, Osama bin Laden, and the 9/11 hijackers. Support for a military response against Afghanistan was high (fig. 6.11), and there were vanishingly few voices of dissent from among the political ranks or within the news media. Even more so than during the debate over an Iraq war, the information environment surrounding a war in Afghanistan was characterized by a singularly one-sided information flow in late 2001 and early 2002 (although criticism mounted over time; Aday 2010).

The elite influence model generates a strong prediction about public opinion on the war in Afghanistan in the fall of 2001 and the spring of 2002: political information should have increased war support among Republicans, independents, and Democrats alike. Discussion of the Afghanistan war was effectively one-sided and lacked a clear political opposition. Only one member of Congress voted against granting President Bush the power to use force in 2001 after the 9/11 attacks.[8] This is very different from the impending war in Iraq, which was characterized by muted Democratic opposition to the war but nonetheless garnered substantial Democratic opposition. Critics of the Afghanistan war such as writer Susan Sontag and comedian Bill Maher were speedily denounced as unpatriotic and effectively silenced. As a consequence, Democrats had few partisan cues that would incline them to oppose the war.

We exploit the one-sided information flow surrounding the war in Afghanistan to pose another challenge to the view that newspaper content drove Democratic opposition to an Iraq war. If knowledgeable Democrats who regularly read newspapers opposed the use of military force in *both* Afghanistan and Iraq, an inherent antiwar bias is suggested on their part.

We used the basic model developed in chapter 5 and expanded in this chapter to examine support for the use of force in Afghanistan (on the basis of the two questions in fig. 6.11, panels A and B).[9] War support was analyzed as a function of information,[10] partisanship, and their interaction, along with the interactions between newspaper reading, information, and partisanship. Estimates for these models are in appendix table A6.3, columns (1) and (3). We first present the effects of partisanship and information on war support in the same form as we did for the Iraq conflict in figure 5.2.[11] These new results are shown in figure 6.12.

Few Americans felt that the US military response to the 9/11 attacks was excessive. This is clear in panel A of figure 6.12, which demonstrates that very few Democrats, Republicans, or independents thought the United States had used too much force in Afghanistan. There are small partisan differences among the most knowledgeable: Democrats and independents are slightly more likely than Republicans to feel that too much force was being used. But even at the highest level of knowledge, it was very unlikely that Democrats would endorse this view.

A somewhat different picture emerges when we turn to the question of *increasing* levels of military action if it means substantial casualties, as shown in panel B of figure 6.12. Among Republicans, increasing information about Afghanistan increased support for expanding military action, whereas Democrats became slightly less supportive of action as they grew more informed. Partisan differences are thus most noticeable at the highest levels of information although still muted by comparison with support for an Iraq war. Overall, Republicans, independents, and Democrats all supported military action in Afghanistan.

There is one other crucial way in which support for the war in Afghanistan differed from that in Iraq. When it comes to newspapers, there is no evidence that they promoted opposition to military action in Afghanistan, bolstering our conclusion that the antiwar content of newspapers was confined to coverage of the war in Iraq. We illustrate this nonfinding with two graphs shown in figure 6.13, which depict predicted support for military

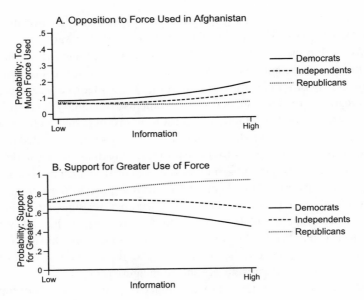

FIGURE 6.12 Partisanship, information, and support for the war in Afghanistan, TNSS, October 2001–March 2002

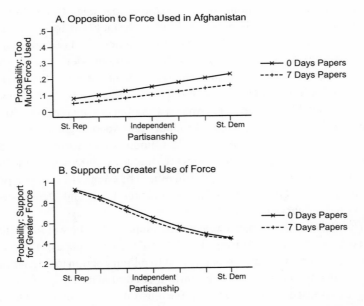

FIGURE 6.13 Newspaper effects on support for the war in Afghanistan, TNSS, October 2001–March 2002

intervention in Afghanistan for those highest in information (where newspaper effects are maximized) across levels of partisanship moving from strong Republicans to strong Democrats (see appendix table A6.3, columns [2] and [4]). Informed Democrats were only slightly more likely than informed Republicans to think too much force had been used in Afghanistan, and this trend was similar among non–and regular newspaper readers. And while there appears to be some difference in the belief that too much force was used in Afghanistan according to levels of newspaper reading, those differences are in the wrong direction—nonreaders are slightly *more* likely to object to the use of force than daily newspaper readers (though the differences are not statistically significant).

Antiwar Attitudes and Support for Military Force in Iraq

Regular newspaper readers are no more opposed than nonreaders to the use of military force, as we demonstrated earlier in this chapter. But we need to ensure that the antiwar influence of newspapers among well-informed Democrats and independents is not conflated with broad antiwar attitudes. We therefore elaborate the Iraq war support model one final time by adding all four wave 1 war variables (see fig. 6.11) as predictors of support for an Iraq war in the fall of 2002 (see appendix table A6.2, column [2]). We also examined possible interactions between each of the wave 1 Afghanistan variables with partisanship and information.

There was absolutely no evidence that Democrats or independents were more likely than Republicans to translate views on the Afghanistan war to Iraq. Nor is there any evidence that well-informed partisans opposed the war on this basis.[12] When taken together, it is very unlikely that the antiwar effects of newspapers can be attributed to greater pacifism among well-informed Democrats and independents. But having opposed the war in Afghanistan and being reluctant to expand the war on terrorism were very good predictors of greater opposition to war in Iraq, regardless of partisanship and knowledge levels.[13] This makes a great deal of sense. The debate about using military force in Iraq was justified, in part, by arguments that Saddam had connections to terrorists (and, possibly, the 9/11 hijackers), and it was relatively clear that it would involve a major commitment of US military forces. Republicans, independents, and Democrats alike who were reticent about expanding the use of military force in the aftermath of 9/11 were significantly less likely to support the proposed Iraq war.

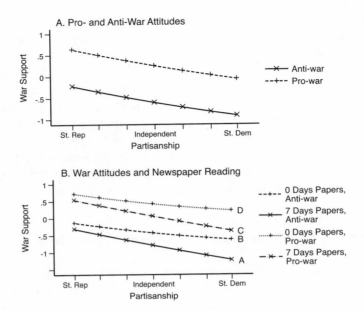

FIGURE 6.14 Effects of pro- and anti-Afghanistan war attitudes in wave 1 on support for war in Iraq in October 2002, TNSS

Having reservations about the war in Afghanistan had sizeable effects on opposition to the war in Iraq. We simulate war support among two diametrically opposed individuals: one who strongly opposed greater military force in Afghanistan and opposed broadening the war and another who strongly favored greater force and wanted to expand the war on terror. This contrast is extreme. Only 5% of the TNSS respondents fall into the antiwar camp and 34% populate the pro-war group. The comparison is depicted in panel A of figure 6.14, showing support for the war in Iraq across the range of partisans who were well-informed and supported military action in Afghanistan and those who were well-informed and opposed it. The differences are large and striking, spanning approximately half the range of the war support scale.

We use this example to gain additional perspective on the magnitude of the antiwar effect of newspaper reading. Panel B of figure 6.14 compares Iraq war support among nonreaders and regular newspaper readers within the most extreme anti- and pro-war respondents on military action in Afghanistan. That panel shows predicted support for the war in Iraq under four conditions: Those with strong antiwar attitudes in wave 1 who were daily newspaper readers (A) and nonreaders (B) and those with strong pro-war attitudes in wave 1 who were daily newspaper readers (C) and nonreaders (D). Comparing predictions A and B, and C and D illustrates the maximum effect of newspaper reading for those most opposed and most supportive of military force in wave 1. Among Democrats, regular newspaper reading (daily vs. nonreaders) had almost as large an effect as the difference between being opposed and supportive of the war in Afghanistan, an admittedly extreme comparison from wave 1. This is a tough yardstick against which to measure the impact of newspaper reading. The two questions asked in wave 1 tap orientations toward the use of force that are clearly linked to the debate over war in Iraq one year later. Yet we find that regular newspaper reading in the fall of 2002 had an almost equally large influence on support for military action in Iraq as these specific war-related attitudes.

A Republican Ceiling?

There is one other aspect of the trends in public opinion presented in chapter 1 (fig. 1.2) that may have seemed a little surprising. Despite unanimous support for the war among Republican elites, rank-and-file Republican support for the war remained flat as the administration launched its case for military action in Iraq in the fall of 2002. As we have seen, an overwhelming majority of Republicans backed the Bush administration on this issue. And support increased very slightly among Republicans as their level of information about Iraq increased. But support remained well short of 100%, and there is absolutely no evidence that the media campaign by prominent Republicans produced any increase in this support.

While partisanship clearly played a major role in the Iraq war debate it is important to recognize that it was not the only factor. We have shown that Americans who were more reluctant to use military force after the 9/11 attacks in wave 1 of the TNSS were also less supportive of the military option in Iraq. Interestingly, some Republicans fell into this isolationist group. For example, when asked whether they favored increased military force in Afghanistan even with substantial US casualties, 14% of Republicans said they were opposed and 40% said they were only somewhat in favor. Many Republicans (31%) also disapproved of the United States taking the leading role in solving international problems. These attitudes are consistent with a long history of isolationist sentiments among some

Republicans. This reluctance could have created a ceiling for Republican support of military action in Iraq.

To test this, we focused on the most direct TNSS question on war support: "How strongly do you favor or oppose U.S. military action against Iraq?" This is the closest question we have to the public opinion data summarized in figure 1.2. We then examined responses to this question, testing the basic model from chapter 5 but with the addition of questions from wave 1 tapping support for increased military force in Afghanistan and approval of the United States taking the leading role in solving international problems. Both variables significantly influenced support for the war among all partisan groups. We then generated predicted probabilities of support for war in Iraq among Republicans who differed (in wave 1) on their response to these two questions.[14]

Among Republicans who strongly supported greater military force in Afghanistan and felt that the United States *should* play a major role in international affairs, the predicted probability of support for the war was .95—virtually complete support. But among isolationist Republicans, those opposed to the United States taking the lead in world affairs and somewhat opposed to increasing troop levels in Afghanistan, the probability of support for an Iraq war was much lower at .64. Even if isolationist Republicans were somewhat supportive of expanding troop force in Afghanistan, the probability that they supported the impending Iraq war was .78. In the aftermath of the 9/11 attacks, there was a minority of rank-and-file Republicans who exhibited these isolationist tendencies. Approximately 17% of Republicans rejected a leading role for the United States in the world *and* opposed or were only weakly supportive of the greater use of force in Afghanistan. Nonetheless, this resistance was sufficient to keep overall Republican support for the proposed Iraq war below 100% and to limit the extent to which the Bush administration's efforts to mobilize support for the war were able to increase support among Republicans.

Conclusions

Those familiar with social science research on selective perception and motivated reasoning could have read chapter 5 and concluded that the antiwar effect of newspapers we report is nothing more than the expression of the more liberal and Democratic profile of newspaper readers. While plausible, this alternative explanation gained no substantial support in the analyses presented in this chapter. Regardless of whether regular newspaper readers were strong or weak Democrats, strong liberals or moderates, liked or disliked George W. Bush, or supported or opposed military action in Afghanistan post-9/11, those who acquired information from newspapers were more opposed to military action in Iraq.

We are now in a better position to evaluate the antiwar effects of newspaper reading within a broader array of factors that influenced support for military intervention in Iraq. The combination of ideology and attitudes toward Bush played a major role in shaping public opinion toward the proposed Iraq war. In the extreme, well-informed liberals who disliked Bush did not require any further information to oppose the war in Iraq. For many Americans, however, these predispositions were insufficient. For them, war opposition depended crucially on the acquisition of information from newspapers. For one group, strong Democrats who felt neutral toward Bush, the information obtained from newspapers aroused strong opposition to the war, but this did not occur if they did not regularly read a newspaper. This meant that newspapers had their maximum effect among Americans who were somewhat predisposed to accept information critical of the Bush administration. Nonetheless, newspapers increased antiwar sentiment across the board even among political independents. In that sense, their modest antiwar content played an important role in providing democratic citizens with critical grist for the mill. Who knows what might have happened if this content had been more pervasive within the news media?

CHAPTER SEVEN

Citizen Competence Reconsidered

"Our liberty cannot be guarded but by the freedom of the press, nor that be limited without danger of losing it." —Thomas Jefferson to John Jay, 1786 (Jefferson 1900, 501)

"I am . . . for freedom of the press, and against all violations of the Constitution to silence by force and not by reason the complaints or criticisms, just or unjust, of our citizens against the conduct of their agents." —Thomas Jefferson to Elbridge Gerry, 1799 (Jefferson 1903–1904, 10:78)

We began with two conundrums. First, why did so many Democrats, in the absence of clear direction from Democratic congressional leadership, move so robustly to reject the Bush administration's Iraq war project in the fall of 2002? And second, why did independents not respond with greater support of the administration's position given that the war was strongly advocated by the Bush administration and Republican politicians and only weakly and inconsistently opposed by congressional Democrats? Before we turn to reviewing our answers, it is worth reflecting on why these are conundrums.

For millennia, scholars have long held that the public is largely incapable of making independent, thoughtful, sound judgments. Philosophers Plato and Thomas Hobbes each advanced this claim. More recently, Walter Lippmann, in the aftermath of World War I, advanced an account of public gullibility in his famous and highly influential book *Public Opinion* (1922). Gustave Gilbert (1950, 278–79), the staff psychologist assigned to oversee the Nazi leadership held in confinement during the Nuremberg trials, recorded an oft-quoted exchange with Hermann Goering in his cell:

> We [Gilbert and Goering] got around to the subject of war again and I said that, contrary to his attitude, I did not think that the common people are very thankful for leaders who bring them war and destruction.

Why, of course, the people don't want war, Goering shrugged. Why would some poor slob on a farm want to risk his life in a war when the best that he can get out of it is to come back to his farm in one piece. Naturally, the common people don't want war; neither in Russia nor in England nor in America, nor for that matter in Germany. That is understood. But, after all, it is the leaders of the country who determine the policy and it is always a simple matter to drag the people along, whether it is a democracy or a fascist dictatorship or a Parliament or a Communist dictatorship.

There is one difference, I [Gilbert] pointed out. In a democracy the people have some say in the matter through their elected representatives, and in the United States only Congress can declare war.

[Goering] Oh, that is all well and good, but, voice or no voice, the people can always be brought to the bidding of the leaders. That is easy. All you have to do is tell them they are being attacked and denounce the pacifists for lack of patriotism and exposing the country to danger. It works the same in any country.

Harold Lasswell (1941) coined the expression "the garrison state" to make much the same point, that any public will readily accept the authority of the state when faced with a purported external threat. George Orwell's dystopic novel *1984* (1949) extends this theme as its central foundation. That the public is gullible and highly influenced by political leaders is a widely accepted truism, especially on matters of war and national security. It became conventional wisdom a long time ago.

John Zaller's classic volume *The Nature and Origins of Mass Opinion* (1992) can be viewed in this long tradition. He offers a formal model, giving metric clarity to the dynamics by which public opinion is formed and changed. But unlike many others, he also offers a means by which the public can be placed in a position of independence. He argues that when elites differ and when those differences are made public, debate can animate the public and offer it real and meaningful choice. The public can play an influential role, become a democratic citizenry, when political elites are publicly divided over matters of public importance.

As we noted in our review of Zaller's model, the concept of "information flow" is central to whether the public is led by elite opinion. When political elites of differing political persuasions share the same view on an issue, the "information flow" is one sided and the public is predicted to fall into line behind the unified elite. When elites are divided and competing political parties offer distinct policy choices, the "information flow" is

two-sided and the public is given alternatives from which to choose. It is a
central axiom of Zaller's thesis that as elites shift from division to consensus, the public will move from a position of choice and judgment to one of
compliance and acceptance.

The period of interest to us, September to October 2002, was dominated by the Bush administration's anti-Saddam, pro-war message and
was thus imbalanced in favor of war, if not a completely one-sided information flow, as documented in chapters 3 and 4. In this instance, both the
long-held view of public gullibility and Zaller's model predict the same
outcome: public endorsement of the Bush administration's policy toward
Iraq. That did not happen for most Democrats and many independents,
hence our two conundrums. But finding conundrums is one thing; offering
explanations is another.

The divergence we uncovered between print and national electronic
news media—especially the degree to which they scrutinized several pivotal claims made by the Bush administration about Iraq—provided us
with unexpected leverage to investigate the basis of our conundrums. In
effect, this gave us something like a natural experiment. The difference in
coverage of two central news stories, one dealing with the alleged link between Saddam Hussein and al Qaeda and the other the supposed use of
aluminum tubes to produce nuclear weapons, belies the popular notion
that the news media as a whole failed to critically evaluate the administration's claims concerning Iraq. As we have shown, newspapers, especially
nonelite papers, and the AP news wire service were far more critical than
other news outlets of the administration's claims. They were also more
likely than TV or elite newspapers to air the views of various experts and
members of the intelligence community who criticized the administration's facts on the aluminum tubes story.

In chapter 5, we addressed the conundrums head-on. We showed that
Democrats and independents who obtained their news from newspapers,
and who were well informed about Iraq, were most opposed to a war in
Iraq and least likely to view Saddam as an imminent threat. We find this
same pattern in two distinct national surveys, increasing our confidence
that the finding is not a chance event. The analyses discussed in chapter 6
show that the antiwar influence of information obtained from newspapers
on public opinion could not be explained by other factors, including the
prior beliefs and characteristics of newspaper readers. We found that it
was Democrats and independents who read newspapers, and were more
likely to be exposed to antiwar information, who ended up questioning

the wisdom of a war in Iraq whereas Democrats and independents who predominantly got their news from television did not.

Findings reported in chapter 6 address one other puzzle. Republicans collectively did not increase their support for military action in the fall of 2002. This arose, as best we can tell, because a small segment of Republicans simply oppose war. These isolationist Republicans opposed the war in Afghanistan and the war in Iraq. Leaving them aside, we see that Republican support for the military action in Iraq was almost unanimous.

At the core of our answer to the conundrums are two fundamental dynamics not previously considered jointly: The public *can learn* about a vital policy choice before them, even in circumstances that largely conform to a one-sided information flow. And their capacity to gain information in order to form an independent judgment depends vitally on the manner by which the press functions. The importance of the press in providing Americans with pivotal antiwar information, documented in chapters 2 through 6, brings us back full circle to our initial concern with the essential ingredients of representative democracy.

The People and the Press

As we noted in chapter 1, the First Amendment of the Bill of Rights binds together the public and the press, emphasizing the public's right to petition, air grievances, protest injustice, and thus influence their government. The First Amendment is based on the implicit assumption that the public would actively engage the government by petitioning it on matters of public import. And as indicated by the quotes that begin this chapter, the Founders, none more so than Thomas Jefferson, regarded the press as a vital empowering link between the public and their elective representatives. The Founders did not envision a passive public mutely awaiting the decisions determined by their elected leaders but rather enacted the Bill of Rights to ensure that the public could, and would, inform their elected representatives of their views on any matter that engaged their interest.

This somewhat ideal view of a "bottom-up" democracy wherein public discussion and deliberation, empowered by a free and open press, drive politics (Barber 1984; Fishkin 2009; Pateman 1970) has largely been replaced by the view that influence flows from elites to the public. The conventional view of elite-driven politics, of which Zaller's account is the best

(Zaller 1992), emphasizes the importance of competing elites who debate policy alternatives so that the public may become informed and is able to decisively choose one side or the other. This view of elite-driven politics is supported by much ancillary evidence including the public's lack of information about public affairs (Delli Carpini and Keeter 1996), especially foreign policy (Lippmann 1922).

Within the popular elite influence model, the news media plays something of a supporting role as the agent responsible for an accurate presentation and full coverage of elite opinion and debate. But this characterization of the press is not what the Founders had in mind in devising the First Amendment to protect the freedom of a far more muscular and contrary news entity. The full meaning of a free press goes well beyond the transmission of a range of elite opinion to include the active revelation of hidden information as exemplified by the publication of the Pentagon Papers during the Vietnam War, WikiLeaks documents pertinent to the war in Afghanistan, Edward Snowden's leaks concerning NSA activities, and intelligence officers' misgivings about the quality of the Bush administration's intelligence on Iraq in the latter part of 2002. In these instances, the press fulfilled its role as envisioned by the Founders, enshrined in the First Amendment, as a fiercely independent government watchdog and a cornerstone of representative democracy.

Likewise, some segments of the public performed better than predicted by the elite influence model in evaluating the wisdom of a war in Iraq, defying much conventional wisdom and political science lore. The Bush administration's proclamation of a proposed new war against Saddam Hussein and Iraq in early September of 2002 gave the public an opportunity to form their own views on the endeavor. They did so in less than ideal conditions: Democratic opposition was muted, the news media conveyed and amplified the administration's position for the most part, government energy scientists were actively muzzled, and some news reporting was plainly false. Even so, many Democrats and political independents rejected the war as they learned more about it.

In retrospect, it seems fair to conclude that the war against Iraq that began in March of 2003 proved to have been ill conceived on many grounds. It was far more difficult, expensive, and destructive of Iraqi society than anticipated and achieved considerably less than promised by the administration.[1] Of course, we cannot blame democratic publics any more than democratic elites for their lack of prescience (Tetlock 2005). What we can say, however, is that news coverage that was critical of the administration's claims appears to have moved certain sectors of the public to oppose the war, a conclusion that applies to both Democrats and political independents. No foresight was needed to know that Saddam Hussein was not in cahoots with al Qaeda or that Iraq was not importing aluminum tubes for use in a nuclear centrifuge. These claims were readily falsifiable at the time they were advanced.

Some news organizations, principally newspapers, embraced their democratic role and challenged the administration's readily disputed facts. But not all news organizations did so. This raises an intriguing question about what might have happened if a greater number and variety of news organizations had given less weight to the administration's claims and greater weight to experts who found them questionable. Would a larger segment of the population have been moved to oppose the war? Would congressional leaders have been less willing to endorse the war if faced with even greater antiwar sentiment? Would the Bush administration have abandoned the war effort as it did with Social Security "reform"? Or would it have shifted its justification for war without altering its policy trajectory, as George H. W. Bush did in the months before the Persian Gulf War.[2] Of course, we cannot know the answers to such questions.

What we can say is that the press plays a vital role in enriching and informing elite and public debate. The public's failure to rally to the president turned on how much information Americans obtained about Iraq and from where. In our analysis, we uncover a critical distinction between print and televised news media, reflecting a difference in reporting practices. Moreover, the key difference in reporting content was not simply focused on whether the news medium was print or electronic because not all newspapers performed equally well. On the issue of WMD and the aluminum tubes, nonelite newspapers provided more critical coverage of the administration's claims than did such papers as the *New York Times* or the *Washington Post*. And while elite papers conveyed false information about Iraq's WMD program (as reflected in the *New York Times* infamous mea culpa for Judith Miller's reporting), they were just as likely as other regional newspapers to publish stories critical of an Iraq–al Qaeda connection. In contrast, television news was far less critical of the administration's claims.

We should add a modest caveat to our analysis. We cannot conclusively demonstrate that newspaper content shaped an individual's opinion on a war with Iraq because we do not know the specific newspaper or TV news outlet each survey respondent regularly relied on. We have done our best in chapter 6 to rule out alternative explanations for our findings such as the greater sophistication, more liberal ideology, or stronger antiwar

proclivities of newspaper readers which might have inclined them to oppose the war in Iraq regardless of the content of news stories. We are heart-
ened by the robustness of our findings: Democrats who regularly read
newspapers and became well informed about Iraq were more opposed to
the war in data drawn from two major national surveys; this finding held
up in analyses that included numerous controls; the finding emerged regardless of whether information was assessed specifically or more generally; findings were strongest among Americans who relied exclusively on
newspapers for their news; findings were diluted among those who consumed both newspapers and TV on a regular basis. The difference between those who consumed news from print and those who relied on TV
news matched well with our content analysis showing that newspapers
provided the public with a stronger factual basis than TV news for skepticism of the Bush administration's claims.

   It is our conclusion that the public is capable of engaging with complex policy issues, including foreign policy, when the press performs well.
When journalists examined more completely the Bush administration's
claims for war in Iraq, well-informed Democrats and independents were
moved to oppose the war. This suggests that the conventional account of
public opinion in political science, which has treated the news as a largely
passive medium through which elite messages and events are transmitted
to the public, is incomplete (as noted by Baum and Groeling [2010]).

   We are not the first to raise questions about the elite influence model
of public opinion. For example, in examining the public's response to
President Clinton's affair with Monica Lewinsky, Zaller documented the
inability of the elite influence model to explain why Clinton became more
popular with the American public at the same time as elite criticism of
the president mounted (Zaller 1998). Additionally, John Aldrich, John
Sullivan, and Eugene Borgida (1989) found that the public is able to sort
out the foreign policy choices before it much as it does for domestic issues. Ben Page and Robert Y. Shapiro (1992) and V. O. Key (1966) are
but a few among many scholars who find the mainstream portrait of an
ill-informed and apathetic public overdrawn. All of this suggests that the
public can make political decisions independently of elites.

The Political Psychology of Media Influence

Of course, media content does not provide a simple conduit for public influence. Republicans had little motivation to carefully consider newspaper

content that was critical of the Bush administration. Rather, they were motivated to defend their party and its standard bearer, George W. Bush. Under strongly partisan circumstances, when political parties send a clear signal on where to stand on an issue, people are driven to defend their partisan beliefs and simply fall back on partisan heuristics to establish their position.

Things get more interesting, and more complicated, however, when one or both parties fail to send a unified and unambiguous signal. This is exactly what we observe for Democrats in the fall of 2002. The party was internally divided on the war. The American public was exposed to anti-war Democratic senators in both print and TV news, yet the vote on the Iraq War Resolution also made clear that this position was not shared by the congressional Democratic leadership or, as it turned out, a majority of Democratic senators. In this situation, we expect Democrats and, as occurred in this case and perhaps others, independents to process information more carefully. It was not entirely easy, even for regular newspaper readers, to learn that credible experts and intelligence officials had doubts about Iraq's links to al Qaeda or the unlikely use of aluminum tubes to make WMD. But Democrats and independents who read newspapers did so.

We thus conclude that some Democrats and independents engaged in effortful thinking about the war and turned against it once they obtained credible antiwar information. Political independents provide a critical test of the influence of newspaper content. It had a decided antiwar thrust among them, leading the majority of well-informed newspaper-reading independents to oppose the war. But Democrats took this information even further, suggesting that once they had a reason to doubt the administration, they were even less supportive of its actions. We believe their reasoning was deliberate but biased in a partisan direction nonetheless. This underscores the difficulty in removing partisan consideration from political reasoning.

One-Sided Elite Information Flow on the Iraq War

We turn finally to consider the third element (in addition to the people and the press) of the elite influence model—political elites. As previously noted, Zaller's (1992, 1996) model outlines two types of information environments that ground many of the analyses in his book: one-sided information flow and two-sided information flow. It is the latter, when elite opinions are divided, that provides the public with a visible choice along familiar political lines.

We need to reflect on a lingering concern about the nature of the information environment in the period from September to October 2002. That period contained at least some partisan division over a possible war in Iraq and is best described as an environment dominated by information heavily skewed in favor of war. Some might argue that there was sufficient, albeit minority, opposition to the war from congressional Democrats which led the best-informed rank-and-file Democrats to oppose it. Moreover, such war opponents appeared in the news more frequently than their congressional Democratic counterparts who supported the war. This complicates the picture of simple one- and two-sided information flows, suggesting that they are not so easy to identify.

What happens, for example, when one side is unified in its support of a policy, such as Republican support for military action in Iraq, but the other side is more divided? Is that an instance of a one- or two-sided information flow? We face some of this complexity in dealing with the information environment in the months before the Iraq War. As we have noted, some Democratic dissent was visible in September and October of 2002, arising from Senators Byrd, Kennedy, and Feingold, among others. In total, 21 Democratic senators (42%) voted against the Iraq War Resolution in October, as did an even greater percentage of House Democrats (59%, or 122 members).

Even if the pre–Iraq War information environment was not completely one-sided, it was heavily skewed toward a pro-war flow of information. This is supported by our media analysis and Hayes and Guardino's (2010, 2011) more comprehensive analysis of TV network news stories. In their data from September and October of 2002, pro-war statements on TV far outweigh those opposed to the war (see Hayes and Guardino 2011, 838, fig. 2). Moreover, in their analysis of the statements made by domestic political elites, the Bush administration's support for the war swamped any opposition from Democrats. We find the same skew in our examination of electronic and print media coverage of the Iraq–al Qaeda and aluminum tubes stories in chapter 4.

In reality, even a one-sided information environment contains at least some political dissent. Consider the Vietnam War, the situation analyzed by Zaller (1992, 1996) as his key example of a one-sided information environment. Zaller analyzed stories on the war that appeared in issues of *Time*, *Newsweek*, and *Life* magazines featuring the Vietnam War on their cover. In 1963–1964, the single-sided or mainstream phase of war cover-age, there was a ratio of 4 pro-war to 1.5 antiwar stories in the three mag-azines, or roughly 27% anti and 73% pro. In our analysis of news media coverage in the months before the Iraq War, assessed in chapter 4, the ratio is a little lower: 46% of articles were coded as pro-war, 30% as an-tiwar, and 23% as neutral across all news sources. Nonetheless, of those that conveyed a direction (pro or anti), 60% were pro-war, only slightly lower than 73% in the initial phase of the Vietnam War, widely regarded as a pro-war information environment.[3]

Elites and Partisan Opinion

As is evident in the two conundrums, the pro-war information environ-ment that existed in the fall of 2002 did not generate uniform war support across partisan lines. As we have noted repeatedly, Democrats and inde-pendents moved to oppose the war as they acquired information about Iraq, especially from newspapers, which would normally be seen as the consequence of an antiwar message from Democratic elites.

The Democratic public's response can be made consistent with the Zaller model only if Democratic opposition to the war appeared exclu-sively in newspapers, but in our media content analysis, Democrats appear with the same frequency in both TV and newspaper stories, especially in the more numerous stories on a link between Iraq and al Qaeda. The key difference between TV and newspaper coverage of both the Iraq–al Qaeda connection and the aluminum tubes story is that newspapers con-veyed greater antiwar content, and this content was more likely to emanate from nonpartisan domestic sources, sources that require careful consid-eration. Nonelite newspapers were even more likely than elite papers to devote space to the views of nonpartisan energy and security experts and intelligence and defense officials who were critical of the administration on Iraq's use of imported aluminum tubes. The kind of information conveyed by these experts, involving technical details on the purpose and structure of the tubes, for example, is not ideological or partisan and provides few cues of the type envisioned by Zaller as the basis for public message ac-ceptance or rejection. Indeed, such technical information requires careful scrutiny and considered thought, which is not accounted for in an elite influence model of public opinion. Instead, facts seemed to have spoken very directly to the public and shaped their opinions independently of par-tisan elites.

Was Iraq a Unique Information Environment?

Do all prewar periods invite the close public scrutiny of facts and information that we have documented in the months before the onset of the Iraq War? America has been involved in many wars since World War II. Some were of the gravest sort; the Korean and Vietnamese Wars come readily to mind. Other wars, such as the invasions of Grenada and Panama, were quite modest and short-lived by comparison. The recent wars in Iraq and Afghanistan fall somewhere in between: long-lived and extremely costly but less grave than others in terms of US casualties. All prewar periods suffer from a lack of information and uncertainty amid a swirl of claims, counterclaims, and rampant speculation. But does this lead to closer public scrutiny of factual information, especially prior to a war's onset? Do our findings generalize beyond the Iraq War?

Much of the conventional wisdom concerning foreign policy opinion derives from public opinion assessed during an ongoing war (Baum and Groeling 2010; Berinsky 2007, 2009; Gelpi, Feaver, and Reifler 2005; Karol and Miguel 2007). If the question is whether the public is willing and able to process factual information about an ongoing war, the answer is yes. In general, public support for war declines as casualties mount, something that likely reflects a direct reaction to facts on the ground (although it might also reflect a reaction cued by growing elite disenchantment with the war—see Berinsky [2009]). Baum and Groeling (2010) and others (e.g., Gelpi 2010) find evidence that the public reacts very directly to ongoing events, especially as a war persists over time. Americans are thus capable of using factual information to form their opinions during an ongoing war. In the current investigation of opinion on a possible war with Iraq, the public was capable of considering the wisdom of going to war before the war had begun, suggesting, as others have (Aldrich, Sullivan, and Borgida 1989), that citizens are not as dependent on elites as conventional wisdom suggests.

All wars exhibit some historically unique features, and in the case of the Iraq War the Bush administration chose to advance claims that were readily refuted or undermined by existing information. This may have increased the public's attention to facts at the expense of elite cues. But the Iraq War is not the only instance in which an administration has made dubious claims in support of war. The supposed attack by the North Vietnamese on a US naval ship in the Gulf of Tonkin in 1964 raises a parallel example, suggesting that the Bush administration was hardly the first to enhance claims that turned out to be far weaker than presented. The public's close scrutiny of factual claims going into or during a war is consistent with democratic citizens' reluctance to engage in war more generally, unless it is clearly in the national interest (Jentleson 1992; Jentleson and Britton 1998).

Elites have certainly disagreed on the utility and wisdom of past wars. For example, the Persian Gulf War Resolution was passed by the US Congress in January 1991 and almost all congressional Republicans voted in favor whereas a majority of Democrats voted against it. Public support for the war at that time was comparably divided (Mueller 1993). In contrast, Zaller characterizes the early stages (1963–1964) of the Vietnam War as devoid of elite disagreement, making clear that Iraq was not the only war to exhibit some degree of partisan uniformity.

Overall, we do not think that the months before the Iraq War were especially unique in terms of the administration's claims or media coverage of them and regard the process we have uncovered—public assimilation of facts presented by a critical press in the absence of strong political signals from at least one political party—as readily generalizable to other situations including war, climate change, disease epidemics, and fiscal policy. From our perspective, an active press remains central to citizens' ability to support or oppose government policy independently of political elites. In drawing this conclusion, we share with Thomas Jefferson the conviction that the press when free and full throated is essential to empowering the public, to converting the public from passive receptor to an active force that makes democracy more than a chimera.[4] The way in which the press conveyed the merits and demerits of the Iraq war project influenced well-informed Americans, especially Democrats. Thus, when the press gives searching examination to an administration's claims, or indeed to any proposed project or policy, the public is empowered to grapple with policy alternatives.

In sum, the ways in which the press took on the task of covering the Bush administration's push for war in Iraq determined the quality of public deliberation. By scrutinizing the administration's claims and relying on objective experts, the local print media highlighted flaws in the administration's intelligence. But coverage of the administration's claims was far more fatuous in other news media. Given the extraordinary ongoing changes currently occurring within the news media business, what we learned is quite revealing. We turn next to those revelations.

Reexamining the News Media: Past, Present, and Future

"The more I view the independence of the press in its principal effects, the more I convince myself that among the moderns the independence of the press is the capital and so to speak constitutive element of freedom. A people that wants to remain free, therefore, has the right to require that one respect it at all costs."—Alexis de Tocqueville, *Democracy in America* (2000, vol. 1, pt. 2, chap. 4)

Declining Newspaper Readership

The news media has changed considerably since we undertook our investigation of public opinion in the months before the Iraq War. At that time, Pew surveys indicated that over 60% of American adults regularly read a newspaper, roughly similar to the number who regularly watched local TV news, and many more than the roughly 30% who regularly watched a national nightly news broadcast (Cohen 2010). Gallup surveys from late 2002 reveal a slightly different picture in which roughly 60% of Americans read a newspaper every day or several times a week, comparable to the frequency with which Americans watched a national nightly network news broadcast, and slightly below the frequency of watching local TV news (Cohen 2010). Nonetheless, the bottom line is that newspaper reading was pervasive in the latter part of 2002.

By mid-2012, however, regular newspaper reading had declined to 49% of American adults in Pew surveys, still high but below numbers observed in 2002 (Rosenstiel and Mitchell 2012). The number who had read a daily newspaper in the previous day had dropped from 39% in November 2002 to 29% in May 2012. Declining newspaper reading is especially worrisome in light of the findings presented in the previous chapters of this book because newspapers stood out as the one news medium that consistently challenged the Bush administration, apparently swaying public opinion in the process.

The Digital News Age

The notion of "the press" has gone through various formulations. It is apparent that the press is going through a major transformation at this juncture, from print to digital. This is hardly the first such transformation. The press at the time of Thomas Jefferson, its fiercest advocate, was nothing like "objective journalism." Notwithstanding these fundamental shifts in the way journalism is institutionalized and practiced, the core purpose of a free press remains largely as Jefferson envisioned it: to empower the public in its role as citizenry.

What will happen to considered democratic decision making as newspaper readership declines? Is this a cause for alarm? As the press changes before our eyes, what the press is means less, at the moment, than what it will become. What we have shown is that when the press is effective, when it is at its best, the public's capacity for thoughtful consideration is considerably enhanced. But when the press acts as a passive conveyor of an administration's claims, it is at its worst. In that instance, the public is left largely bereft of the tools it needs to arrive at reasoned policy decisions.

This particular conclusion has considerable significance at this point in time because the press is in the midst of a remarkable transition as print news declines and digital forms increase. We cannot claim to be experts on the news. We are not professors of journalism or communications, and we have not been journalists and so have no craft or experience to rely on. But we can lay out some of the democratic pros and cons surrounding the emergent digital news environment, and speculate on the likelihood that this environment can sustain a free press as envisioned by the country's founders.

The decline of print and rise of digital news has numerous positive aspects (Fuller 2010; Shirky 2010). First, the cost of distributing, as distinct from the cost of gathering, the news has benefited enormously from the development of the Internet. This has allowed a greater number of news organizations to emerge online, in the absence of traditional publishing and distribution costs. Second, the Internet, as current events constantly remind us, has sped up and enriched the news with the use of digital cameras in public and private places. It has become far more difficult for national armies and government security forces to impose secrecy and censorship as many recent and not so recent events remind us (Klee, Dressen, and Riess 1988). Consider media reactions to the claim by the Bush administration that it had received "intelligence" from the British suggesting that the Iraqi regime had been seeking to purchase uranium from an African nation.[5] That claim turned quickly into farce as the "intelligence" supposedly obtained by the Americans from the British was in fact given to the British by the Italian security organization and the supportive documents, once placed online, were shown quickly to be forgeries. In that sense, the development of the Internet is a transformative innovation in precisely the manner that Tocqueville foresaw.[6]

But not everyone is sanguine about the future digital news environment (Jones 2009). The Internet can distribute any information, from the most hyperbolic to the most incredulous. While it is important to recognize that research on the growth and impact of the Internet as a news venue is preliminary (Neuman 2007; Neuman, Bimber, and Hindman 2011), we think we can safely advance three key points. First, while the cost of producing and distributing digital news may be decreasing, computers, smartphones, tablets, and e-readers cost money and can prevent someone from accessing news online. In other words, the divide in access to technology may be amplified in the realm of political knowledge, enhancing a political knowledge gap between the "haves" and "have nots."

Second as the information environment becomes increasingly fragmented, it may become easier for citizens to tune out news altogether or simply tune in to sites that confirm their political views (Bennett and Iyengar 2010; Gaines et al. 2007; Iyengar and Hahn 2009; Iyengar et al. 2008). For example, Clay Shirky (2010) notes the loss of incidental news exposure that had created a moderately informed group of citizens in the past, saying "The big thing we lose with the continuing shrinking of the importance of newspapers is having a place where news junkies and sports fans both occasionally see the same front page."[7] There is no question that the presence of a daily statewide or citywide newspaper with decent penetration achieves that goal.

Economics of News Production

The biggest threat to a free press, however, and the third item on our list, is the precarious economic health of current news organizations. The loss of classified advertising revenue destroyed newspapers' traditional business model and the fragmented and multifarious news environment weakened advertising revenues for news organizations across the board. Alex Jones (2009) underscores the critical role played by newspapers in generating news. Traditionally, they have been far more likely to investigate and break news stories than TV, explaining why newspapers need substantial revenues in order to fulfill their democratic mission, on which not only newspapers but the entire news production process hinges. We take a slight detour into Jones's typology of news activity to understand why newspapers, or comparably well-funded news organization, are essential to a healthy democracy.

Jones (2009) identifies four types of news activities that range from less to more costly in terms of resources and journalistic expertise. The first tier, "bearing witness," is clearly well and truly changed by the digital age. The widespread availability of phones with digital cameras, often capable of capturing video, enables reporters, and individuals, to capture spontaneous events, document their occurrence, and rapidly disseminate them to their home bureaus, and to various social media. Whether it be a road accident, a conflict at a picket line, a police action against an individual (think Rodney King), actions by guards against prisoners in a secret facility (such as Abu Ghraib), or actions by government security forces against public demonstrators, there is an ever-increasing likelihood that someone will capture and disseminate the sound and images associated with such an event on his or her phone. Of course, TV frequently conveys news of this kind, placing a reporter at the scene of an event such as an extreme weather event or a political demonstration. But digital news goes further and in the process radically alters the relationship between those who hold authoritative positions and those who do not. As we noted earlier in discussing the positives of digital news, it is becoming increasingly difficult for governments to keep secrets or to ensure that their version of events is uncontested.

The second tier of news activity, "following up," is doing more than just observing and reporting. As Jones notes, this involves finding out what happened before and after an event and discovering who was responsible, and requires craft, persistence, and some resources. Citizens walking about, observing, and recording what they see is simply inadequate. Following up requires skill, determination, knowledge, and the existence of reporters who are able to persist on a story well after its immediate impact has dissipated. It also involves money.

Realizing the requirements of tiers three and four places even greater financial burden on news organizations in order to achieve a truly free press. "Explanatory journalism," Jones's third tier of news activity, requires journalists to become masters of a subject, well acquainted with relevant governmental, industrial, and academic experts who can offer insight into a situation or event. When the Bush administration advanced the claim that Iraq was importing aluminum tubes to produce the centrifuges necessary for extracting purified uranium for nuclear weapons production, it seemed on its face to be a plausible accusation to those who knew little about such centrifuges. How many reporters sought out experts in nuclear engineering to see if the aluminum tubes were of the correct alloy, the correct tube thickness and dimension to be suitable for that purpose? Those that did were practicing tier three, explanatory journalism. The *San Jose Mercury News'* revelation that government energy scientists were prevented from speaking with journalists on the topic underscores the challenges faced by journalists. Journalists that did not directly seek out experts were simply bearing witness by directly conveying the administration's message. Those that did seek out experts were in a position to challenge the credibility of that story if they were sufficiently experienced and resourceful to find an expert able and willing to talk.[8]

Finally, Jones notes that tier four, "investigative journalism," is the most intensive in terms of journalistic skill, craft, and resources. It can involve the exploration of a story before it has become a matter of public note, and requires lengthy training of reporters, considerable persistence in examining source credibility, and the assessment of multiple, often conflicting accounts meant to hide, or reveal, or distort, or correct what is going on. Examples of good American investigative journalism are many, extending back in time. We can begin with Upton Sinclair's influential examination of the meat slaughter industry in the United States as practiced in the beginning of the last century (Sinclair 1906), or we can point to Bob Woodward and Carl Bernstein's investigation, lasting months, of the Nixon Watergate events. But here we also find relevant examples in Knight Ridder's ability to secure interviews with midlevel intelligence officials in the months before the Iraq War. Such investigations require ample financial resources because a journalist must be allocated to a story for some time even knowing that the investigation may not bear fruit. It also requires persistence because such in-depth journalistic investigations are required precisely when considerable effort is made by governmental or other authorities to keep the public from knowing what has happened.

This sort of investigative journalism is extraordinarily expensive, and may require months of work by talented journalists, legal resources, and a publisher able and devoted to sustaining the practice. It is important to note here that the public is often interested in topics of quite transitory nature. Which celebrity is in need of anger management training, or sobriety, often leads the news and happily such stories are cheap and readily available since they require only the most casual commitment of resources (indeed, in many instances the sources themselves promote the story for various reasons). The commitment of the considerable resources required to engage in tier-four journalism are valued by the public only after its fruits are harvested, but not all such investigations come to fruition, which makes it even more difficult to marshal the resources required to carry it out.[9]

Traditional journalism, Jones (2009) argues, ought to pursue profitability as well as essential journalistic standards, notably accuracy, balance, accountability, and independence. Jones explicitly excludes from this list news "objectivity," which he regards as largely misunderstood and frequently equated with an uncritical account of the opinions held by competing elites. In contrast, Jones (2009) regards objective claims as those that weigh competing accounts against evidence. If the evidence is inadequate, more evidence must be obtained. The practice of objectivity involves getting it right, obtaining definitive evidence, seeing something that has been missed, checking the credibility of various claims, and as-sessing the veracity of competing sources. When objectivity is redefined in this way, it more closely resembles investigative journalism, although that is not the way in which it is currently practiced.

Of the various goals pursued by news organizations, Jones argues that profit should be last because good journalism requires financial resources that should not be squeezed in order to maximize profit. Of course, in the absence of sufficient income to sustain news organizations, the issue of profit becomes moot. And declining revenues remain a very real problem for all media outlets, especially newspapers. There are some glimmers of hope as newspaper distribution figures stabilize and online revenues pro-vided by paywalls, e-subscriptions, and advertising increase. But none of this replaces the massive loss of classified and print advertising (Rosens-tiel and Mitchell 2012). Who pays for a free press moving forward into the future? What audience exists in a segmented world for all four tiers of journalism? To those questions, we have no definitive answers.

Finding a suitable business model to secure the revenues needed to sustain a free press committed to all levels of journalism, including inves-tigative journalism, is vital. But a strong financial basis is a necessary but insufficient condition for the development of a free and well-functioning press. Funds ensure the press and specific news organizations survive. But what ensures the survival of a free and open press willing to engage in costly and painstaking investigative journalism? Democratic citizens place their trust in their elected leaders on an election day when some are elected and others rejected. But trust is not the only linkage between the public and their governing leaders. When the public are enabled by a free press to grasp details of a proposed policy or governmental action, they become instrumental agents who can also engage actively in the process of governance.

It is difficult to imagine how fragmented digital news (with modest on-line advertising revenues) could successfully undertake the expensive and time-consuming task of investigative journalism. One bright spot in the darkness that is the current news business is subscriber-supported news organizations. Public radio and television (NPR and PBS) frequently win Peabody awards for their high-quality programming and investigation. This is one possible way forward. Newspapers may also reinvent themselves financially to continue their time-honored role as the generators of news within the news business. Or some new and until now unimagined form of financing may emerge to fund different kinds of news organizations. There is much about the future of news that remains in flux. One thing, however, remains clear. If future news media cannot engage in the kind of investigative journalism typically undertaken by newspapers, the result will be an enfeebled democracy.

Going to War: The Next Time

Going to war against Iraq in 2003 was not the last time America was thrust into war. It has since been followed by renewed efforts in Afghanistan and the use of air power in Libya and against the Islamic State forces in Syria and Iraq. No doubt other wars loom in the near or more distant future. We do know that future wars and military entanglements will pose a challenge to the news industry as a whole because powerful elites, often governments, work actively to promote public support for military action to counteract citizens' distaste for military adventurism. It has ever been thus.

Today Americans face the looming prospect of engagement with wars of various kinds in various parts of the world even as the nation extracts itself from Iraq and Afghanistan. Syria, Ukraine, and terrorism in central Africa are just a few of the current "hot spots" that might spark American debate about the use of American military might. The Enlightenment dream of perpetual peace (Kant 1970) seems remote as the greater horrors of World Wars I and II recede in memory.

Democracies rely on public debate to assess the strengths and weaknesses of any project placed before the public. The development of the Internet and nonelite actors, such as WikiLeaks and Edward Snowden, show that much can be done to inform the public outside of the premier news organizations. New sources of news from non-American organizations, such as Al Jazeera or the *Guardian*, can do much to enrich the array of sources that the public can draw on. But nonetheless, much depends on the ability and willingness of elites, in and out of government, to accurately convey information and foster debate. If the government is allowed to dominate the news, by silencing or seducing opposition elites, then a vital democratic element is lost. Elite debate offers a spectacle— something worth looking at, something that compels the public's attention, and something that merits coverage by the news. It is essential to democratic deliberation. But how elite debate is conveyed to the public by the news media matters as well.

If the news media simply conveys elite messages absent scrutiny, it is essentially engaging in a news activity akin to Jones's bearing witness, much as TV news did in the months before the Iraq War. If, on the other hand, the news media engages in the full array of news manufacture, tiers one through four, everything from bearing witness to investigative journalism, as did some of the print press in the months of September and October in 2002, then in addition to receiving elite messages, the public will be empowered to thoroughly engage with the news and formulate its own policy judgments. If democracy is to mean more than citizens as a passive audience subject to elite persuasion, then a free and fulsome press is required.

Who will make the effort in the days ahead to give the public the full press it requires? Who will make the effort to generate news, beyond just reporting what like-minded audiences wish to hear? Who will commit to objectivity as method? We do not have answers to these questions. What we can say is that a public left with news that is poorly vetted, false, sensational, gossipy, overwhelming, and partisan can do little more than either trust its leaders or withdraw into alienation.

We introduced this chapter with two quotes from Thomas Jefferson. The first makes mention of liberty, not the liberty of the government to do as it will, but rather the liberty of a free people to use the press to enable the people to control the government, to make it "their" government. Absent the press, governments are free to do what they will without much concern for public resistance and without public approval.

Appendix

The Threat and National Security Survey (TNSS)

The core data for this book are drawn from the Threat and National Security Survey (TNSS), a three-wave national panel study. The analyses are based largely on the second wave of the study, which focused on political reactions to the impending Iraq war. The first wave of the survey was conducted via telephone with a national sample of 1,549 adults over age eighteen between early October 2001 and early March 2002, focusing on psychological reactions to 9/11 and support for government antiterrorism policy. The initial sample was drawn as a weekly rolling cross section with roughly 100 individuals interviewed each week throughout this period.[1]

The second wave of data collection occurred in October of 2002 after congressional debate on the Iraq War Resolution had ended. Of the original interviewees, 858 were reinterviewed between seven and twelve months later for a reinterview rate of 55%. An additional 221 respondents were added to the panel from a fresh random digit dial (RDD) sample drawn to the same specifications as the original. This new component was designed to serve as a check on panel effects, attrition, and composition. The cooperation rate for this new component was 56%.

A more complex, third wave of data collection occurred in 2003. Half the sample was recontacted during the Iraq War, starting on the day after the war's onset (March 20, 2003) and continuing until April 10, 2003, roughly at the official end of the war as announced by George W. Bush. The other half was interviewed sometime after the war had "ended," from May 20, 2003, until June 18, 2003. We were able to reinterview 612 individuals from the original panel and 117 of those introduced in wave 2 for a reinterview rate of 68% between waves 2 and 3. All three waves of

TABLE A4.1 **Coded newspapers**

Database	Rank, 2002	Newspaper	Weekday circulation
		Top thirty newspapers by circulation, March 2002	
Lexis-Nexis	1	*USA Today*	2,136,068
Wall Street Journal	2	*Wall Street Journal*	1,800,607
Lexis-Nexis	3	*New York Times*	1,113,000
Access World News	4	*Los Angeles Times*	965,633
Lexis-Nexis	5	*Washington Post*	746,724
Lexis-Nexis	6	*New York Daily News*	715,070
Proquest	7	*Chicago Tribune*	613,429
Lexis-Nexis	8	*New York Post*	590,061
Newsday	9	*Newsday*	578,809
Newspaper Source Plus	10	*Houston Chronicle*	552,052
Newspaper Source Plus	11	*Dallas Morning News*	521,956
Newspaper Source Plus	12	*San Francisco Chronicle*	512,129
Access World News	13	*Chicago Sun-Times*	479,584
Factiva	14	*Boston Globe*	463,113
Proquest	15	*Arizona Republic*	448,782
Access World News	16	*Newark Star-Ledger*	408,557
Lexis-Nexis	17	*Atlanta Journal-Constitution*	381,833
Lexis-Nexis	18	*Minneapolis Star Tribune*	379,139
Lexis-Nexis	19	*Philadelphia Inquirer*	373,892
Proquest	20	*Detroit Free Press*	368,839
Access World News	21	*Cleveland Plain Dealer*	363,750
Access World News	22	*San Diego Union-Tribune*	357,896
Access World News	23	*Portland Oregonian*	342,789
Factiva	24	*St. Petersburg Times*	314,337
Lexis-Nexis	25	*Denver Post*	305,060
Infotrac, Business Insights	26	*Rocky Mountain News*	304,949
Access World News	27	*Miami Herald*	303,575
Lexis-Nexis	28	*Orange County Register*	300,888
Lexis-Nexis	29	*St. Louis Post-Dispatch*	287,424
Lexis-Nexis	30	*Baltimore Sun*	284,753
Total circulation			17,314,698

the survey were roughly twenty minutes in length. The second and third waves focused on reactions to terrorism and support for the Iraq War.

News Content Coding Scheme

Sentence Valence

WEAKLY CRITICAL

1. Statement of doubt/skepticism over the administration's claims.
    a. Any time a reporter indicates that a group or individual is skeptical or unconvinced by the administration's case.

    b. Any time an individual expresses skepticism over the administration's case or expresses doubt about the sufficiency of information as a case for war.

    c. Statements such as "I am not yet convinced by the evidence."

    d. Statements that recognize general dissent or conflict over the administration's claims.

        i. There are a lot of skeptics.

        ii. There is a lot of conflict over this among UN countries.

        iii. The Security Council is divided over the issue.

2. Any statement of a preference for, or the preferable nature of, a go-slow approach, either as a direct quote by an individual, a paraphrasing of a quote by a reporter, or a reporter's reference to an individual's or group's preference to go slow.

    a. "Go slow" may include any of the following:

        i. Actual reference to a go-slow approach.

        ii. Expression of preference for diplomacy.

        iii. Expression of preference for allowing the UN to

            1. take the lead or

            2. continue weapons inspections.

        iv. Expression of preference for waiting for an international coalition/the world community.

            1. Shouldn't go it alone.

        v. War should be the last resort.

        vi. Saddam is allowing weapons inspections/opening his country to inspections. Thus, allow inspections/the UN/diplomacy to work.

3. Statements expressing doubts over positive consequences of going to war.

    a. Democracy won't spread throughout the Middle East.

4. General negative comments about war without explicit reference to consequences of *this* war

    a. War is evil.

    b. Nothing positive comes from war.

    c. Our country has never benefited from going to war.

    d. Remember what happened in Vietnam.

STRONGLY CRITICAL

1. Statements of doubt explicitly referencing source information.

    a. Any time an individual references the lack of/reliability of/or small number of sources for the information presented by the administration as an argument against the information itself.

        i. This will thus exclude any individuals referencing the above in the context of clarifying a *pro-administration* position.

1. E.g., Rumsfeld acknowledging only one source for his claim.
2. E.g., An individual acknowledging that information is not perfect/ isn't proof positive/etc.
   a. These would *not* be coded as a con.
2. Statements about the lack of credibility of members of the Bush administration.
   a. They will/do mislead/lie/distort evidence.
   b. They are untrustworthy.
   c. They have gone back and forth in their information/statements.
      i. They said one thing before and now say something different.
      ii. They contradict themselves.
      iii. They're inconsistent with information/claims.
3. Statements that directly contradict the administration's claims *with* evidence.
   a. Individuals claiming access to identical information and different interpretations/conclusions.
   b. Individuals claiming any evidence against an administration position.
      i. E.g., On the Al Qaeda link, WMD in Iraq, etc.
4. Direct statements that contradict the administration's claims.
   a. Saddam is not an imminent threat.
   b. Al Qaeda is not in Iraq, or Saddam wasn't involved in 9/11.
   c. These are distinguished from statements simply expressing doubt about the case for war.
      i. They are direct statements against the case to go to war.
5. Any statements that talk about the negative consequences of going to war, such as
   a. high casualties, both US and Iraqi, or
   b. high cost.
      i. E.g., monetary,
      ii. world opinion/standing,
      iii. lives lost,
      iv. displaced priorities,
      v. increased terrorism/hatred of the United States, or
      vi. time.

WEAKLY PRO

1. Any general statements of support for the administration's case.
   a. These are statements that simply express agreement *without* evidence or logical reasoning accompanying them.
   b. Congress will approve the war measure.
   c. We will speak with one voice in support of war.

2. Statements of increasing information over time.
   a. When an individual claims that we are still learning more over time.
   b. More information is coming in.
   c. These are statements of increasing evidence without any explicit reference to the evidence itself.
3. General negative statements about Saddam that *do not* include references to evidence in support of going to war.
   a. He is a bad guy.
   b. He is evil.
   c. He is a dictator/ruthless.
   d. He has done bad things in the past.
      i. He hurt his own people.
      ii. He gassed the Kurds.
      iii. He tried to kill my dad.
   e. He hates us.
   f. His hatred is directed at us.
   g. He hates our freedom.
4. Expressions of doubt over ability of the UN to be successful.
   a. Doubt over UN ability to disarm Saddam.
   b. Doubt that it will find the weapons of mass destruction.
   c. Doubt that Saddam is willing to disarm.
   d. Doubt that the international community will come to a consensus in time/ at all.
5. Statements that claim support from other countries to go to war.
   a. If we go to war, there will be international support/an international coalition.
   b. Countries have offered unsolicited help.
   c. I have no doubt we will have an international coalition.
6. Statements of evidence in favor of going to war that are accompanied *in the same sentence* with caveats/clarifications.
   a. When an individual acknowledges that evidence is weak in the context of a pro-administration position.
      i. This will only include sentences that contain the caveat with the evidence.
         1. In other words, a sentence such as "That evidence came from a limited number of sources" following a statement of evidence is coded neutral; while a statement such as "There is intelligence that supports the claim of Al-Qaeda in Iraq, but the sources are not completely reliable" is coded weakly pro.

     2. All statements, in the context of pro-administration positions, that are simply acknowledging the imperfect nature of intelligence are coded neutral.

7. Statements that express the credibility of the administration in general.
   a. E.g., It is not in our interest to deceive the American public.
8. Statements that claim the illegitimacy of opposition to the president/administration in the case for war.
   a. Questioning the president's credibility is wrong/unpatriotic/counterproductive/emboldens enemy.
   b. Just placating the Iraqi regime.
   c. Giving Iraq more time to build up weapons.

STRONGLY PRO

1. Statements of evidence that support the administration's position for war.
   a. Links/contacts between Iraq/Saddam/senior Iraqi officials and al Qaeda members/top officials.
   b. Any time a mention is made of single/multiple al Qaeda members seeking refuge in Iraq/in Baghdad/with Saddam.
   c. Training of al Qaeda in Iraq/Baghdad or from Saddam/Iraqis.
   d. Al Qaeda seeking WMD/chemical or biological weapons/general weapons/general training from Iraqis/Saddam.
   e. Iraq seeking weapons/WMD/nuclear material or supplies for building nuclear weapons/reactors.
   f. Iraq having chemical weapons/biological weapons/WMD in general/nuclear weapons/nuclear material/secret weapons sites/hidden stockpiles of weapons.
2. Any statement that claims a previous statement is factual/perfectly credible.
   a. E.g., It's not a question; it's a fact.
      i. This is a separate sentence, but it is referencing the validity of evidence being talked about.
   b. The information is perfectly credible.
3. Statements about the negative consequences of *not* going to war.
   a. Smoking gun will be a mushroom cloud.
   b. Saddam will use Al Qaeda to hurt America/the Middle East/the world.
   c. Saddam/Iraq will give Al Qaeda/terrorists WMD/chemical or biological weapons/training.
   d. Saddam/Iraq will get WMD/take over Middle East/attack Israel/attack its neighbors.

e. Saddam/Iraq will gain ability to attack Europe/the United States (long-distance capabilities).

f. We will always have to fear an attack as long as he is in power.

4. Statements about positive consequences of going to war.

a. E.g., democracy in Iraq,

b. free Iraqi people,

c. stabilized Middle East, or

d. democracy spreading throughout the Middle East.

5. Statements that portray the administration's war position as inevitable/inherently correct.

a. E.g., If Saddam does not disarm, we will disarm him by force.

i. This statement assumes (1) that Saddam is armed and (2) that Congress will approve the war measure.

b. E.g., Saddam needs to disarm.

c. These statements all assume what needs to be proven and thus create a strong argument in favor of war.

GENERAL STATEMENTS OF STRATEGY FOR CODING

1. Sentences are taken as the unit of analysis in terms of what is coded.

a. However, for purposes of external validity, sentences should not be completely removed from their context.

i. Generally, a statement will explain itself in terms of coding.

ii. This will not always be the case, and when confusion as to the positive/neutral nature of the sentence is in question, context may be necessary to determine this.

1. When the subject is defined in an earlier sentence and thus is not mentioned in the sentence of interest directly (e.g., he, they, etc.).

2. This information came from a limited number of sources.

a. This can be critical in some contexts or neutral in others.

i. If Rumsfeld is simply acknowledging the imperfect nature of intelligence in general, this would be neutral.

ii. If a Democrat is arguing that the information presented by the administration is invalid, then this would be evidence against the position itself.

iii. Context should be used when necessary to understand the meaning of the statement.

2. If an individual asks himself or herself a question and then answers it, this is coded as one sentence.

a. Can we prove this connection? No.

3. A sentence is defined as beginning after a period and ending with a period (except in the one situation [no. 2]).
4. All sentences are coded.
   a. These include single-word sentences and greetings/good-byes/etc.
5. Only content directly related to the war in Iraq should be coded.
   a. Agree on beginnings and endings of relevant content and record word start and word end.

TABLE A4.2 **News source coding scheme**

Category	Specific examples
Bush administration	George W. Bush, Donald Rumsfeld, Dick Cheney, Condoleezza Rice, other administration officials or aides (cabinet secretaries, Colin Powell, White House; "Team Bush," hard-liners in the government, administration experts)
Republicans	Republican senators, Republican members of the House, other Republican figures (governors, state legislators, etc.)
Democrats	Tom Daschle, Ted Kennedy, Joe Biden, Russ Feingold, Democratic senators, Democratic members of the House, other Democratic figures (governors, state legislators, etc.), unnamed Democrats, former Clinton cabinet secretaries/officials
General members of Congress	Members of Congress, party unlisted/independent; bipartisan members of Congress (e.g., Biden and Hagel)
Intelligence officials	Intelligence officials (CIA/FBI, American intelligence, intelligence sources)
State Department	State Department officials (diplomats, senior US/American officials, US government analysts)
Military/defense	Defense Department, hard-liners in the Pentagon
Experts	Experts (academics, analysts, intelligence experts, think tanks, David Albright)
News media	Journalists, reporters, news media outlet
US public	Domestic protesters, American public opinion
Iraqi foreign sources	Iraqi officials, Saddam Hussein, Iraqi defector(s) (Iraqi opposition movements/groups, Iraqi opposition leaders)
British foreign sources	Blair, other British sources (British intelligence, British historians, *not* experts)
Other foreign sources	Other countries (Europe/European countries, foreign leaders, Arab nations, heads of state, foreign ministers, Israeli intelligence), foreign protesters, world leaders (unnamed), US allies, humanitarian groups/NGOs, unnamed foreign intelligence officials
United Nations	United Nations (UN spokesperson Kofi Annan, UN agencies, current UN inspectors), Scott Ritter, International Atomic Energy Agency, former UN weapons inspectors

Intercoder Reliability Ratings: News Content Coding

Intercoder reliability was assessed for a number of attributes coded for each sentence: neutral versus pro/antiwar sentence, strength of pro- or antiwar sentence valence (strongly anti- to strongly pro-war), and the nature of the source who made a pro- or antiwar statement within each sentence. Coder reliability was also assessed for the overall pro- or antiwar thrust of the article (ranging from strongly antiwar to strongly pro-war). Five PhD students each coded the same ten news articles or segments, which contained a total of 277 sentences. One of the first judgments made by each coder was whether each sentence could be considered neutral in terms of the war or had a pro- or antiwar thrust. Of the 277 sentences cross-coded, the number deemed to have a pro- or antiwar valence ranged from a low of 97 (35% of all sentences) for one coder to a high of 116 (42%) for another.

Half of the ten articles or segments were TV transcripts and half were from the *New York Times* and the *Washington Post*. All stories dealt with the link between Iraq and al Qaeda, the more numerous of the two cases analyzed in chapter 4.

Intercoder reliability was assessed using Krippendorff's alpha (using the krippalpha ado file within Stata). Krippendorff's alpha is a reliability coefficient designed to measure agreement among coders adjusting for the level of agreement that would occur due to chance. Intercoder reliability is acceptably high for the following variables presented and discussed in chapter 4: sentence valence ($\alpha = 0.83$), specific source code (for the full scheme with roughly fifty categories; $\alpha = 0.80$), source categories (the fourteen categories shown earlier in the appendix; $\alpha = 0.87$). Judgments concerning whether a specific sentence was neutral or had a pro- or antiwar thrust were somewhat less reliable ($\alpha = 0.66$). Intercoder reliability was acceptably high for the pro- or antiwar thrust of the article as a whole ($\alpha = 0.79$) but was somewhat less reliable for the ratio of pro- to pro- and antiwar sentences in the article ($\alpha = 0.66$). Overall, coders were quite reliable in judging the presence of different sources in each article and its overall thrust.

Model Specification and Estimates for Chapters 5 and 6

The basic statistical model we used to examine the determinants of Iraq war support and perceived Saddam threat was designed to capture several important aspects of the dynamics of public opinion. The theory and analyses reported by John Zaller (1992) demonstrate that information often has nonlinear effects on public opinion conditional on predispositions such as partisanship. To capture this, we included terms for information and information squared and the interactions between those information terms and partisanship. Our model specification went one step beyond this. If partisanship had been simply treated as a linear variable (as predispositions typically are in Zaller's models), it would have constrained the effect of information among independents to be exactly halfway between that of strong Democrats and strong Republicans. Since we are particularly interested in the dynamics of war support among independents, we wanted to release that constraint. We did so by also including a squared term for partisanship. We thus estimated models that included nonlinear effects for both information and partisanship.

In all models we estimated the interaction, squared terms, and all the constituent components of these terms. In other words, all models included a linear term for both information and partisanship, a squared term for both, an interaction between each linear term and TV viewing and newspaper reading, an interaction between partisanship squared and information, and a three-way interaction between partisanship squared, linear information, and TV and newspaper consumption.[2]

This is a complex model and its effects are difficult to understand from coefficients alone, which is why we present the findings in chapters 5 and 6 in a series of graphs. To provide an economical presentation of the key results in tabular form, we do not show in the tables constituent terms that were estimated to be virtually zero. Even if we reestimate the models with those terms excluded, the results reported here do not change in any significant way.

The source for each graph in chapters 5 and 6 is noted in the text. Unless stated otherwise, values are estimated for white women, at the mean value of age and mean (TNSS) or modal (ANES) value of education.

TABLE A5.I **Information, partisanship, and media effects on war support**

| | TNSS | | | | ANES | |
| | War support | | Saddam threat | | War support | |
Predictor variables	(1)	(2)	(3)	(4)	(5)	(6)
Age (10 yrs.)	-.04 (.01)	-.05 (.01)	-.00 (.01)	-.00 (.01)	-.09 (.03)	-.12 (.04)
Female	-.25 (.04)	-.24 (.04)	.03 (.01)	.03 (.01)	-.21 (.10)	-.22 (.10)
Education (yrs.)	-.017 (.008)	-.017 (.008)	-.003 (.003)	-.003 (.002)		
High school					-.20 (.13)	-.20 (.14)
2 yrs. college					-.23 (.17)	-.22 (.17)
BA					-.55 (.14)	-.54 (.14)
Advanced degree					-.54 (.16)	-.53 (.17)
Black	-.42 (.07)	-.45 (.07)	-.11 (.03)	-.12 (.03)	-.48 (.17)	-.48 (.17)
Hispanic	-.29 (.08)	-.30 (.08)	-.09 (.03)	-.09 (.03)	-.05 (.20)	-.03 (.20)
Other	-.32 (.09)	-.32 (.09)	-.11 (.03)	-.10 (.03)		
Information	-.86 (.21)	-.84 (.23)	-.14 (.08)	-.13 (.08)	-1.30 (.62)	-1.50 (1.06)
Party identification (Republican)	.40 (.08)	.36 (.13)	.04 (.03)	.12 (.05)	.63 (.24)	.81 (.31)
Information^2	.34 (.21)	.54 (.31)	-.17 (.08)	.03 (.12)	-.18 (.77)	1.41 (.94)
Party × Information^2	-.02 (.42)	-.50 (.56)	.19 (.15)	-.16 (.23)	-.94 (1.03)	-2.47 (1.46)
Information × Party^2	.88 (.36)	.85 (.42)	.09 (.13)	.27 (.15)	2.74 (.86)	3.20 (.95)
Newspaper		-.00 (.01)		-.00 (.01)		.09 (.04)
Television		-.00 (.01)		.01 (.01)		.03 (.04)
Newspaper × Information		-.09 (.03)		-.03 (.01)		-.23 (.10)
Newspaper × Party^2		-.02 (.03)		-.01 (.01)		-.16 (.08)
Paper × Information × Party		.10 (.05)		.03 (.02)		.23 (.17)
TV × Information		.05 (.03)		-.01 (.01)		-.01 (.10)
TV × Party^2		.03 (.02)		-.01 (.01)		.03 (.09)
TV × Information × Party		.04 (.06)		.01 (.02)		.06 (.18)
Constant	.52 (.13)	.56 (.14)	.82 (.04)	.77 (.05)	1.21 (.24)	1.06 (.28)
N	1044	1039	1040	1034	946	944
Pseudo/adjusted R^2	.27	.28	.14	.15	.19	.21

Note: Entries in columns (1) through (4) are regression coefficients with standard errors in parentheses. Entries in columns (5) and (6) are maximum likelihood probit coefficients with standard errors in parentheses. The dependent variable for the ANES data is a dichotomous support versus oppose Iraq war variable. The four-item Iraq war support measure defined in chapter 2. The dependent variable in columns (1) and (2) is the four-item Iraq war support measure defined in chapter 2. The dependent variable in columns (3) and (4) is the three-item Saddam threat measure defined in chapter 2. An empty cell indicates when a variable was not included in an equation.

TABLE A6.1 **Predictors of newspaper reading and television news viewing**

| | TNSS | | | | ANES | |
| | Papers | | TV | | Papers | TV |
Predictor variables	(1)	(2)	(3)	(4)	(5)	(6)
Age (10 yrs.)	.22 (.02)	.22 (.03)	.29 (.03)	.36 (.03)	.21 (.02)	.27 (.02)
Female	−.41 (.07)	−.40 (.09)	−.27 (.07)	−.18 (.09)	−.28 (.07)	−.03 (.07)
Education (yrs.)	.08 (.02)	.09 (.02)	.02 (.02)	.02 (.02)		
High school					.24 (.09)	.05 (.09)
2 yrs. college					.32 (.12)	.09 (.12)
BA					.40 (.09)	.12 (.08)
Advanced degree					.50 (.11)	.12 (.11)
Black	−.14 (.14)	−.04 (.18)	.46 (.14)	.47 (.18)	−.31 (.12)	.30 (.12)
Hispanic	−.06 (.16)	.17 (.21)	.26 (.16)	.51 (.21)	−.01 (.14)	−.03 (.14)
Other	−.09 (.17)	−.06 (.22)	.06 (.17)	.25 (.22)		
Party identification (Republican)	−.35 (.21)	−.07 (.26)	.05 (.21)	.09 (.27)	.12 (.27)	−.08 (.26)
Ideology (Conservative)	−.51 (.18)	−.39 (.23)	−.05 (.18)	−.00 (.23)	−.03 (.23)	.17 (.23)
Party × Ideology	.70 (.30)	.37 (.37)	.15 (.31)	−.04 (.38)	−.35 (.40)	−.11 (.40)
Support force in Afghanistan		.07 (.10)		−.08 (.10)		
More force in Afghanistan		.01 (.05)		.21 (.06)		
Broaden war on terror		−.09 (.13)		−.06 (.14)		
United States take leading role		.12 (.09)		−.08 (.10)		
Threshold						
1	1.07	1.39	.51	.96	.18	.55
2	1.33	1.66	.74	1.23	.56	.82
3	1.58	1.93	1.04	1.55	.83	1.13
4	1.76	2.08	1.30	1.80	1.05	1.44
5	1.88	2.20	1.47	2.00	1.18	1.64
6	2.01	2.34	1.68	2.22	1.36	1.94
7	2.07	2.40	1.75	2.29	1.45	2.03
N	1053	666	1050	664	1135	1134
Pseudo R^2	.04	.04	.04	.06	.04	.04

Note: Entries are maximum likelihood ordered probit coefficients with standard errors in parentheses. The dependent variables are the reported frequency of reading about politics in newspapers and watching television news in the past week ranging from never to seven days a week. An empty cell indicates when a variable was not included in an equation.

TABLE A6.2 **Determinants of war support: Ideology, antiwar attitudes, and Bush feelings**

Predictor variables	TNSS		ANES	
	(1)	(2)	(3)	(4)
Information	−1.03 (.28)	−.75 (.31)	−2.54 (1.29)	−3.84 (1.46)
Party identification (Republican)	.31 (.20)	.30 (.23)	1.78 (.82)	.04 (.98)
Information^2	.61 (.32)	.66 (.35)	2.37 (1.12)	2.37 (1.15)
Party x Information^2	−1.14 (.66)	−.72 (.72)	−3.96 (1.85)	−3.55 (1.91)
Information × Party^2	1.47 (.66)	.95 (.63)	4.59 (1.51)	4.07 (1.64)
Newspaper	−.00 (.01)	−.00 (.01)	.65 (.30)	.69 (.30)
Television	.00 (.01)	.00 (.01)	.02 (.04)	.02 (.04)
Newspaper × Information	−.07 (.03)	−.08 (.04)	−1.93 (.76)	−1.86 (.80)
Newspaper × Party^2	−.01 (.03)	−.02 (.03)	−1.12 (.58)	−1.21 (.62)
Paper × Information × Party	.06 (.05)	.08 (.06)	2.20 (1.27)	2.11 (1.36)
TV × Information	.02 (.04)	.00 (.04)	−.04 (.11)	−.02 (.12)
TV × Party^2	.02 (.03)	.01 (.03)	.03 (.09)	.05 (.10)
TV × Information x Party	.05 (.06)	.03 (.06)	.10 (.18)	.05 (.20)
Ideology (Conservative)	.08 (.14)	−.09 (.15)	.30 (.56)	.62 (.59)
Ideology × Information	1.10 (.38)	.93 (.43)	3.17 (1.44)	1.98 (1.52)
Ideology × Party	.14 (.25)	.24 (.27)	−1.44 (1.10)	−2.51 (1.22)
Ideology × Information × Party	−1.12 (.68)	−1.23 (.76)	−.94 (1.10)	1.34 (2.74)
Support force in Afghanistan		.03 (.04)		
More force in Afghanistan		.19 (.02)		
Broaden war on terror		.13 (.06)		
International coalition		.20 (.04)		
Bush feelings				−.69 (.63)
Bush × Information				3.56 (1.50)
Bush × Party				3.79 (1.24)
Bush × Information × Party				−7.08 (2.77)
Constant	.48 (.16)	−.34 (.22)	.85 (.43)	1.16 (.52)
N	1039	661	924	915
Pseudo/adjusted R^2	.30	.50	.22	.25

Note: Entries in columns (1) and (2) are regression coefficients with standard errors in parentheses. Entries in columns (3) and (4) are maximum likelihood probit coefficients. The dependent variable in columns (1) and (2) is the four-item Iraq war support measure defined in chapter 2. The dependent variable for columns (3) and (4) is a dichotomous support versus oppose Iraq war variable. These statistical models also included the same demographic variables reported in tables A5.1 and A6.1: gender, age, education, and race/ethnicity. These did not change significantly from those reported in table A6.1 and were excluded from this table to save space. An empty cell indicates when a variable was not included in an equation.

TABLE A6.3 **Determinants of support for the war in Afghanistan**

Predictor variables	Support Afghan war		More force in Afghanistan	
	(1)	(2)	(3)	(4)
Age (10 yrs.)	−.02(.02)	−.03 (.02)	.02 (.03)	−.00 (.03)
Female	−.33 (.07)	−.32 (.07)	−.31 (.08)	−.32 (.08)
Education (yrs.)	−.01 (.02)	−.01 (.02)	.01 (.02)	.01 (.02)
Black	−.27 (.12)	−.29 (.13)	−.53 (.14)	−.56 (.14)
Hispanic	−.19 (.14)	−.21 (.14)	−.37 (.15)	−.45 (.15)
Other	−.02 (.16)	−.03 (.16)	−.32 (.17)	−.36 (.17)
Information	−.30 (.13)	−.33 (.13)	−.28 (.16)	−.28 (.16)
Party identification (Republican)	.20 (.17)	.47 (.23)	.32 (.19)	.63 (.28)
Information^2	−.48 (.20)	−.67 (.38)	−.25 (.22)	−.82 (.45)
Party × Information^2	.32 (.51)	.17 (.79)	−1.11 (.61)	−.85 (.45)
Information × Party^2	.10 (.43)	.49 (.49)	2.11 (.54)	2.27 (.63)
Newspaper		.00 (.03)		−.00 (.03)
Television		.04 (.03)		.03 (.04)
Newspaper × Information		.02 (.06)		−.03 (.07)
Newspaper × Party^2		−.01 (.06)		.04 (.07)
Paper × Information × Party		.03 (.10)		.10 (.12)
TV × Information		.03 (.06)		.13 (.07)
TV × Party^2		−.06 (.06)		−.03 (.07)
TV × Information × Party		−.05 (.10)		−.15 (.12)
Threshold				
1	−1.99	−1.82	−.51	−.40
2	.39	.58		
N	1401	1386	1327	1313
Pseudo R^2	.03	.03	.10	.11

Note: Entries are maximum likelihood probit coefficients with standard errors in parentheses. The dependent variable in columns (1) and (2) is a three-category variable that asked respondents whether there was too little, too much, or the right amount of force used in Afghanistan. The dependent variable in columns (3) and (4) is a dichotomous measure of support or opposition to increasing the use of military force in Afghanistan even if it leads to more US casualties. An empty cell indicates when a variable was not included in an equation.

Notes

Chapter One

1. John F. Kennedy, address before the American Newspaper Publishers Association, April 27, 1961, John F. Kennedy Presidential Library and Museum, accessed February 9, 2015, http://www.jfklibrary.org/Asset-Viewer/Archives/JFKPOF-034-021.aspx.

2. A good introduction into the various claims advanced as to why democracy is ill-advised can be found in Don Herzog's *Poisoning the Minds of the Lower Orders* (1998).

3. And as our colleague John L. Sullivan showed some time ago, the greater the difference among contending parties' policy positions during election campaigns, the larger the turnout of voters (Sullivan and O'Connor 1972).

4. Some may wish to argue that a regime can remain democratic without these elements and we have no wish to preclude that argument. Nonetheless, there must be some minimal conditions required for public sovereignty and we hold these to be among them. There are many factors that influence the ability of the electorate to successfully perform its democratic role, such as access to a system of public education that provides the foundation for learning much that would be useful in making collective decisions. There are, of course, other factors that can promote or inhibit democracy, such as the laws that grant, or restrict, suffrage or that make voting difficult by mandating strict registration requirements. The entire corpus of research on the competence of the electorate is vast. Later in this chapter we will take up some pertinent aspects.

5. For a wide-ranging portrait of the history and variety of democratic regimes, see Held (2006).

6. American history reveals that it has been quite common to treat criticism of government in periods of war as seditious, if not outright treasonous, a practice strengthened by the force of law, in spite of the explicit prohibitions contained in the Bill of Rights. Governments often impose formal and informal rules of

censorship on the press at such times. And heightened patriotism has often led the news media to practice self-censorship.

7. A garrison town or city is a fortified community, often walled, on a border confronting a hostile neighbor in which the military holds final say on all matters related to security, including trade, border crossing, and matters otherwise normally under civilian rule. Such towns might have a mayor or an elected council but the authority of such offices is always subordinate to that of the military. Lasswell extended this definition to apply not just to one town but to the entire nation, warning that in times of perpetual war the military would have expanded and perhaps even final say on all national matters, using external threat as its principal claim to legitimacy.

8. There is some research showing that democratic publics when confronted by a substantial external threat place greater value on authority, security, and authoritarian leadership, and less value on democratic debate and civil liberties (Landau et al. 2004; McCann 1997).

9. Whether generals are capable, or not, whether battles were won, or lost, whether victory is approaching as a "light at the end of the tunnel," for the answers to all such vital questions, and more, the public are reliant on what their leaders and the press tells them. And because events quickly change, some of these answers can change rapidly as well. Saddam Hussein was a favored US ally, and portrayed as such, in the 1980s when he was a useful check against Iran, but he was quickly transformed into an enemy following Iraq's invasion of Kuwait.

10. Converse and others note that on topics such as the estate tax, as well as other fiscal matters, the public can rely on their direct experience as a basis for policy positions. But on matters of foreign affairs, few will have ever visited a potential enemy nation and, thus, have no experiential basis on which to accept or reject an administration's claims.

11. Republicans present a possible additional puzzle. They do not respond to the Iraq initiative with increased support. Instead their level of support seems to hold steady during this period. We might have expected Republicans to show even greater support for the proposed Iraq war given the powerful pro-war message issued by the Bush administration. But there is no evidence of that in figure 1.2.

12. Berinsky's approach is heavily indebted to social psychologist Fritz Heider (1958) and hedonic balance theory.

13. Baum and Groeling (2010) also add nuance to the elite influence model of war opinion by demonstrating that the news media does not simply index the existing range of elite opinion, a topic to which we return in chapter 3. The researchers also identify different phases of war opinion and find that partisan elites are most influential in the early stages of a conflict whereas events such as mounting casualties are influential in later stages. Their revised model thus does little to alter expectations of the standard elite influence model concerning public opinion in the lead-up to the Iraq War. Given the weight of pro-war elite sentiment at that time, the public should have endorsed the war.

14. Because other, though unspecified, foundations of resistance may be at work, John Zaller (2012, 598), in reviewing the same pattern of public support for the Iraq War shown in figure 1.2, concludes, "I do not see a violation of any argument in *Nature and Origins* in this pattern."

15. For those interested in the dual process model of judgment, Haidt (2001) and Kahneman (2011) provide excellent introductions.

16. A number of factors have been proposed to explain when and why people move from the default judgment orientation, reliance on established loyalties, to reflective deliberation. Evans (2008) and Chaiken and Trope (1999) provide reviews of this research.

17. We, of course, acknowledge, that the press as it existed in Jefferson's time was quite different than that which emerged in the late 1800s and into our time. We reference Jefferson's view to shed light on the press's broad and enduring democratic role and responsibilities.

Chapter Two

1. "Americans Thinking about Iraq, but Focused on the Economy: Midterm Election Preview," October 10, 2001, Pew Research Center for the People and the Press, accessed December 12, 2014, http://www.people-press.org/2002/10/10/americans-thinking-about-iraq-but-focused-on-the-economy/.

2. News consumption patterns, especially TV viewing, differed over time in the TNSS panel, indicating the link between heightened TV viewing and ongoing events. When analyses are confined to individuals who participated in all three waves, the percentage who watched national TV news daily was at a high of 62% in wave 1 (post-9/11), dropped to 44% in wave 2 (October 2002), and increased again to 51% in wave 3 (after the war's onset). Newspaper reading was more stable; 44% of panel respondents read a newspaper every day in wave 1, 36% in wave 2, and 36% in wave 3.

3. We treat those who said that they were independents but "leaned" toward the Republican or Democratic Parties as partisans. This is consistent with prior research that has found that "leaners" are essentially weak partisans (Keith et al. 1997). Removing "leaners" from the Republican and Democratic categories has little effect on our results.

4. In addition, 17% of independents volunteered that they "didn't know" whether George Bush had explained the reasons for going to war clearly enough.

5. Responses to this question were also more weakly correlated with the other four war support questions.

6. The mean interitem correlation of the four scale items is .76 and the estimated scale reliability (coefficient α) is .93, indicating an excellent and reliable scale of war opinion.

7. The mean interitem correlation among these three questions is .45. The scale has an estimated reliability of (coefficient α) .71.

Chapter Three

1. Hayes and Guardino (2011) further divide this time period from September 2002 to March 2003 into four subphases: the administration's case for war in September, the congressional debate in the first two weeks of October, the focus on UN inspections from late October until Powell's UN speech in early February, and the military buildup from February to March 2003. Our focus is on the first two of those periods because this was when the public had their only formal opportunity to influence the vote of their congressional representatives.

2. "Fools on the Hill," *Washington Times*, February 2, 2002.

3. "Vermont Senators Urge Bush to Consult Congress, Allies before Going after Saddam," Gannett News Service, June 18, 2002.

4. We assess the volume of news in each phase by examining the average number of stories per month containing the terms "Iraq" and either "Democrat" or "Republican" in several prominent electronic (ABC, CBS, CNN) and newsprint (*New York Times* and *USA Today*) sources included in Lexis-Nexis Academic. The number of monthly stories on television was lowest in the first two phases (until June), increased in July and August, and then increased even further from September to December. For example, CNN carried roughly 70 stories per month in January and February; 54 stories each month in March, April, May and June; 105 per month in July and August; and then 223 per month from September to December. A similar trend was observed in the *New York Times*, which published roughly 20 stories per month each month until June, roughly 50 per month in July and August, and 156 per month from September to December. Hayes and Guardino (2011) document a similar spike in the number of stories on Iraq in network evening news in September 2002.

5. "Call in Congress for Full Airing of Iraq Policy," *New York Times*, July 18, 2002; "Debating Preemptive War," *Washington Post*, August 21, 2002; "Senator Has 'No Doubt' Iraq Would Use 'Every Weapon,'" *Washington Post*, August 4, 2002.

6. "Senators Want a Say in Iraq Decision," *USA Today*, August 1, 2002.

7. "Top Democrats Say Congress Must OK War; Debate on Iraq Had Been among the GOP. Two Key Democrats Said the Constitution Requires Bush to Consult Lawmakers," *Philadelphia Inquirer*, August 30, 2002.

8. "Senate Hearings Begin on Iraq War," *Boston Globe*, August 1, 2002.

9. "Top Democrats Say Congress Must OK War; Debate on Iraq Had Been among the GOP. Two Key Democrats Said the Constitution Requires Bush to Consult Lawmakers," *Philadelphia Inquirer*, August 30, 2002.

10. "Specter, Bayh Discuss War on Terror; Butler, Lang Talk about War with Iraq; Interview with Daniel Ayalon," *CNN Late Edition*, August 4, 2002.

11. The numbers of stories aired or printed were obtained from searches conducted in Lexis-Nexis Academic.

12. "Specter, Bayh Discuss War on Terror; Butler, Lang Talk about War with Iraq; Interview with Daniel Ayalon," *CNN Late Edition*, August 4, 2002.

13. Alison Mitchell and Carl Hulse, "Lop-sided Victory: G.O.P. Backing is Solid—Democrats' Votes are Sharply Split," *New York Times*, October 11, 2002.

14. The tenor of Democratic congressional debate reversed in the next two weeks, running roughly two to one for war in the first two weeks of October.

15. Robinson et al. (2010), however, argues that humanitarian concerns replaced left-right ideology as a framework for British news of the 2003 Iraq invasion, resulting in elite-driven and pro-war coverage.

16. We have an added concern about the robustness of Hayes and Guardino's (2011) analysis because of its complexity and numerous terms. The key analysis (in table 2) contains ten three-way interactions and fifteen two-way interactions, leading to some unusual coefficients. For example, well-educated Democrats appear to support the war when it is opposed by domestic sources, a finding that does not make much sense. This coefficient is not significant due to a high standard error undoubtedly linked to the small number of domestic antiwar sources in the data. But the coefficient is roughly the same absolute size as the effects of foreign news sources (.33 vs. −.38). Moreover, there is a puzzling and large negative coefficient for the three-way interaction between Democratic Party identification, education, and Iraqi war support. In essence, when Ahmed Chalabi (former Iraqi exile and later politician in the post-Saddam regime) made pro-war statements on TV, well-educated Democrats dramatically increased their opposition to the war. The effect of such pro-war Iraqi statements had reduced impact on less well-educated Democrats but was also negative. The negative effect of pro-war Iraqi statements was even more dramatic among well-educated independents. Again, this is a counterintuitive finding. Why would pro-war Iraqi statements boomerang when antiwar Iraqi statements from Hussein had no impact on public opinion (as shown in table 2). When taken together, these findings raise further questions for us as to what the media variables in Hayes and Guardino's analysis measure and the robustness of their findings to alternative model specification.

Chapter Four

1. The Knight Ridder team was initially marginalized but later recognized for its excellent coverage. In early 2003, Warren Strobel and Jonathan Landay received the Raymond Clapper Memorial Award from the Senate Press Gallery (Ritea 2004). And they were subsequently featured in a *Bill Moyers Journal* program aired on April 25, 2007. The transcript of that program can be found at http://www.pbs.org/moyers/journal/btw/transcript1.html (accessed January 16, 2015).

2. Wolfowitz was interviewed by Sam Tanenhaus for the July 2003 issue of *Vanity Fair*, noting that weapons of mass destruction was the one issue everyone in

the administration could agree on as a basis for war in Iraq. Transcripts of this interview were initially available online at the Department of Defense and snippets remain online. In the interview, Wolfowitz rejected terrorism as an explicit basis for the war, saying "That second issue about links to terrorism is the one about which there's the most disagreement within the bureaucracy" ("Deputy Secretary Wolfowitz on the Reasons for Iraq War: Excerpts from the News Transcript of Sam Tannenbaus' *Vanity Fair* Interview with Paul Wolfowitz, U.S. Department of Defense: News Transcript, May 9, 2003," *Caltech Peace and Justice News*, June 30, 2003, accessed January 16, 2015, http://peacefuljustice.caltech.edu/0630/5.shtml).

3. "Hijack Suspect Met Iraqi Intelligence, Sources Say," Reuters, September 18, 2001; "Justice Drafts New Rules for Deportation; Terrorist Suspects Would Be Removed," *Washington Post*, September 18, 2001.

4. "Threats and Responses: The View from Prague; Prague Discounts an Iraqi Meeting," *New York Times*, October 21, 2002; "Threats and Responses; Havel Denies Telephoning U.S. on Iraq Meeting," *New York Times*, October 23, 2002.

5. "Interview with John McLaughlin," January 11, 2006, *Frontline*, accessed January 16, 2015, http://www.pbs.org/wgbh/pages/frontline/darkside/interviews/mclaughlin.html.

6. We searched the online databases Lexis-Nexis, Infotrac, Factiva, Business Insights, Trac Newsstand, Newspaper Source Plus, *Newsday*, *New York Times*, *Wall Street Journal*, and Access World News for newspaper stories on the Iraq-al Qaeda link, searching for articles within each newspaper.

7. We coded evening news broadcasts to make network and cable news as comparable as possible but read a broader array of TV programming, including interviews and lengthier segments, and newspaper stories to obtain additional qualitative material for this chapter.

8. "Transcript of President's Remarks on Iraq Resolution," *New York Times*, September 27, 2002.

9. "New Bush Accusations/Iraq Is Supposedly Connected to al Qaeda," *ABC World News Tonight*, September 26, 2002.

10. "Is the White House Successfully Making the Case for an Iraq–al Qaeda Connection?," *CNN Wolf Blitzer Reports*, September 26, 2002.

11. "Reality Check: No Evidence Whatsoever of Iraq-Al Qaeda Connection," *ABC World News Tonight*, September 26, 2002; "Senate Set to Begin Formal Debate on Resolution to Authorize Military Action against Iraq," *CBS Evening News*, September 27, 2002.

12. "Bush Addresses Nation on Iraq," CNN live event/special, October 7, 2002.

13. "Pentagon Looks at Terror States," *Fox Special Report with Brit Hume*, October 24, 2002.

14. "Interview with James Woolsey," Fox News' *On the Record with Greta Van Susteren*, October 2, 2002; "Interview with Kay Bailey Hutchinson," Fox News' *On*

the Record with Greta Van Susteren, October 2, 2002; "Interview with Sen. Richard Shelby," Fox News' *The Big Story with John Gibson,* October 15, 2002. TV interview programs are included in qualitative analyses but omitted from quantitative analyses to make news stories comparable across media outlets.

15. "Interview with Jeff Sessions, Loretta Sanchez," Fox News' *Fox Wire,* September 29, 2002; "Reality Check Bush Iraq Plan," *ABC World News Tonight,* October 8, 2002; "Showdown: Iraq," *CNN Late Edition with Wolf Blitzer,* October 6, 2002; "Showdown Iraq: Should Diplomacy be Given a Bigger Chance?," CNN live event/special, October 18, 2002.

16. "Little Evidence to Support Bush Administration Claim of Working Relationship between al-Qaeda and Saddam Hussein," *NBC World News Tonight,* October 21, 2002.

17. Many of the coded sentences referred to the war more generally, although all coded articles made at least some mention of the Iraq–al Qaeda connection. See the appendix for details.

18. Each nonneutral (positive or negative) sentence was coded in greater detail for the broad meaning of the sentence, whether a person was quoted or paraphrased, and the sentence's placement in the overall story. Sentence-level codes were collapsed into key article-level variables including the average sentence valence; the number of sentences supportive, critical, and neutral of the war; and the presence in nonneutral sentences of Bush administration officials, Republican congressional leaders, Democratic congressional leaders, foreign officials (e.g., Iraqi, French), officials of other US governmental agencies, and groups of other individuals who spoke out for or against the administration's position. A total of five coders coded the stories. Ten articles were coded by all coders to determine intercoder reliability (for details, see the appendix).

19. "Interview with Jeff Sessions, Loretta Sanchez," Fox News' *Fox Wire,* September 29, 2002; "Interview with John McCain; McDermott, Thompson Discuss Their Trip to Iraq; Should Congress Give President Authority to Wage War?," *CNN Late Edition with Wolf Blitzer,* September 29, 2002; "Iraqi Weapons Inspections Discussion with Representatives McDermott, Bonior," *ABC World News Tonight,* September 29, 2002.

20. The *New York Times* story also contained a discussion of chemical weapons, including a lengthy series of quotes from an Iraqi exile, Ahmed al-Shemri, later identified as Ahmed Chalabi (former Iraqi exile and later politician), who erroneously claimed that Saddam had continued to produce nerve gas between 1994 and 1998 in locations that were remote from UN weapons inspectors and had invented a new and even more deadly form of such gas. Chalabi also claimed that Iraq continued to hold large reserves of biological weapons. These claims were very difficult to assess at the time and indeed were only discredited after the war's onset and an extensive search for such weapons stockpiles.

21. "Administration Officials Echo Bush's Message on Iraq," *CNN Sunday*

Morning, September 8, 2002; "Interview with Condoleezza Rice; Pataki Talks about 9-11; Graham, Shelby Discuss War on Terrorism," *CNN Late Edition with Wolf Blitzer*, September 8, 2002.

22. "Interview with Scott Ritter," *CNN Saturday*, September 7, 2002; "New Report from London Could Shed Light on How Deadly Hussein's Arsenal Really Is", *CNN American Morning with Paula Zahn*, September 9, 2002; "Scott Ritter Discusses Weapons Inspections in Iraq," *CBS The Early Show*, September 9, 2002; "Interview with Scott Ritter," *CNN American Morning with Paula Zahn*, September 9, 2002; "Top Story, Interview with Stephen Hayes," *The O'Reilly Factor*, September 9, 2002.

23. "Interview with Scott Ritter," *CNN American Morning with Paula Zahn*, September 9, 2002; "Provoking Concern," *ABC Nightline*, September 9, 2002.

24. News stories were obtained by conducting a search using the following parameters: "Iraq AND aluminum AND/OR tubes." Just as we did for the Iraq–al Qaeda link, we searched Lexis-Nexis, Infotrac, Factiva, Business Insights, Trac Newsstand, Newspaper Source Plus, *Newsday, New York Times, Wall Street Journal*, and Access World News for stories on aluminum tubes in each newspaper.

25. There was additional news content that we did not code; for example, there were roughly thirty-five additional TV segments that mentioned the tubes but were not coded because the issue arose in the context of an interview segment, making comparisons with newspaper stories difficult.

26. "Experts Question if Tubes Were Meant for Weapons Program," *Washington Post*, September 19, 2002.

27. "Energy Dept Tells Scientists to Hush on Iraq," *Secrecy News*, October 15, 2002, FAS Project on Government Secrecy, accessed January 15, 2015, http://www .fas.org/sgp/news/secrecy/2002/10/101502.html.

28. "Former UN Chief Weapons Inspector in Iraq, Richard Butler, Discusses Iraq's Weapons and the Possibility of War," NBC's *The Today Show*, September 13, 2002; "Former U.N. Weapons Inspector Accused of Spying for the U.S.; Bush Calls for Action on Iraq's Refusal to Obey Resolutions," *CNN NewsNight with Aaron Brown*, September 12, 2002.

29. "Administration Lays Out Evidence against Hussein," *CNN Talkback Live*, September 9, 2002.

Chapter Five

1. The mean interitem tetrachoric correlation for the five knowledge questions is .77.

2. Research in political communication has demonstrated a clear association between political knowledge and greater awareness and exposure to the ongoing flow of news stories (see Price and Zaller 1993).

3. The simple correlation between the two knowledge measures is .51. The correlation between the measures in a two-factor latent variable model is .71. This model is estimated with Mplus, and individual knowledge items are treated as categorical indicators. A simple two-factor model fit the data extremely well, indicating that information about Afghanistan and about Iraq, while correlated, are somewhat distinguishable (CFI/TLI = .98, RMSEA = .05).

4. The regression models in this chapter were designed to test the nonlinear effect of information on war support, consistent with Zaller's (1992) model in which information can have reduced effects at higher levels of partisanship because of greater message resistance to contrary arguments. In addition, we allow partisanship to have a nonlinear effect on war support. The latter step removes the constraint that independents follow a path exactly midway between Democrats and Republicans. For details, see the appendix.

5. The Iraq information scale is clearly categorical, not continuous. We conducted a series of analyses to determine whether its effects on war support and other dependent variables were linear or deviated from linearity. We found no substantial evidence of nonlinearity. Since several models include important interaction terms, it was more straightforward to present these complex interactions in linear form.

6. Unless stated otherwise, all graphs are estimated for white women at the mean sample value of age and education (or modal value of two years of college in the American National Election Studies [ANES] data).

7. The mean interitem correlation for the eight information items is .33. The estimated reliability of the scale (coefficient alpha) is .80. With the measure coded to range from a low of 0 to a high score of 1, the mean for the ANES sample is .39, suggesting moderate to low levels of general political knowledge.

8. The dependent variable in the ANES data is dichotomous (favor or oppose), and we analyzed it with a probit estimator (see table A5.1 in the appendix).

9. The single dichotomous dependent variable leaves little room for any substantial increase in war support among Republicans.

10. There is one modest difference in findings from the two data sets. All partisan groups, especially Republicans, are more supportive of military action in Iraq in the analysis using ANES data than in the TNSS data. This is almost certainly a function of the differences in how war support was measured in the two data sets. As we showed in chapter 2, the single question on war support reported in most national surveys, and the measure included in the 2002 ANES, substantially underestimates concerns about a war in Iraq, including considerable opposition among Democrats and independents to placing large numbers of ground troops in harm's way.

11. Measurement error in the frequency of news media consumption is likely to lead to an underestimate of the effect of news consumption on war support.

12. For practical reasons, we assumed that TV and newspaper consumption had

independent effects on public opinion. It is not possible to reliably assess the joint effects of the two media sources on war support, which would require the inclusion of a four-way interaction in the model between information, TV viewing, newspaper consumption, and partisanship. Information on exact model specification can be found in the appendix.

13. Predicted values are generated for a white female at mean levels of age, education, and TV viewing.

14. Since war support is dichotomous in the ANES, we estimate a probit regression, which is shown in appendix table A5.1, column (6). Predicted values are generated for a white female at mean levels of age, education, and TV viewing.

15. The strength of the newspaper effect is less obvious in figure 5.6 than in figure 5.5 because of surprisingly strong war support among Democrats who read a newspaper every day but knew nothing about Iraq. Since there are not many people who read newspapers daily and score at the lowest levels of information, we are careful not to overinterpret this finding and focus instead on the effect of information on war support for those who never read a newspaper and those who read one daily.

16. The different results on the effect of television news on war support in the TNSS and ANES data are not simply a function of the different dependent variables in the two data sets. When we repeat the analysis in the TNSS data after constructing a single dichotomous dependent variable comparable to the measure of war support in the ANES data, we still get significant effects of TV news. Those who obtained their news from TV became more supportive of the war.

Chapter Six

1. "Gore Vidal Quotes: 26 of the Best," *Guardian*, August 1, 2012.

2. These probabilities are computed for a white female at the means for age and education.

3. To be precise, the values shown in figure 6.2 are the predicted change in war support (or, in the ANES data, the probability of war support) as newspaper reading moves from zero days per week to seven days per week at the highest level of information and holding all else constant.

4. There are very few conservative Democrats and liberal Republicans in either data set, and we do not plot values for them. Similarly, there are few strong liberals or strong conservatives among independents, and we plot values for the less extreme categories of liberal and conservative (2 and 6 on the 1 to 7 ideological self-placement scale).

5. An obvious problem with Berinsky's explanation is that it assumes only well-informed Democrats would have known President Bush's position on the war well enough to use that as a cue to oppose military action. But given the prominence

of Bush administration officials in the news at this time, it is difficult to believe that even relatively uninformed Democrats were ignorant of Bush's position on the war. Moreover, this argument has difficulty explaining opposition to the war among well-informed independents.

6. The interview period for wave 1 was from early October 2001 through early March 2002. Two hundred new participants were added to the survey in the fall of 2002. There is no evidence that the two hundred new interviewees differed from those who were reinterviewed. However, these added participants cannot be included in any analyses that make use of the post-9/11 interviews.

7. This may help explain why the Bush administration waited as long as it did for an endorsement from the UN Security Council before launching the war. As we showed in chapter 2, although rank-and-file Republicans generally supported the use of military force in Iraq in the fall of 2002, many wanted to wait for support from the UN before going ahead. Those reservations largely disappeared once the war started in March 2003.

8. Democratic Congresswoman Barbara Lee from Berkeley, California.

9. The first question asks whether the level of US military action in response to the terrorist attacks is too little, just about right, or too much. Since it has three categories, it is estimated as an ordered probit. The second question asks whether the respondent favors or opposes increasing the level of military action "even if it means that U.S. armed forces might suffer a substantial number of casualties." The four response categories ranged from strongly favor to strongly oppose. Since we are interested in opposition to the use of force, we recoded the variable to have two categories—favor and oppose—and estimates are derived using dichotomous probit. Estimation of the four-category ordered probit model yields very similar results.

10. Information in wave 1 was measured with the following four factual questions about Afghanistan and al Qaeda: "Can you tell me the name of the Muslim holy book?"; "Can you tell me the name of *one* country that shares a border with Afghanistan?"; "Is Afghanistan an Arab country?"; and "Can you name the country that Osama bin Laden is originally from?"

11. The estimates for this model and the model including the media effects are shown in appendix table A6.3.

12. Although we do not present these models, interaction terms between each of the wave 1 variables with both partisanship and information were statistically insignificant and substantively trivial. As opposed to the effects of ideology and anti-Bush attitudes, there is no evidence that the effects of preexisting antiwar feelings on Iraq war support depended on either partisanship or levels of information.

13. These two variables were modestly correlated ($r = .31$).

14. These analyses are available from the authors on request. The probabilities were computed for white females with mean levels of education, age, and information.

Chapter Seven

1. For example, the war enhanced substantially Iranian influence in Iraq and the region. And while nominally a democratic republic, the new regime has much distance to cover before, if ever, it realizes the fuller meaning of that designation.

2. The initial efforts to secure public support for the Persian Gulf War and reverse Iraq's invasion of Kuwait were based on jobs and the securing of an important oil supplier. But this initial effort failed. It was only when Saddam Hussein, our then principal ally in the region, was depicted as a mini-Hitler that public support was forthcoming.

3. And as in the case of the Iraq War run-up, when Senators Kennedy, Feingold, and Byrd, among others, raised alarms, in the case of Vietnam there were a cadre of Democratic senators who expressed early public misgivings about that war, among them Senators Gore, Church, Nelson, McGovern, Morse, Gruening, Ellender, Johnston, and Eastland (Stone 2007). This led to several references to partisan division on the war in the news media, including an article in *US News and World Report*, which suggested that the "debate over U.S. foreign policy, more and more, looks like an intraparty row" (Johnson 2005, 108).

4. Benjamin Ginsberg (1986), along with others (Sartori 1987; Schumpeter 1943), gives little credence to the possibility or desirability of an independent public.

5. This story played out after the period we examine. President Bush made claims concerning the uranium in his State of the Union Speech in January of 2003.

6. With the invention and then application of photography by, among others, Matthew Brady during the American Civil War publics could see for themselves what bullets, bayonets, missiles, bombs, and other weapons did to human bodies. Ever since, governments have sought to control information to mask the true costs of war by, among other things, censoring letters back home. The German army, during World War II, forbade its soldiers from sending photos to their loved ones back home about what they saw taking place in the various roundups and killings of Jews that took place during the invasion of Russia (Klee, Dressen, and Riess 1988). For example, actual footage of the D-Day invasion was not made available for decades (it was the movie *Saving Private Ryan* in 1998 that presented the reality of that war in fictionalized form). The images of the treatment of prisoners at Abu Ghraib showed the public another view into the Iraq project. In all these ways, technology has the capacity to challenge authority.

7. "Clay Shirky on the Internet as a Distractor and Disruptor," The Atlantic, November 5, 2012, accessed February 2, 2015, http://finance.yahoo.com/news/clay-shirky-internet-distractor-disruptor-130953879.html.

8. This reinforces Jones's overarching point that news requires a combination of resources, among them, expertise, intention, and resources.

9. In a world where the fight for "eyeballs" dominates, tier four is likely to be quite unattractive in the digital age, for beyond the issue of expense—months of

labor by groups of journalists and many associated costs—there are two risks. First, the story may not pan out. Second, the story must attract interest in a world when an unexpected event, a tsunami, a rebellion, another outbreak of a new deadly disease, or some scandal will dominate the news. In a world where such events are often unpredictable, it is likely that editors and publishers will find tier one activity not only far less expensive but also far less risky in securing the desired audience.

Appendix

1. To get into the field rapidly, the first month of data was collected by the firm Schulman, Ronca, and Bukuvalas; the remainder of the data (including waves 2 and 3) was collected by the Stony Brook University Center for Survey Research. The cooperation rate for the survey was 52% (AAPOR COOP3, the ratio of completed interviews to all completed interviews plus households that refused to participate; see https://www.aapor.org/AAPORKentico/AAPOR_Main/media/MainSiteFiles/Standard_Definitions_07_08_Final.pdf). There was no difference in response rate between the two survey organizations, and response rates were similar to those obtained in random digit dial (RDD) surveys conducted at the same time using a different geographic sampling frame but similar methodology (Losch et al. 2002; Steeh et al. 2001). For more detail on the panel study, see Huddy et al. (2005) and Huddy, Feldman, and Cassese (2007).

2. We removed information squared in interaction with the news consumption variables in the following tables because in no instance was its coefficient significant. Including it has no effect on the estimated coefficients we report here.

References

Aday, Sean. 2010. "Leading the Charge: Media, Elites, and the Use of Emotion in Stimulating Rally Effects in Wartime." *Journal of Communication* 60:440–65.

Aldrich, John H., Christopher Gelpi, Peter Feaver, Jason Reifler, and Kristin Thompson Sharp. 2006. "Foreign Policy and the Electoral Connection." *Annual Review of Political Science* 9:477–502.

Aldrich, John H., John L. Sullivan, and Eugene Borgida. 1989. "Foreign Affairs and Issue Voting: Do Presidential Candidates 'Waltz Before a Blind Audience?'" *American Political Science Review* 83:123–41.

Althaus, Scott L. 2003. "When News Norms Collide, Follow the Lead: New Evidence for Press Independence." *Political Communication* 20 (4): 381–414.

Althaus, Scott L., and Devon M. Largio. 2004. "When Osama Became Saddam: Origins and Consequences of the Change in America's Public Enemy #1." *PS: Political Science and Politics* 37:795–99.

Andrews, Robert. 1993. *The Columbia Dictionary of Quotations*. New York: Columbia University Press.

Baker, James A., III. 2002. "The Right Way to Change a Regime." *New York Times*, August 25.

Balz, Dan. 2002a. "Democrats Assail Bush on Economy and Foreign Policy." *Washington Post*, July 30.

———. 2002b. "Gore Supports 'Final Reckoning' with Iraq; Former Vice President Urges Administration to Avoid 'Go It Alone' Approach" *Washington Post*, February 13.

Bamford, James. 2002. "Maintain CIA's Independence," *USA Today*, October 24, 2002.

Barber, Benjamin. 1984. *Strong Democracy: Participatory Politics for a New Age*. Berkeley: University of California Press.

Baum, Matthew A., and Tim J. Groeling. 2010. *War Stories: The Causes and Consequences of Public Views of War*. Princeton, NJ: Princeton University Press.

Benhabib, Seyla. 1996. "Toward a Deliberative Model of Democratic Legitimacy." In *Democracy and Difference: Contesting the Boundaries of the Political*, edited by Seyla Benhabib, 67–94. Princeton, NJ: University of Princeton
Press.

Bennett, W. Lance. 1990. "Toward a Theory of Press-State Relations in the United
States." *Journal of Communication* 40 (2): 103–27.

Bennett, W. Lance, and Shanto Iyengar. 2008. "A New Era of Minimal Effects?
The Changing Foundations of Political Communication." *Journal of Communication* 58 (4): 707–31.

———. 2010. "The Shifting Foundations of Political Communication: Respond-
ing to a Defense of the Media Effects Paradigm." *Journal of Communication*
60:35–39.

Bennett, W. Lance, Regina G. Lawrence, and Steven Livingston. 2006. "None
Dare Call It Torture: Indexing and the Limits of Press Independence in the
Abu Ghraib Scandal." *Journal of Communication* 56 (3): 467–85.

———. 2007. *When the Press Fails: Political Power and the News Media from Iraq
to Katrina*. Chicago: University of Chicago Press.

Bennett, W. Lance, and Steven Livingston. 2003. "Editors' Introduction: A Semi-
Independent Press: Government Control and Journalistic Autonomy in the
Political Construction of News." *Political Communication* 4: 359–62.

Bennett, Stephen E., and David Resnick. 1990. "The Implications of Nonvoting
for Democracy in the United States." *American Journal of Political Science*
34:771–802.

Berinsky, Adam J. 2007. "Assuming the Costs of War: Events, Elites, and American Public Support for Military Conflict." *Journal of Politics* 69:975–97.

———. 2009. *In Time of War: Understanding American Public Opinion from
World War I to Iraq*. Chicago: University of Chicago Press.

Bishop, George F. 2005. *The Illusion of Public Opinion: Fact and Artifact in American Public Opinion Polls*. Lanham, MD: Rowman and Littlefield.

Boettcher, William A., III, and Michael D. Cobb. 2006. "Echoes of Vietnam? Casualty Framing and Public Perceptions of Success and Failure in Iraq." *Journal
of Conflict Resolution* 50 (5): 831–54.

———. 2009. "'Don't Let Them Die in Vain': Casualty Frames and Public Tolerance for Escalating Commitment in Iraq." *Journal of Conflict Resolution* 53
(6): 677–97.

Bolsen, Toby, James N. Druckman, and Fay Lomax Cook. 2014. "The Influence of
Partisan Motivated Reasoning on Public Opinion." *Political Behavior* 36 (2):
235–62.

Borjesson, Kristina. 2005. *Feet to the Fire: The Media After 9/11: Top Journalists
Speak Out*. Amherts, NY: Prometheus Books.

Brody, Richard A. 1991. *Assessing Presidential Character: The Media, Elite Opinion, and Public Support*. Stanford, CA: Stanford University Press.

Bumiller, Elisabeth. 2002. "Traces of Terror: The Strategy; Bush Aides Set Strategy to Sell Policy on Iraq." *New York Times*, September 7.

Bumiller, Elisabeth, and James Dao. 2002. "Eyes on Iraq; Cheney Says Peril of a Nuclear Iraq Justifies Attack." *New York Times*, August 27.

Campbell, Angus, Philip E. Converse, Warren E. Miller, and Donald E. Stokes. 1960. *The American Voter*. New York: John Wiley and Sons.

Carpenter, Serena. 2007. "U.S. Elite and Non-Elite Newspapers' Portrayal of the Iraq War: A Comparison of Frames and Source Use." *Journalism & Mass Communication Quarterly* 84 (4): 761–76.

Chaiken, Shelly, and Yaacov Trope, eds. 1999. *Dual Process Models in Social Psychology*. New York: Guilford Press.

Chen, Serena, Kimberly Duckworth, and Shelley Chaiken. 1999. "Motivated Heuristic and Systematic Processing." *Psychological Inquiry* 10 (1): 44–49.

Chong, Dennis. 2013. "Rational Choice Theory and Political Psychology." In *The Oxford Handbook of Political Psychology*, 2nd ed., edited by Leonie Huddy, David O. Sears, and Jack Levy, 96–129. New York: Oxford University Press.

Churchill, Winston S. 1974. *His Complete Speeches, 1897–1963*. Edited by Robert Rhodes James. 8 vols. New York: Chelsea House.

Cohen, Jeffery E. 2010. *Going Local: Presidential Leadership in the Post-Broadcast Age*. New York: Cambridge University Press.

Converse, Philip E. 1964. "The Nature of Belief Systems in Mass Publics." In *Ideology and Discontent*, edited by David Apter, 206–61. New York: Free Press.

———. 1966. "The Concept of the Normal Vote." In *Elections and the Political Order*, edited by Angus Campbell, Philip E. Converse, Warren E. Miller, and Donald E. Stokes, 9–39. New York: Wiley.

———. 1970. "Attitudes and Non-attitudes: Continuation of a Dialogue." In *The Quantitative Analysis of Social Problems*, edited by Edward F. Tufte, 168–89. Reading, MA: Addison-Wesley.

———. 2006. "Democratic Theory and Electoral Reality." *Critical Review* 18:297–329.

Cunningham, B. 2003. "Re-thinking Objectivity." *Columbia Journalism Review* 42 (2): 24–32.

Daley, Suzanne. 2002. "A Nation Challenged: The Allies; Many in Europe Voice Worry U.S. Will Not Consult Them." *New York Times*, January 31.

Dao, James. 2002a. "Call in Congress for Full Airing of Iraq Policy." *New York Times*, July 18.

———. 2002b. "Powell Charts Low-Key Path in Iraq Debate." *New York Times*, September 2.

Delli Carpini, Michael X., and Scott Keeter. 1996. *What Americans Know about Politics and Why It Matters*. New Haven, CT: Yale University Press.

Elkin, Stephen L., and Karl Edward Soltan, eds. 1999. *Citizen Competence and Democratic Institutions*. University Park: Pennsylvania State University Press.

Entman, Robert M. 2003. "Cascading Activation: Contesting the White House's Frame after 9/11." *Political Communication* 20 (4): 415–32.

———. 2004. *Projections of Power: Framing News, Public Opinion, and US Foreign Policy.* Chicago: University of Chicago Press.

Entman, Robert M., and Benjamin Page. 1994. "The News before the Storm." In *Taken by Storm: The Media, Public Opinion, and US Foreign Policy in the Gulf War,* edited by W. Lance Bennett and David L. Paletz, 82–101. Chicago: University of Chicago Press.

Evans, Jonathan St. B. T. 2008. "Dual-Processing Accounts of Reasoning, Judgment, and Social Cognition." *Annual Review of Psychology* 59:255–78.

Everts, P., and P. Isernia. 2005. "The War in Iraq." *Public Opinion Quarterly* 69 (2): 264–323.

Feldman, Stanley. 2003. "Enforcing Social Conformity: A Theory of Authoritarianism." *Political Psychology* 24:41–74.

Feldman, Stanley, and Karen Stenner. 1997. "Perceived Threat and Authoritarianism." *Political Psychology* 18:741–70.

Fishkin, James S. 1991. *Democracy and Deliberation.* New Haven, CT: Yale University Press.

———. 2009. *When the People Speak: Deliberative Democracy and Public Consultation.* Oxford: Oxford University Press.

Fromm, Erich. 1965. *Escape from Freedom.* New York: Avon.

Fuller, Jack. 2010. *What Is Happening to News: The Information Explosion and the Crisis in Journalism.* Chicago: University of Chicago Press.

Gadarian, Shana Kushner. 2010. "The Politics of Threat: How Terrorism News Shapes Foreign Policy Attitudes." *Journal of Politics* 72:469–83.

Gaines, Brian J., James H. Kuklinski, Paul J. Quirk, Buddy Peyton, and Jay Verkuilen. 2007. "Same Facts, Different Interpretations: Partisan Motivation and Opinion on Iraq." *Journal of Politics* 69:957–74.

Gans, Herbert J. 1979. *Deciding What's News: A Study of "CBS Evening News," "NBC Nightly News," "Newsweek," and "Time."* Evanston, IL: Northwestern University Press.

Gartner, Scott Sigmund. 2008. "The Multiple Effects of Casualties on Public Support for War: An Experimental Approach." *American Political Science Review* 102:95–106.

Gartner, Scott Sigmund, and Gary M. Segura. 1998. "War, Casualties, and Public Opinion." *Journal of Conflict Resolution* 42 (3): 278–300.

Gelpi, Christopher. 2010. "Performing on Cue? The Formation of Public Opinion toward War." *Journal of Conflict Resolution* 54 (1): 88–116.

Gelpi, Christopher, Peter D. Feaver, and Jason Reifler. 2005. "Success Matters: Casualty Sensitivity and the War in Iraq." *International Security* 30:7–46.

Gelpi, Christopher, Jason Reifler, and Peter Feaver. 2007. "Iraq the Vote: Retrospective and Prospective Foreign Policy Judgments on Candidate Choice and Casualty Tolerance." *Political Behavior* 29 (2): 151–74.

Gershkoff, Amy, and Shana Kushner. 2005. "Shaping Public Opinion: The 9/11-Iraq Connection in the Bush Administration's Rhetoric." *Perspectives on Politics* 3 (3): 525–37.

Getler, Michael. 2004. "Looking Back before the War." *Washington Post*, June 20.

Gilbert, Gustave M. 1950. *The Psychology of Dictatorship*. New York: Ronald Press.

Ginsberg, Benjamin. 1986. *The Captive Public: How Mass Opinion Promotes State Power*. New York: Basic Books.

Glazier, Rebecca A., and Amber E. Boydstun. 2012. "The President, the Press, and the War: A Tale of Two Framing Agendas." *Political Communication* 29 (4): 428–46.

Green, Donald, Bradley Palmquist, and Eric Schickler. 2002. *Partisan Hearts and Minds: Political Parties and the Social Identity of Voters*. New Haven, CT: Yale University Press.

Groeling, Tim, and Matthew A. Baum. 2008. "Crossing the Water's Edge: Elite Rhetoric, Media Coverage, and the Rally-Round-the-Flag Phenomenon." *Journal of Politics* 70:1065–85.

Habermas, Jürgen. 1989. *The Structural Transformation of the Public Sphere: An Inquiry into a Category of Bourgeois Society*. Cambridge, MA: MIT Press.

Haidt, Jonathan. 2001. "The Emotional Dog and Its Rational Tail: A Social Intuitionist Approach to Moral Judgment." *Psychological Review* 108:814–34.

Hayes, Danny, and Matt Guardino. 2010. "Whose Views Made the News? Media Coverage and the March to War in Iraq." *Political Communication* 27:59–87.

———. 2011. "The Influence of Foreign Voices on U.S. Public Opinion." *American Journal of Political Science* 55:830–50.

———. 2013. *Influence from Abroad: Foreign Voices, the Media, and U.S. Public Opinion*. New York: Cambridge University Press.

Heider, Fritz. 1958. *The Psychology of Interpersonal Relations*. New York: John Wiley and Sons.

Held, David. 2006. *Models of Democracy*. Cambridge: Polity.

Herrmann, Richard K., Philip E. Tetlock, and Penny S. Visser. 1999. "Mass Public Decisions to Go to War: A Cognitive-Interactionist Framework." *American Political Science Review* 93:533–73.

Herzog, Don. 1998. *Poisoning the Minds of the Lower Orders*. Princeton, NJ: Princeton University Press.

Hobbes, Thomas. 1968. *Leviathan*. London: Penguin.

Howell, William G., and Jon C. Pevehouse. 2007. *While Dangers Gather: Congressional Checks on Presidential War Powers*. Princeton, NJ: Princeton University Press.

Hoyle, Russ. 2008. *Going to War: How Misinformation, Disinformation, and Arrogance Led America into Iraq*. New York: Thomas Dunne Books.

Huddy, Leonie. 2013. "Translating Group Identity into Political Cohesion and Commitment." In *The Oxford Handbook of Political Psychology*, 2nd. ed., edited by Leonie Huddy, David O. Sears, and Jack Levy, 737–73. New York: Oxford University Press.

Huddy, Leonie, Stanley Feldman, and Erin Cassese. 2007. "On the Distinct Political Effects of Anxiety and Anger." In *The Affect Effect: Dynamics of Emotion in Political Thinking and Behavior*, edited by W. Russell Neuman, George E. Marcus, Ann Crigler, and Michael MacKuen, 202–30. Chicago: University of Chicago Press.

Huddy, Leonie, Stanley Feldman, Charles Taber, and Gallya Lahav. 2005. "Threat, Anxiety, and Support of Antiterrorism Policies." *American Journal of Political Science* 49 (3): 593–608.

Isikoff, Michael, and David Corn. 2006. *Hubris: The Inside Story of Spin, Scandal, and the Selling of the Iraq War.* New York: Crown.

Iyengar, Shanto, and Kyu S. Hahn. 2009. "Red Media, Blue Media: Evidence of Ideological Selectivity in Media Use." *Journal of Communication* 59:19–39.

Iyengar, Shanto, Kyu S. Hahn, Jon A. Krosnick, and John Walker. 2008. "Selective Exposure to Campaign Communication: The Role of Anticipated Agreement and Issue Public Membership." *Journal of Politics* 70:186–200.

Jacobson, Gary C. 2007. *A Divider, Not a Uniter: George W. Bush and the American People, the 2006 Election and Beyond.* Great Questions in Politics. New York: Longman.

Jefferson, Thomas. 1900. *The Jeffersonian Cyclopedia: A Comprehensive Collection of the Views of Thomas Jefferson Classified and Arranged in Alphabetical Order under Nine Thousand Titles Relating to Government, Politics, Law, Education, Political Economy, Finance, Science, Art, Literature, Religious Freedom, Morals, Etc.* New York: Funk & Wagnalls.

———. 1903–1904. *The Writings of Thomas Jefferson.* Memorial Edition. Edited by Andrew A. Lipscomb and Albert Ellery Bergh. 20 Vols. Washington, DC.: Thomas Jefferson Memorial Association of the United States.

Jentleson, Bruce W. 1992. "The Pretty Prudent Public: Post Post-Vietnam American Opinion on the Use of Military Force." *International Studies Quarterly* 36:49–74.

Jentleson, Bruce W., and Rebecca L. Britton. 1998. "Still Pretty Prudent: Post–Cold War American Public Opinion on the Use of Military Force." *Journal of Conflict Resolution* 42:395–417.

Johnson, Robert David. 2005. *Congress and the Cold War.* Cambridge: Cambridge University Press.

Jones, Alex S. 2009. *Losing the News: The Future of the News That Feeds Democracy.* New York: Oxford University Press.

Jordan, Donald L., and Benjamin I. Page. 1992. "Shaping Foreign Policy Opinions." *Journal of Conflict Resolution* 36 (2): 227–41.

Kahneman, Daniel. 2011. *Thinking, Fast and Slow.* New York: Farrar, Straus and Giroux.

Kant, Immanuel. 1970. "Perpetual Peace: A Philosophical Sketch." In *Kant's Political Writings*, edited by Hans Reiss, 93–130. Cambridge: Cambridge University Press.

Karol, David, and Edward Miguel. 2007. "The Electoral Costs of War: Casualties and the 2004 U.S. Presidential Election." *Journal of Politics* 69:633–48.

Keith, B. E., D. B. Magleby, C. J. Nelson, E. Orr, and M. C. Westlye. 1992. *The Myth of the Independent Voter*. Berkeley: University of California Press.

Key, V. O., Jr. 1966. *The Responsible Electorate: Rationality in Presidential Voting, 1936–1960*. With the assistance of Milton C. Cummings, Jr. New York: Vintage Books.

Kinder, Donald R. 2003. "Belief Systems after Converse." In *Electoral Democracy*, edited by Michael B. MacKuen and George B. Rabinowitz, 13–47. Ann Arbor: University of Michigan Press.

———. 2006. "Belief Systems Today." *Critical Review* 18:197–216.

Klee, Ernst, Willi Dressen, and Volker Riess, eds. 1988. *"The Good Old Days": The Holocaust as Seen by Its Perpetrators and Bystanders*. New York: Free Press.

Knowlton, Brian. 2002. "Bush's 'Axis of Evil' Draws Fire; But Congress Backs Warning." *International Herald Tribune*, January 31.

Kriner, Douglas L., and Francis X. Shen. 2014. "Reassessing American Casualty Sensitivity: The Mediating Influence of Inequality." *Journal of Conflict Resolution* 58 (7): 1174–201.

Kull, Steven, Clay Ramsay, and Evan Lewis. 2003. "Misperceptions, the Media, and the Iraq War." *Political Science Quarterly* 118 (4): 569–98.

Kunda, Ziva. 1990. "The Case for Motivated Reason." *Psychological Bulletin* 108:480–98.

Kurtz, Howard. 2004. "The *Post* on WMDs: An Inside Story. Prewar Articles Questioning Threat Often Didn't Make Front Page." *Washington Post*, August 12.

Lacy, Stephen, Tsan-Kuo Chang, and Tuen-yu Lau. 1989. "Impact of Allocation Decisions and Market Factors on Foreign News Coverage." *Newspaper Research Journal* 10 (1): 23–32.

Ladd, Everett C. 1978. *Where Have All the Voters Gone?* New York: Norton.

Lancaster, John. 2002. "'Halo' Cows Democrats; Popular Support for Bush, Republicans Makes Mounting Challenges Difficult" *Washington Post*, February 11.

Landau, Mark J., Sheldon Solomon, Jeff Greenberg, Florette Cohen, Tom Pyszczynski, Jamie Arndt, Dale T. Miller, Daniel M. Ogilvie, and Alison Cook. 2004. "Deliver Us from Evil: The Effects of Mortality Salience and Reminders of 9/11 on Support for President George W. Bush." *Personality and Social Psychology Bulletin* 30:1136–50.

Larson, Eric V. 1996. *Casualties and Consensus: The Historical Role of Casualties in Domestic Support for US Military Operations*. Santa Monica, CA: Rand Corporation.

Lasswell, Harold D. 1941. "The Garrison State." *American Journal of Sociology* 46:455–68.

Lavine, Howard., Christopher D. Johnston, and Marco R. Steenbergen. 2012. *The Ambivalent Partisan: How Critical Loyalty Promotes Democracy*. New York: Oxford University Press.

Lawrence, Regina G. 2000. *The Politics of Force: Media and the Construction of Police Brutality*. Berkeley: University of California Press.

Leeper, Thomas J., and Rune Slothuus. 2014. "Political Parties, Motivated Reasoning, and Public Opinion Formation." Supplement, *Advances in Political Psychology* 35 (S1): 129–56.

Lenz, Gabriel S. 2012. *Follow the Leader? How Voters Respond to Politicians' Policies and Performance*. Chicago: University of Chicago Press.

Lewis, Neil A., with David E. Sanger. 2002. "Bush May Request Congress Backing on Iraq, Aides Say." *New York Times*, August 29.

Lewis-Beck, Michael S., William G. Jacoby, Helmut Norpoth, and Herbert F. Weisberg. 2008. *The American Voter Revisited*. Ann Arbor: University of Michigan Press.

Lincoln, Abraham. 1953. *The Collected Works of Abraham Lincoln*. New Brunswick, NJ: Rutgers University Press.

Lippmann, Walter. 1922. *Public Opinion*. New York: Macmillan.

Livingston, Steven, and W. Lance Bennett. 2003. "Gatekeeping, Indexing, and Live-Event News: Is Technology Altering the Construction of News?" *Political Communication* 20 (4): 363–80.

Lodge, Milton G., and Charles Taber. 2000. "Three Steps toward a Theory of Motivated Political Reasoning." In *Elements of Political Reason: Understanding and Expanding the Limits of Rationality*, edited by Arthur Lupia, Mathew D. McCubbins, and Samuel L. Popkin, 183–213. New York: Cambridge University Press.

———. 2013. *The Rationalizing Voter*. New York: Cambridge University Press.

Losch, Mary E., Aaron Maitland, Gene Lutz, Peter Mariolis, and Steven C. Gleason. 2002. "The Effect of Time of Year of Data Collection on Sample Efficiency: An Analysis of Behavioral Risk Factor Surveillance Survey Data." *Public Opinion Quarterly* 66 (4): 594–607.

Massing, Michael. "Now They Tell Us." 2004. *New York Review of Books*, February 26. http://www.nybooks.com/articles/archives/2004/feb/26/now-they-tell-us/.

McCann, Stewart J. H. 1997. "Threatening Times, 'Strong' Presidential Popular Vote Winners, and the Victory Margin, 1924–1964." *Journal of Personality and Social Psychology* 73:160–70.

McClellan, Scott. 2008. *What Happened: Inside the Bush White House and Washington's Culture of Deception*. New York: Public Affairs.

McGuire, William J. 1969. "The Nature of Attitudes and Attitude Change." In *The Handbook of Social Psychology*, edited by G. Lindzey, and E. Aronson, 136–314. Reading, MA: Addison-Wesley.

Mencken, H. L. 1949. *A Mencken Chrestomathy*. New York: A. A. Knopf.

Moyers, Bill. 2007. "Buying the War." http://www.pbs.org/moyers/journal/btw /watch.html.

Mueller, John. 1973. *War Presidents and Public Opinion*. New York: Wiley and Sons.

———. 1993. "American Public Opinion and the Gulf War: Some Polling Issues." *Public Opinion Quarterly* 57:80–91.

———. 1999. *Capitalism, Democracy, and Ralph's Pretty Good Grocery*. Princeton, NJ: Princeton University Press.

———. 2011. "Public Opinion, the Media and War." In *The Oxford Handbook of American Public Opinion and the Media*, edited by Robert Y. Shapiro and Lawrence Jacobs, 675–89. New York: Oxford University Press.

Nacos, Brigitte L., Yaeli Bloch-Elkon, and Robert Y. Shapiro. 2011. *Selling Fear: Counterterrorism, the Media, and Public Opinion*. Chicago: University of Chicago Press.

Nagourney, Adam. 2002. "A Nation Challenged: The Democrat; Gore, Championing Bush, Calls for a 'Final Reckoning' with Iraq." *New York Times*, February 13.

Neuman, W. Russell. 2007. "Globalization and the New Media." In *The Politics of News: The News of Politics*, edited by Doris Graber, Denis McQuail, and Pippa Norris, 230–46. Washington, DC: Congressional Quarterly Press.

Neuman, W. Russell, Bruce Bimber, and Matthew Hindman. 2011. "The Internet and Four Dimensions of Citizenship." In *The Oxford Handbook of American Public Opinion and the Media*, edited by Robert Y. Shapiro and Lawrence R. Jacobs, 22–42. New York: Oxford University Press.

Oppel, Richard A., Jr., with Julia Preston. 2002. "Administration Seeking to Build Support in Congress on Iraq Issue." *New York Times*, August 30.

Orwell, George. 1949. *1984*. New York: Harcourt, Brace.

Page, Benjamin, and Robert Y. Shapiro. 1992. *The Rational Public*. Chicago: University of Chicago Press.

Paine, Thomas. 1776. *Common Sense: Addressed to the Inhabitants of America on the Following Interesting Subjects*. Philadelphia.

Pateman, Carol. 1970. *Participation and Democratic Theory*. Cambridge: Cambridge University Press.

Petty, Richard E., and John T. Cacioppo. 1986. *Communication and Persuasion: Central and Peripheral Routes to Attitude Change*. New York: Springer-Verlag.

Plato. 1974. *The Republic*. New York: Penguin.

Polenberg, Richard. 1987. *Fighting Faiths: The Abrams Case, the Supreme Court, and Free Speech*. New York: Viking.

Price, Vincent, and John Zaller. 1993. "Who Gets the News? Alternative Measures of News Reception and Their Implications for Research." *Public Opinion Quarterly* 57 (2): 133–64.

Prior, Markus. 2009. "Improving Media Effects Research through Better Measurement of News Exposure." *Journal of Politics* 71 (3): 893–908.

Purdum, Todd S. 2002. "A Nation Challenged: Congress; Democrats Starting to Fault President on the War's Future." *New York Times*, March 1.

Purdum, Todd S., and Patrick E. Tyler. 2002. "Top Republicans Break with Bush on Iraq Strategy." *New York Times*, August 16.

Rainie, Lee, Susannah Fox, and Deborah Fallows. 2003. "The Internet and the Iraq War: How Online Americans Have Used the Internet to Learn War News, Understand Events, and Promote Their Views." Pew Internet and American Life Project. Accessed October 28, 2014. http://www.pewinternet.org/2003/04/01/the-internet-and-the-iraq-war/.

Rawls, John. 1971. *A Theory of Justice*. Cambridge, MA: Harvard University Press.

Redlawsk, David P. 2002. "Hot Cognition or Cool Consideration? Testing the Effects of Motivated Reasoning on Political Decision Making." *Journal of Politics* 64 (4): 1021–44.

Rendall, Steve. 2006. "Wrong on Iraq? Not Everyone: Four in the Mainstream Media Who Got It Right." Fairness and Accuracy In Reporting (FAIR). April 1. http://www.fair.org/index.php?page=2847.

Ricchiardi, Sherry. 2008. "Whatever Happened to Iraq? How the Media Lost Interest in a Long-Running War with No End in Sight." *American Journalism Review*, June/July. http://www.ajr.org/article.asp?id=4515.

Rich, Frank. 2006. *The Greatest Story Ever Sold: The Decline and Fall of Truth—From 9/11 to Katrina*. New York: Penguin.

Ricks, Thomas E. 2006. *Fiasco: The American Military Adventure in Iraq*. New York: Penguin.

Ritea, Steve. 2004. "Going It Alone: Accolades Now Come to Knight Ridder for Its Prescient Reports Expressing Skepticism about Claims That Iraq Had Weapons of Mass Destruction." *American Journalism Review*, August/September. http://www.ajr.org/article_printable.asp?id=3725.

Robinson, Piers, Peter Goddard, Katy Parry, and Craig Murray, with Philip M. Taylor. 2010. *Pockets of Resistance: British News Media, War and Theory in the 2003 Invasion of Iraq*. Manchester, UK: Manchester University Press.

Rojecki, Andrew. 2005. "Media Discourse on Globalization and Terror." *Political Communication* 22 (1): 63–81.

———. 2008. "Rhetorical Alchemy: American Exceptionalism and the War on Terror." *Political Communication* 25 (1): 67–88.

Rosenbaum, David E. 2002. "Threats and Responses: The Democrats; United Voice on Iraq Eludes Majority Leader." *New York Times*, October 4.

Rosenstiel, Tom, and Amy Mitchell. 2012. *The State of the News Media 2012*. Washington, DC: Pew Research Center's Project for Excellence in Journalism.

Sartori, Giovanni. 1987. *The Theory of Democracy Revisited*. Chatham, NJ: Chatham House Publishers.

Schattschneider, E. E. 1960. *The Semi-Sovereign People*. New York: Holt, Rinehart, and Winston.

Schumpeter, Joseph A. 1943. *Capitalism, Socialism and Democracy*. London: George Allen and Unwin.

Scowcroft, Brent. 2002. "Don't Attack Saddam: It Would Undermine Our Antiterror Efforts." *Wall Street Journal*, August 15.

Shapiro, Robert Y., and Yaeli Bloch-Elkon. 2008. "Do the Facts Speak for Themselves? Partisan Disagreement as a Challenge to Democratic Competence." *Critical Review* 20 (1–2): 115–39.

Shapiro, Walter. 2002. "Time for 'Loyal Opposition' to Break Vow of Silence." *USA Today*, February 15.

Shirky, Clay. 2010. *Cognitive Surplus: Creativity and Generosity in a Connected Age*. New York: Penguin.

Sigal, Leon V. 1973. *Reporters and Officials: The Organization and Politics of Newsmaking*. Lexington, MA: D. C. Heath.

Sinclair, Upton. 1906. *The Jungle*. New York: Doubleday, Page.

Steeh, C., N. Kirgis, B. Cannon, and J. DeWitt. 2001. "Are They Really as Bad as They Seem? Nonresponse Rates at the End of the Twentieth Century." *Journal of Official Statistics* 17 (2): 227–48.

Stone, Gary. 2007. *Elites for Peace: The Senate and the Vietnam War, 1964–1968*. Knoxville: University of Tennessee Press.

Sullivan, John L., and Robert E. O'Connor. 1972. "Electoral Choice and Popular Control of Public Policy." *American Political Science Review* 66:1256–68.

Suskind, Ron. 2006. *The One Percent Doctrine: Deep Inside America's Pursuit of Its Enemies Since 9/11*. 1st ed. New York: Simon Schuster.

Swoger, Kate. 2002. "Intelligence Chief Casts Doubt on Atta Meeting." *Prague Post*. August 8.

Taber, Charles S., and Milton Lodge. 2006. "Motivated Skepticism in the Evaluation of Political Beliefs." *American Journal of Political Science* 50 (3): 755–69.

Taber, Charles S., and Everett Young. 2013. "Political Information Processing." In *The Oxford Handbook of Political Psychology*, 2nd ed., edited by Leonie Huddy, David O. Sears, and Jack Levy, 525–58. New York: Oxford University Press.

Tetlock, Philip E. 2005. *Expert Political Judgment: How Good Is It? How Can We Know?* Princeton, NJ: Princeton University Press.

Tocqueville, Alexis de. 2000. *Democracy in America*. Chicago: University of Chicago Press.

Warren, Mark E. 1996. "Deliberative Democracy and Authority." *American Political Science Review* 90:46–60.

Wills, Garry. 2010. *Bomb Power: The Modern Presidency and the National Security State*. New York: Penguin.

Wolfsfeld, Gadi. 2004. *Media and the Path to Peace*. New York: Cambridge University Press.

Wolfsfeld, Gadi, and Tamir Sheafer. 2006. "Competing Actors and the Construction of Political News: The Contest over Waves in Israel." *Political Communication* 23 (3): 333–54.

Zaller, John R. 1991. "Information, Values, and Opinion." *American Political Science Review* 85 (4): 1215–37.

———. 1992. *The Nature and Origins of Mass Opinion.* New York: Cambridge University Press.

———. 1996. "The Myth of Massive Media Impact Revived: New Support for a Discredited Idea." In *Political Persuasion and Attitude Change*, edited by Diane C. Mutz, Paul M. Sniderman, and Richard A. Brody, 17–78. Ann Arbor: University of Michigan Press.

———. 1998. "Monica Lewinsky's Contribution to Political Science." *PS: Political Science & Politics* 31:182–89.

_____. 2012. "What *Nature and Origins* Leaves Out." *Critical Review* 24:569–642.

Index

Page numbers followed by the letter *f* indicate figures. Those followed by the letter *t* indicate tables.